100

Learn why more than a million children are excelling!

In *Real-Life Homeschooling*, you'll discover how:

- you can incorporate homeschooling into your daily life
- successful homeschoolers come up with new ideas and strategies and solve problems
- homeschoolers thrive in a variety of geographic settings and special circumstances
- families with one child or even eleven children are making it work
- teaching at home means lots of exciting options for your children and you!

Real-Life Homeschooling

The Stories of 21 Families
Who Make it Work

Rhonda Barfield

FIRESIDE
New York   London   Toronto   Sydney   Singapore

FIRESIDE
Rockefeller Center
1230 Avenue of the Americas
New York, NY 10020

FIRESIDE and colophon are registered trademarks
of Simon & Schuster, Inc.

Designed by Kris Tobiassen

Manufactured in the United States of America

10   9   8   7   6   5   4   3   2   1

ISBN 0-7434-4229-6

For information regarding special discounts for bulk purchases,
please contact Simon & Schuster Special Sales at 1-800-456-6798
or business@simonandschuster.com

I'd like to thank Michael, my husband of twenty-eight years and my best friend; Eric, Christian, Lisa, and Mary, our children and next-best friends; Toni Lopopolo, my extremely competent agent; and Tracy Bernstein and Wendy Walker, my editors, who shared the vision for this book and had the skill to help bring it to fruition.

Real-Life Homeschooling is dedicated to my late mother, Lois Price, who supported me 100 percent in teaching her beloved grandchildren at home.

Contents

INTRODUCTION

It's only 7:00 A.M. on Monday morning, but already little Bobby and Susie are sitting at their desks in the cozy kitchen, sharpened pencils in hand, workbooks opened, eagerly anticipating the day. Dad has left for work. Mother's finishing up the breakfast dishes, but Bobby and Susie don't mind; they know their assignments and are ready to start work on their own.

Mother wipes her hands on her embroidered apron. "Are we ready to begin our homeschool today?" she asks with a twinkle in her eye. "Yes!" the children chorus enthusiastically. "I can hardly wait to take that long-division test," says Bobby. "I know I can make a hundred on it!" Little Bobby is only in kindergarten, but already he's completed thirteen math workbooks.

Eight-year-old Susie opens her folder and points to a complicated algebra problem. "Mommy, could you please help me with this, just a little?" "Of course," Mother smiles. "I'm all finished with my house cleaning, the dishes, the laundry, and the bill paying, and our six-course supper is prepared and in the 'fridge. I can sit here with you and Bobby all the rest of the morning." Susie throws her arms around Mother's neck and hugs her tight. "Oh Mommy," she exclaims. "I just love homeschooling!"

*   *   *

If you think this is a description of a typical day in the life of a homeschooling family, you're not alone. Many prospective homeschoolers daydream about it, and scores of veterans have a vaguely uneasy notion that this is probably how other, better-prepared homeschoolers really live.

Nothing could be further from the truth. Home-schooled children, like any others, get grouchy, rebellious, and sometimes sullen. Parents struggle with balancing the demands of house-work, running errands, chauffeuring and for-pay work with the challenging task of homeschooling. There are many, many good days, including thrilling experiences of a child finally "getting" a concept, and warm moments of family sharing. But there are also dark times of great discouragement, days when both parent and kids may feel like running out of the house screaming.

When someone says, "I homeschool," what does that really mean? In spite of a number of books written on the subject, most people have no clue what it's like to live and work, day after day, teaching from home. While we might not buy the Bobby-and-Susie scenario, it's still hard to imagine what homeschooled children are like and how they spend their days. Do they sit at desks in their rooms, filling out worksheets from 9:00 A.M. to 3:00 P.M., Monday through Friday? Do they romp in the backyard for hours on end with no supervision? How do homeschooled children become "socialized"? Are homeschooling parents superhuman, always patient June and Ward Cleaver types? What motivates these parents to go to such great lengths to teach their children at home?

The answers will surprise you, as they have surprised me. A homeschooler myself, with four children—Eric, fifteen, Christian, fourteen, Lisa, twelve, and Mary, ten—I imagined that most homeschool life-styles were similar to my own. Not so. In interviewing families all across the country, I have been astonished to discover a variety of life-styles and teaching philosophies that are just about as diverse as you can get.

Some of the homeschooling families featured in *Real-Life Home-schooling: The Stories of 21 Families Who Make It Work* live in the country, some in towns, and others in cities. They may be devoutly religious or they may practice no religion. Some stress history subjects in their teaching, others the arts, literature, or practical skills. Many have home businesses, and a few work outside the home. These twenty-one families include those who have always homeschooled and others who have sometimes homeschooled. They come from a variety of ethnic backgrounds, and from eighteen different states plus a military base on a Pacific island. Some prefer quiet, simple living, and others are constantly on the go. Two of the featured families have eleven children, two have just one.

Regardless of this staggering diversity, homeschoolers are producing solid academic results nationwide. In his comprehensive study, *Homeschooling on the Threshold: A Survey of Research at the Dawn of the New Millennium*, Dr. Brian Ray has found, "These [homeschooling] students consistently score above the national average in various academic areas, with the median score at about the 67th percentile [compared to the 50th percentile for public school children] on national norms."

Home-schoolers' numbers are growing, too. According to Dr. Ray, there are currently 1.2 to 1.6 million homeschooled children in the United States alone. With an estimated 7 percent annual growth rate, Dr. Ray predicts three million homeschooled children by 2010.

I suppose, by 2010, I can write a least a dozen sequels to this book, or perhaps one enormous volume called *Real-Life Home-schooling: A Million Families Who Make It Work*. I doubt that I could find a single family that includes children like the fictionally perfect Bobby and Susie. Still, each homeschooling family has a fascinating story to tell. I hope you enjoy each of those profiled in this book. Better still, may each story give you a better idea of what it really means to homeschool.

Rebecca and sister Judith reading.

One

Running for the School Board

Family:
Glenn (53), Ann (52), Judith (18), Rebecca (10).

Location:
Alexandria, Virginia.

Best advice:
Relax and make learning fun.

Worst advice:
Follow the steps in *The Well-Trained Mind*. (This is not to discount the many useful resources and ideas in the book; just to say that while the theory is enticing, the practice is overwhelming.)

Favorite quote:
"To laugh often and much, to win the respect of intelligent people and the affection of children, to earn the appreciation of honest critics and endure the betrayal of false friends, to appreciate

beauty, to find the best in others, to leave the world a bit better, whether by a healthy child, a garden patch, or a redeemed social condition: to know even one life has breathed easier because you have lived. This is to have succeeded." (Ralph Waldo Emerson)

Favorite resources:
Saxon Math by Hake and Saxon, Saxon Publishing.
History of US series by Joy Hakim, Oxford University Press Children's Books.
Literature-Based Reading series, International Fair (Grand Rapids, Michigan).
Critical Thinking Skills series, Remedia Publications (Scottsdale, Arizona).
"Real books" from the public library.

Some people leave their public school system and never look back; this wasn't true for Glenn S. and his wife, Ann. The couple fought to keep their daughter in their neighborhood school until they finally felt forced out by bureaucratic indifference.

The family had long been at odds with their local public school administration, beginning with its push to create full-day kindergarten classes several years previously. The pervasive attitude at that time was summed up in a quote from the then head of early childhood education: "No matter how enriching the home environment, the public schools still know best how to educate your child." Ann and Glenn thought that they, as parents, should judge what was best for their daughter, and firmly believed that a five-year-old child with a parent at home did not need to be in school all day. When the school converted to full-day kindergarten, the couple worked with a sympathetic principal and together arranged a half-day program for Rebecca within the system.

By the time Rebecca was ready to enter third grade, "some administrative personnel had changed, but the attitudes hadn't," Ann says. "Because of redistricting, many in our daughter's rising third-grade class were slated to attend three different elementary schools in three years." The prevailing quote now became, "Only parents are bothered by such moves; the children adjust fine."

After several attempts to work with the school, Ann and Glenn pulled Rebecca out of her class. "Children are not ping-pong balls, to be batted about at will," says Glenn. "Our efforts to put some common sense into administrative decisions affecting the education of children became time consuming and frustratingly unsuccessful. It was time to go. But we loved Alexandria and didn't want to move, and we couldn't afford the private schools in the area. So homeschooling became our only alternative."

Rather than simply walk away, though, Glenn ran for the school board. He felt he couldn't leave without making a statement about how the city's schools were chasing good people away and failing those who remained.

"The decision to homeschool our daughter after second grade was for her sake," Ann says. "The decision to run for school board was for the sake of others who didn't have that option." Glenn's slogan was "Put children first." His goals were to increase the administration's responsiveness to parental concerns, to heighten the role of parents as partners—rather than as enemies—in the education process, and to awaken the community to the detrimental effects that frequent school changes have on student achievement. While Glenn lost the race, through his efforts and that of others, positive changes were made. Children in Alexandria are no longer required, for example, to switch schools between second and third grades.

Ann, a freelance writer for the *Washington Post*, educational associations, and other clients, is now Rebecca's primary teacher. Glenn continues in his work for the General Services Administration in Washington, D.C., where he is a writer and editor who works on internal communications; he also has the role of Rebecca's history teacher. Big sister Judith, who graduated from a private school and is attending college, helps teach when she is available.

Rebecca, ten, is "the proverbial little girl with a touch of tomboy," Ann says as she smiles. "She loves dolls and anything pink, but she says her goal is to become a catcher for the Baltimore Orioles." Rebecca is in fourth grade of the Perky Pelican School, her self-named homeschool, complete with flag and stationery. The school song, composed by Rebecca, is sung to the tune of "You Are My Sunshine":

I love my homeschool,
My Perky Pelican School
I'm learning new things
All day long.

I love my homeschool
My Perky Pelican School
It's fun, it's cool, and it's
Why I sing this song.

I do experiments
And I learn history
I read a lot
Which makes me glad!

I'm taught by Mommy,
And my sister, Judy,
And even my
Grumpy ol' dad.

As Ann began her second year of teaching in the Perky Pelican School, her said goals remained the same as when she began.

"All education should be geared to helping children become in-dependent, lifelong learners," she says. "Rather than memorizing a bunch of disconnected facts, children should be taught how to find any information they need and how to tell *when* they need more information. In addition, my job is to show my daughter the myriad of wonders that are out there; hers is to latch on to her passion and take it as far as she can."

Rebecca enjoys homeschool. "She likes the fact that she can stay with a subject," Ann says. "In public school she said that as soon as they got into something interesting, it was time to rush off to another activity."

They do maintain a daily routine, however. "My daughter gets up around six A.M. on her own, so I have an assignment waiting on her bulletin board," Ann says. "Morning homework, we call it. I'm up by seven, and we must be dressed before the school day starts: no lessons in p.j.s." Mom and daughter take a brisk walk to get their circulation going, and then return to "work." This might include reading about a particular topic, doing experiments, writing for Rebecca's monthly newsletter, or filling out work sheets.

"Work sheets have never been a learning tool that worked for me, but Rebecca loves them," Ann says. "I've made it a point to seek out the most challenging in various subjects. For example, I shy away from the fill-in-the-blank reading comprehension work-books, where the answer is found word for word in the accompa-nying passage. Rebecca needs to be encouraged to think and read between the lines."

Ann has found tools such as the *Literature-Based Reading* series, books that base questions and activities on well-loved books at each grade level, to be a good compromise between her desire for discussion-oriented learning and Rebecca's love of workbooks. Ann also likes the *Critical Thinking Skills* series. "Their exercises in com-parison, analysis, and application fit in well with our goals for Re-becca," she says.

The family enjoys playing games with an educational twist, such as Chronology, in which players demonstrate their knowledge of when things happened in history; Made For Trade, a game about buying, selling, and bartering in colonial days; and Chatter Matters, to help stimulate conversation on family traditions, goals, and special moments.

Rather than following a packaged curriculum, Ann assembles a variety of tools to help Rebecca grasp a concept or subject. "We use our computer through all subject areas to research specific topics and narrow down good resources," she says. "We belong to several homeschooling boards and find the interactions between members to be invaluable in exploring effective ways to approach any subject." Ann also pulls resources from the library and a local teacher's store. Virginia's Standards of Learning serve as a guide to what is covered in each grade, but Ann thinks of them only as a guide. She uses one textbook, Saxon Math.

Many activities are hands-on, accommodating Rebecca's visual learning style. One of her favorite parts of her language arts program, for example, is diagramming sentences. "Her writing has improved tremendously because of the way she can visualize how words relate to each other," Ann says. "We use the Frank Schaeffer *Basics First* series. The exercises are clear and easy to follow."

Instead of simply reading about geography, Ann and Rebecca use globes and maps regularly each day. "Rebecca automatically looks up places we hear or read about, and she is the navigator on all road trips—whether around town, to a nearby community, or to another state," Ann says. "One of the most enjoyable resources we used was a free 'What Do Maps Show' program offered by the US Geological Survey in Washington, D.C. A variety of excellent maps give students experience in reading different types of maps—topographic, road, or relief."

Rebecca studies Hebrew in her twice-a-week Sunday school classes. "We practice Reform Judaism and find homeschooling to be a natural extension of the faith," Ann says. "A basic tenet of Judaism is to question in order to understand, to look at ideas from many different perspectives. We encourage our daughters to think it through to reach a genuine understanding of the subject at hand."

"We don't want our children to accept things blindly," Ann continues, "but rather, as Judaism teaches, to reach for the real meaning of things." The family studies religions other than their own, as well. "Both girls have found it fascinating to see what others believe and what binds them to their individual faiths," Ann says. "We've taught our daughters that the religious label one claims is not as important as the way one lives. My favorite illustration is from the Hindu philosophy, that religion is like a giant mountain. There are hundreds of paths up the mountain, all leading in the same direction, so it doesn't matter which path you take. The only one wasting time is the one who runs around and around the mountain, telling everyone else that his or her path is wrong."

One of Glenn's passions is history, and he is very active in homeschooling his younger daughter in the subject. His schedule allows him to have one day off every other week, so he uses that day for Rebecca's history lessons. "Glenn really makes the subject come alive," Ann says. "He has studied extensively and has an envious ability to recall unique facts about historical figures, with descriptions of—and insights into—significant moments and people in mankind's past. For example, rather than just talk about Longstreet's role in the Civil War, Glenn can visually put you there with his description of the general's hulking bear size and piercing blue eyes." Glenn has found this descriptiveness, plus reading some of the best historical fiction, helps Rebecca grasp not only historical concepts, but the emotions, fears, and triumphs of each time period.

Ann thinks traditional history textbooks are deadly. Instead, to instill a passion for the subject in the girls, Ann and Glenn have relied on historical fiction and classics such as *Johnny Tremain*.

They use primary sources found in local museums and collections, as well as history anthologies such as *The Story of Mankind* by Hendrik Willem Van Loon and a 1951 version of *The Heritage of America* by Henry Commager and Allan Nevins. Rebecca enjoys the writing in the *History of US* series by Joy Hakim. A typical ten-year-old, she likes to let her imagination flow back through time by curling up with one of the books in the *Dear America* or *Royal Diary* series.

The family spent six months studying colonial history from Roanoke up to the Declaration of Independence. "Our location in the mid-Atlantic region is a big plus, because there are countless places to go to walk in the footsteps of historical figures," Ann says. "We have Jamestown, Williamsburg, Valley Forge, Independence Hall, the Smithsonian, National Geographic, the National Archives, and a myriad of other museums and art galleries, all within easy reach."

During their first summer homeschooling, Ann and Glenn concentrated on visiting places that helped bring their history studies alive. Rebecca became involved with a local living history group and participated in colonial reenactment programs. Alexandria offers a living history camp, taught by two women who call themselves "The Little Maids of History." Bonnie Fairbank, one of the partners, says, "We're not little, and we're not maids, but we are here to clean up after bad history." During weeklong sessions, the two women don the outfits and mannerisms of various personalities in American history and take campers through a hands-on program that highlights the political and social activities of a particular era, including its art, music, and customs. Students enjoy walking tours around Alexandria, one day learning about the first fire engines, another learning the difference between colonial, Georgian, and Victorian architecture, and so on.

Glenn and Ann cover history sequentially. "One thing that always troubled us about the public school approach to history was its disconnected thread," Ann says. "In Virginia, third graders study ancient Egypt, Greece, and colonial Jamestown! Some classes cover Jamestown at the beginning of the year, others at the end. The natural flow of history is lost. We believe it's important in the younger years to give a child a sense of continuity, how one event or period in history led to another. We may not be on the same page with our school system, but we are striving to give Rebecca an in-depth look at the causes and results of historical events."

With all of the family's study and activities, Ann has little problem keeping up with state regulations. "They're very basic, no-sweat requirements," she says. "I have a B.A. degree and that's all the state requires. When asked what curriculum I'd follow, I said, 'the Virginia Standards of Learning, state-mandated tests, and common sense.' No further questions were asked." Ann makes sure that Rebecca is tested yearly. "I need to know where she stands in relation to her grade and I think testing is an important skill for kids to learn. There will be many times when children may have to be tested in life."

Academic skills are important, but so are socialization skills. "I always laugh when people ask about socialization," Ann says. "The hardest part about homeschooling in our area is *limiting* the group activities. Between Girl Scouts, dance, a choral group, pottery lessons, and her twice-weekly classes at our temple, she certainly doesn't lack for interaction." Rebecca just finished a Toastmasters public speaking course, where she gained confidence talking in front of a group. In the spring she plays softball with a local recreation team, and in the summer looks forward to a week or two of Girl Scout camp.

Rebecca interacts with more diverse ages and backgrounds now than she did in school. "Her second-grade class was seventy-five percent low-income minority, but as hard as we tried, we could not get any real interaction after hours," Ann says. "Groups stayed in their own neighborhoods. Now my daughter doesn't see that division. Her 'school' group is comprised of children of many different ethnic and economic backgrounds," ranging in age from six to the teens."

The local homeschool support groups are very casual. That's fine with Ann, who prefers not to get into the regulation and formal structure of one particular organization. "Here in the northern Virginia area we have numerous groups who share resources and event ideas, and who open their activities to all homeschoolers, regardless of 'style,' " Ann says. "All it takes is for someone to have an idea and take the lead in organizing an event."

With other homeschoolers, the family has attended both theatrical and musical programs at the Kennedy Center (about ten times a year rather than the one or two Rebecca got in public school), nature outings, or special classes that are hard for individual parents to conduct. Home-schoolers have organized pottery classes, salamander counts, tall-ship visits, camp-outs, and study skills groups. "It's very easy for any parent who has a particular interest to post it on the computer boards, giving others who share the interest a chance to pool resources," Ann says. "We're currently hoping to organize a camp-out geared to eighteenth-century living, with no modern clothing or conveniences allowed."

One thing that has troubled Ann in her still fledgling foray into homeschooling is the drop-off in participation during long-term activities. "Because homeschooling parents tend to be free-spirited, it seems that many sign up for an activitiy, only to abandon it when another interest takes root," she observes. "That may be the down side to homeschooling: not giving children a sense of commitment to a group or activitiy. Some homeschoolers' propensity to go with the flow—to drop an interest the minute it's not exciting—may come back to haunt those children later in life."

To cope with this, Ann and Glenn work hard to help Rebecca make choices, and to understand her responsibility to carry out her activities to their proper conclusion. Ann says piano lessons have helped tremendously in giving her daughter the ability to stick to it even through the tedious or slow times.

Ann finds homeschool "fabulous—exhausting but fabulous. It's been more than I expected. I've been surprised at how much we accomplish in a short period. And I've been able to help my daughter, who is very shy, to gain a sense of control and confidence. We do all the same things we did while she was in school. The only difference is that now we have time to enjoy them."

The homeschooling life-style can be a challenge for Ann. "One of my biggest problem areas is that I have no time for other things, like basic chores," she says. "Fortunately, I have a very helpful husband. Also, there are times when I don't want the responsibility, when I have doubts about doing things right. But these are short-lived when I see how well my daughter is doing and how much she has grown intellectually. We will continue to homeschool until we think it's not working."

For support, Glenn and Ann rely on "great friends over the past thirty years who are thrilled with our adventure into homeschooling," Ann says. Extended family are either deceased or absent from the family's life, but "friends and former teachers support us enthusiastically, because they know what we went through in the school system. Ironically, some of our biggest supporters are the teachers and staff from our public school days—many are on the mailing list for Rebecca's newsletter, and take the time to write her encouraging notes after each issue. So far, the fact that we are homeschooling has received minimal growls, maximum applause."

When Ann and Glenn pulled Rebecca out of public school, their lives took a very different turn. Glenn's run for the school board was based on the hope that one voice could help change a system badly in need of repair. Instead, the school system inadvertently did the family a favor. "We never would have considered homeschooling if we hadn't been pushed into it," Ann says.

Front row: Matt, Gabe, Drew. Back row: Kevin, Teri, Josh.

Two

Homeschool to Public School and Back to Homeschool Again

Family:
Kevin (41), Teri (38), Joshua (13), Matthew (11), Gabriel (8), Drew (5).

Location:
St. Peters, Missouri (St. Louis suburb).

Best advice:
Enjoy the process rather than always striving for the product, whether in homeschooling, daily life, or the training and development of your children.

Worst advice:
Maybe public school would be better for your children than homeschooling.

Favorite quote: ————————

"Love is never lost. If not reciprocated, it will flow back and soften and purify the heart." (Washington Irving)

Favorite resources:

The Bible.

The Well-Trained Mind by Jessie Wise and Susan Wise Bauer, W. W. Norton and Company.

The Well-Trained Mind website: www.welltrainedmind.com

Books and music by Michael Card.

Christian Home Educators' Curriculum Manual by Cathy Duffy, Grove Publishing.

Teri T. decided to homeschool her children the first time she heard Dr. Raymond Moore, noted homeschool author and speaker, on a radio program. "The whole concept of home-schooling made a lot of sense to me," says Teri. "It appealed to my sense of doing the right thing for my children."

Five years later, though, Teri and her husband Kevin, a computer programmer and analyst, agreed to send their two oldest to public school. "When I started homeschooling I didn't have strong enough convictions about it," Teri says. "I was beginning to have doubts about whether or not my boys were getting all they needed academically and socially, and I thought maybe the public schools would be able to offer them more than I could offer them at home."

Josh and Matt made the switch, while Gabe and Drew stayed home. This was a time of reflection for Teri. "During the three years the older two were in school, I did a lot of praying, thinking, observing, and reading on the subject of homeschooling. I discovered that there were many philosophies of education, many methods that I hadn't even considered the first time around. I learned a lot about myself and why homeschooling was important to me, and gained convictions that were lacking at the beginning."

In the summer of 1999, Josh and Matt rejoined their two younger brothers in homeschool. Teri says she started homeschooling the second time around "with fresh perspectives and determination, and it made a tremendous difference in every way."

Teri sees homeschooling as "a process of growing and maturing and experiencing that I believe takes place more authentically in a nurturing home environment." To this end, she prefers a schedule that allows for flexibility. "My goal for our mornings is a relaxed, peaceful easing into the day," she says. Teri is usually the first one up, at six A.M., to spend time praying and reading both the Bible and spiritual, homeschooling and/or homemaking books. Kevin leaves for work around 6:30, before the boys awaken and just before Teri (usually) exercises. Then, "I try to create a peaceful environment for us by playing classical or worship music, having the blinds open to let the sun in and perhaps have a good breakfast waiting," Teri says.

School officially begins between 9:00 and 9:30, when Teri and the boys gather in the living room to open their day with prayer and Bible reading. Next comes *Latina Christiana*, a Latin course that includes listening to tapes, oral quizzes from the manual, and writing exercises. Mid-morning break is chore time; the family cleans one floor of their three-level house a day, dividing and alternating duties. The rest of the morning is spent on individual math from textbooks and language arts assignments from workbooks. Each child checks his own work from an answer key, but must report to Teri what he missed and why he missed it, as well as explaining the correct answer.

Teri expects the boys to be productive, but they are free to complete schoolwork wherever they like, whether at the dining room or kitchen table or stretched out on their own beds. If someone needs help while Mom is busy with another child, he's free to start on a new project or get on the computer while waiting. Josh and Matt often begin a game of chess and move a man or two during spare moments.

Lunch is followed by a short period of free time for play or recreation. Then Teri and the boys gather in the living room again for either science or history, with more reading, discussion, or activities that relate to the topic. When they studied Egypt, they read Old Testament (Bible) history related to Egypt, including the story of Moses and his encounter with Pharoah. Teri thinks it's important to "examine a topic through books, videos, or actual on-site places," so she and the boys checked out every exciting, relevant book they could find at the local library. They watched a video of an Egyptologist and a construction worker building a pyramid. The family visited the St. Louis Art Museum to see an authentic mummy and sarcophagus, and the St. Louis Science Center's Omnimax Theater for a special presentation on ancient Egypt. Since they happened to be in Colorado vacationing during their four-month study of Egypt, they also made it a point to view Egyptian artifacts at the Denver Museum of Natural History.

After this early afternoon time of intensely examining a topic "through many different perspectives and methods," as Teri puts it, she and the boys relax with a good read-aloud book. They recently finished *Johnny Tremain*. "This is a story time that we all share for pure enjoyment," says Teri. "It's usually the highlight of our day."

All four boys learn together in Bible study, Latin, current events, history, science, poetry reading, art, and both music and art appreciation—every subject except language arts and math. "I make allowances for the younger ones," Teri says, "taking into consideration their needs and abilities." The questions and stimulating discussions that arise naturally each day help the younger boys learn from the older. Drew, an active five-year-old, "can be a distraction sometimes," Teri says. "But he has learned to occupy himself when what we're doing doesn't interest him."

Teri goes for a mid-afternoon walk while the boys do silent reading from their library books, each in his own room. Everyone regroups with work on a weekly project; at this writing, for example, the boys are composing a short story and drawing a comic strip of their own invention. "This pretty much sums up our daily schedule," says Teri. "Soon afterward, the neighborhood kids will show up at our door."

When Teri decided to homeschool the second time around, she struggled to find a schedule that was workable. "This year I really had to get something out of my system," she says, "so midstream into our second month of homeschooling, we stopped what we were doing to try 'unschooling' [see Chapter Fourteen] for three weeks. It was a very fruitful experiment, because through it I found the balance that works for us. We definitely need more structure than the typical unschooler."

Now Teri sees her schedule as part of a "full and basically satisfying day, although we don't always accomplish it all. I strive for a simple flow, and I'd rather do less and try to squeeze the essence out of a topic than cram too much in."

To fit her flexible homeschooling style, Teri prefers an eclectic assortment of curricula, including Greenleaf Press, Beautiful Feet History of Science, Saxon Math, and Alpha Omega Language Arts. The boys are also on the computer daily and often watch educational videos. "I'm planning to use something different next year for language arts," Teri says, "and take advantage of lots of good literature, poetry, music, and places that St. Louis has to offer. The sky is the limit, really."

Dad comes home between 5:00 and 5:30 P.M., Monday through Friday, and has every other Friday off from work. After a relaxed dinner together comes a family time of prayer, Bible reading, and discussion.

Kevin is primarily a support person for Teri as teacher, readily listening if she's struggling with a particular problem, and willing to offer suggestions or advice. "His presence is very helpful in maintaining discipline," Teri says. "He reinforces what I'm trying to do, and makes sure the boys are listening to me." Sometimes Kevin provides logic problems for the older boys to solve. He is also the driver for various family educational trips.

By and large, Teri and Kevin's decision to homeschool has been supported by their families and friends. Teri's sister is especially sympathetic and is considering homeschooling her own daughter. Teri notes, "I find that, for the most part, the least supportive people are those who know the least about homeschooling."

"What about socialization?" is a question that's asked of nearly every homeschooler. Teri replies that her sons "play organized sports as well as spontaneous neighborhood games. They also attend church, youth group and church functions, and spend time with family and family friends."

They meet three Friday mornings each month in a science cooperative with four other homeschooling mothers and a total of fifteen children. Teri calls it "a tremendous blessing. It satisfies not only academic needs but socialization and support as well." Science club focuses on one subject each month, with intense, two-hour, hands-on classes for two consecutive Fridays and a field trip on the third Friday. The children in the class have studied subjects such as insects, Missouri in the fall, the solar system, and oceans. At noon, when science club ends, Josh, Matt, and Gabe like to join some of the other boys in a game of touch football while Drew plays with toy trucks or explores the host family's yard with the younger children.

In addition to academic subjects, Teri puts a priority on teaching practical skills. "Our sons receive an allowance each week for jobs done at home," Teri says. "We require that they save a portion and give a portion as well as have some to spend. My oldest son, Josh, also has an outside job cleaning at an autobody shop near our home twice a week with another homeschooled friend. This has allowed him valuable experience, independence, and a sense of accomplishment."

In spite of plenty of support, a good schedule, and generally cooperative students, Teri finds herself fighting discouragement. "Often it's because I have unrealistic expectations for either myself or my children," Teri says. "So I try to keep things in proper perspective and pray a lot." Teri also finds herself returning to the best advice she ever received: "To enjoy the process of each day and each year of homeschooling rather than always looking for a product-type result." Teri says this is hard for her "because I tend to be performance-oriented in my thinking. Enjoying the process rather than the product so much gives me permission to relax along the way."

Teri regrets it when she puts pressure on herself "to be like So-and-So and do things like her instead of finding out what works best for us." Her moments of solitude, plus hours spent with friends, are a priority. But she has little free time for herself. An LPN, she works four days a month in a nursing home in addition to homeschooling her children. She is also responsible for logging homeschool hours and lesson plans as required by the state of Missouri, which she records in a daily journal.

Teaching at home has been more challenging and complex than Teri had expected, even the second time around. Still, she says the payoff definitely has been worth it. "My children enjoy homeschooling overall. The older two prefer it to public school, though they both say that they miss being with all of their friends."

Teri and Kevin certainly don't miss the changes they observed in Josh and Matt when the older boys were in public school. "There was a certain amount of physical alienation," Teri says. "My sons would come home from school and immediately want to leave and go to a classmate's home. I worried because they were becoming more and more outward-oriented. I felt like I was losing connections."

Besides spending more time together, Teri also hoped to reverse some bad attitudes—and instill good ones—when she began homeschooling again. "Kevin and I wanted to be role models for our sons, rather than their peers being the models," she says. "I wanted to train the boys in character traits like serving, and that's taken time. I've learned that I can't always expect immediate success. But I'm encouraged by glimpses of effort in the right direction, like Josh helping to unload groceries from the van without being asked. All the boys are offering to carry big stacks of library books, opening doors, that sort of thing . . . the fruit of thoughtfulness."

Teri thinks the homeschooling experience has been a positive educational experience for her as well as for her sons. "It has challenged me to use all of my organizational skills, to be creative. I've also been surprised at how enjoyable tackling history and science is, and how wondrous the whole process of learning and discovering is; I don't recall it ever being so exciting during my own school years. The distractions of peer pressure and school sociability are removed, so much more priority is given to learning for its own sake."

"I see my role as more of a facilitator and fellow-learner than a teacher," Teri continues. "My goals are to provide the environment, time, and space for my sons to be themselves and learn to develop and walk in all of the gifts, talents, and abilities God has put within them. I want them to become people of integrity and of godly character. Therefore, the hard lessons of life, plus what one can glean from the difficult, is as important as mastering, say, writing skills. Education to me envelops all of life and its experiences. Home-schooling allows the room and time to weave all this into academics."

While some parents might think of this all-day sharing with

their children as a negative, Teri disagrees. "By being together so much, we tend to see the worst in each other, but then we learn to forgive and show mercy for each other's shortcomings and move on. I see it as a growing time." Teri thinks the family has definitely become closer. "Most of all," she says, "it's been good for me to not be alienated from my children. I have begun the rewarding process of getting to know my sons by virtue of the sheer number of hours we spend together. We share many experiences and these become an ongoing conversation with ever-changing subject matter."

There's also a lot of laughter. "Sometimes we have funny moments during the day," Teri says, "when I'm so very intent on having the boys' attention, and one or the other of them gets the giggles. The harder I try to keep a straight face, the more difficult it becomes, until a smile is starting—while trying to look stern—and then we're all collapsing with laughter."

When asked if she's glad she's homeschooling now, Teri says, "Absolutely. I realized what I first thought were advantages of public schooling really turned out to be more like conveniences. Honestly, the only so-called advantages that I could think of for sending my children to school were that I didn't have to prepare lessons for them, facilitate their education, or deal with conflicts. I also had more time for me. The advantages soon became disadvantages when I began to feel alienated from my children. So I see these more as conveniences and am now willing to do with less convenience."

From oldest to youngest: Bobby, Nina, Virginia, Rachel, Bobby John, Lori, Ben, Billy, Bonnie, Timmy, Emily, Tommy, Katie.

Three

Arrested for Homeschooling

Family:
Bobby (47), Nina (45), Virginia (23), Rachel (22), Bobby John (21), Lori Ann (18), Benjamin (17), Billy (16), Bonnie (16), Tim (14), Emily (12), Tommy (9), Katie (6).

Location:
Huntsville, Alabama.

Best advice:
Think/teach. As you think about things throughout the day, teach your children accordingly. When you're driving down the road, for example, and your child wants to know the meaning of something, explain it right then.

Worst advice:
Put your children in school this year; you can homeschool *next* year.

Favorite saying:
Civilization exists for the sole purpose of impeding progress.

Favorite resources:
The Word of God (the Bible).
The library.
Biographies and autobiographies of great men and women.
The Prayer Organizer by Jim Richards, Impact Ministries, 1-800-
     284-9402.
Basic Youth Conflict material by Bill Gothard, www.iblp.org,
     1-800-398-1290.

B obby L. is an ardent believer in homeschooling. So ardent,
in fact, that he was willing to go to jail to confirm his right to
educate his own children. And in 1983, he did just that.

Like many other homeschoolers, Bobby had felt increasingly
uncomfortable with sending his children to school. "Years before
I became a father, I recognized the unique difference between
what God was speaking to my heart about raising children and
how children were normally raised," Bobby says. "Also, public
school was not a pleasant experience for me. That in itself made
me consider an alternative."

In 1976, when Bobby and Nina's oldest child, Virginia, was
born, homeschooling was virtually nonexistent in their city,
Huntsville, Alabama. This was also the case in Pensacola,
Florida, where the family moved so Bobby could attend Bible
college. It was a matter of course, when Virginia turned four, to
send her to the early kindergarten program of a highly recom-
mended Christian school. By then, Virginia had a sister, Rachel,
and a brother, Bobby John, and Nina was expecting a fourth
child.

Bobby and Nina were, at first, very excited about Virginia's
enrollment in such an outstanding school. But their enthusiasm

dimmed as they began to notice certain aspects of the school that bothered them. Bobby once brought in a book and suggested the teacher use it as part of the curriculum. The teacher replied, "I have to use whatever the administration says I have to use. I couldn't use this without their permission." Bobby began to realize that "the best teacher in the world, with the best ability and character, can only function within the system to the degree that the system allows her to function. She's not autonomous."

Red flags were going up, but Bobby and Nina remained idealistic. Then one day, when Virginia and her father were working together on her homework, they had a disagreement. Virginia explained that her teacher had said that a certain fact was correct. Bobby said it wasn't correct. "Virginia and I went back and forth," Bobby says, "until I had to explain firmly that *this was not correct!* Then I realized, I'm expecting a four-year-old child to make a judgment. Whenever there is a contradiction between two authorities, the teacher and me, she has to decide which one is right. That was asking too much."

At that point Bobby realized he had to make a choice, and his choice was not, at first, in accordance with Nina's. "My wife, like most mothers of young children, looked forward to getting the children out of the house. I told her, 'Hon, I'm really uncomfortable with this school situation.' Little by little I exposed my wife to my need to bring Virginia home." When kindergarten finished for the year, Virginia was not reenrolled in Christian school.

In Florida at the time, children were not required to attend school until they were seven years old. By the following fall, Virginia was only five, but Bobby enrolled her in a home study program called Christian Liberty Academy of Satellite Schools. The couple received their curriculum from CLA and occasionally sent in reports. They also read books aloud, memorized chapters from the Bible, used readers purchased from the school, and taught beginning math and reading skills.

The family moved into a large two-story house in Pensacola, Florida, the following September. Shortly after Thanksgiving, when Virginia had just turned seven, the children noticed a man in a jeep who would often pull up and park close to the house, and then sit there. "My wife is a very private person and was concerned," Bobby says, "especially when this man called the children by name. In the course of time he finally came to the door and asked why the children were not in school. Nina said, 'They are; we teach them here at home.'" Shortly afterward, a visiting teacher came to the door and asked what school the children attended. Nina again answered, "Christian Liberty Academy," explaining that the school was located in the home. When the man asked who was doing the teaching, Nina suggested he speak directly to Bobby. The man left, at least for the time being.

Nina and Bobby could see that difficult times were ahead, and little support was available. "We didn't know of any homeschoolers other than one friend," Bobby says. Even more frightening, "I had heard of a case in Decatur, Alabama, where a husband and wife had been incarcerated because they hid their homeschooled children," Bobby says.

Back in Pensacola, a truant officer from the local school system came to speak with Bobby. "I remember him asking the same basic questions Nina was asked," Bobby says. "He wanted to know if our school was under the auspices of any local church. I said, 'No, it's a program that's based out of Illinois.' He said, 'You do understand that your children will need to be enrolled in a state-approved school.' And I answered, 'They *are* in school, and if the state chooses not to recognize what we do, then that poses a problem, because we're doing what God has spoken to our hearts to do.' The truant officer said, 'I'll give you two days to put your children in school, and if they're not in school, we're going to proceed with disciplinary action.'"

Bobby and Nina called Christian Liberty Academy's legal department for advice and were told to follow certain procedures. Meanwhile, someone gave Bobby a newspaper article about a couple in South Carolina who had been arrested for homeschooling. "This man and wife were taken to police headquarters at 3:00 A.M. for interrogation," Bobby remembers. "Their children went into foster homes for forty-eight hours before being returned to their parents." Bobby and Nina didn't want this to happen to them. "We kept a car full of gas and clothes packed," Bobby says. "And we had a place designated where Nina and the children could go. We had an exit plan." Bobby and Nina had begun to realize that most people were oblivious to their constitutional rights. "We knew parents had a choice in their right to home educate," Bobby says. "But the school system did not seem to understand this. Authority in the hands of people with an agenda can be misused for intimidation."

Two days later, the truant officer returned with a deputy sheriff. "We went through the same questions again," Bobby recalls. "When he asked, 'Are you going to put your children in school?,' I said, 'Sir, they *are* in school.' He said, 'I'm going to give you two more days to put your children in school.' Then he and the sheriff left."

Bobby tried to keep up his business of repairing appliances and doing plumbing and heating/cooling work. He was also worship leader at a church of three thousand people. He suspected that someone from the church had reported his homeschooling to the authorities, and wanted to set the record straight. "When I went to the leaders of the church for prayers, they told me to either put my children in school or step down," Bobby says. "So I stepped down. Out of our church's fifteen pastors, not one recognized either that I had the right to do what I was doing or that there was any scriptural basis for what I was doing. They thought I was in rebellion and/or deceived."

The people of the church had no idea of what was really going on. "I couldn't go to them for help because it would have looked like I was inspiring an insurrection," Bobby says. "The pastor stood up in church and announced that I needed to spend more time with my family, and that's why I was stepping down." It was the same kind of announcement that had been made when a former church leader had a moral problem. Fellow parishioners suspected that Bobby and Nina were experiencing marital turmoil, or worse.

As promised, the truant officer and the deputy sheriff returned after two more days, this time with a summons for Bobby to appear in court for violation of the compulsory school attendance statute. "I had never been in jail and never had a need for a lawyer, so I was perplexed," Bobby remembers. "I never thought it would come to this. It seemed like a dream."

Within a week of the visit by the truant officer, a plain-clothes detective came to pick up Bobby, take him downtown, and book him. "I asked the detective if I could go to a back room and call a friend who was a lawyer, to ask what my rights were," Bobby says, "and he agreed. I had just picked up the bedroom phone and turned back toward door, when the man came around the corner with his gun drawn. I remember looking up with the phone in my hand and thinking, 'He's got his gun pulled and *this is not a dream.*' I was a little shaky at that point."

Since Bobby couldn't reach his lawyer friend, he decided to cooperate. The detective escorted Bobby to the car. "Now, I have always believed that whoever you are, you need to know your position toward eternity," Bobby says. "So I said to the detective, 'Do you have the peace and joy that comes from knowing your sins have been washed away by the death, burial, and resurrection of Jesus?' It got quiet. The man pulled over to the side of the road and began to weep. He said, 'I'm not right with God. This is an experience that makes me really examine my heart.' I prayed with him and then we drove on to the station."

Bobby was booked and placed in the "drunk tank," a holding

section of the jail set aside for processing. "I was there for two or three hours," Bobby says. "The police finally came in and took me out and the detective brought me home; he had stayed around purposely so he could drive me."

The pretrial hearing was set for December, and Bobby needed a professional who understood the issues involved in home-schooling. He recalled a fellow Bible college student who was a lawyer. "I made an appointment with Paul, and the secretary said, 'Your consultation will cost you forty-five dollars,' " Bobby recalls. "I didn't have any money. I had just relocated and my clientele had changed, and money was not readily available. Still, I went out and worked hard for a week to get it. Then Nina and I took all the homeschooling books we had and left them with Paul and his son, who was just about ready to graduate from law school. He said they'd take the material and look at it."

A week later, Bobby was called in for a conference. "Paul and his son were at the conference table with our books piled every-where," Bobby remembers, smiling. "He told me, 'Bobby, I never knew homeschooling existed. I've never heard of anything like this.' His son added that he wished his father had home-schooled him. In such a hostile environment, those words were very encouraging."

Paul agreed to take the case, but needed two hundred dollars up-front. "That was a lot of money in 1983, especially for us," Bobby says. "I had no way to get enough cash that fast. I couldn't appeal to my church for funds, my parents were oblivious to what was going on, and every pastor we knew had labeled me a rebel. At least once a day somebody would come to the house and encourage me to see the light."

Nina was also questioning her husband's decision. "I was pregnant at the time, trying to keep up the house and take care of five young children," she says. "The stress was tremendous. I knew I loved my husband, and my husband loved God. But I wondered how he could be right while all these other men were wrong." Bobby replied that he wasn't accusing his friends of being wrong. "I'm just saying I don't have a peace about turning the education of my children over to someone else," he told Nina, "and as much as I want to please the pastors, I can't do that and still do what God wants me to do."

One night Bobby went into a side room of the house, shut the door, and prayed earnestly. " 'God,' I asked, 'Are you sure you've got the right guy?' And God said, 'I chose you because I know you will obey me.' So I asked, 'Lord, have I got a rich uncle who's going to die and leave me some money?' And God said, 'No, I'm going to take care of you.' "

The next day Bobby got a call from a laundry owner. "This businessman asked me to lower the water levels in all his machines," Bobby says. "The amount, at my hourly rate of twenty-five dollars plus the cost per machine, added up to exactly two hundred dollars. Back then, I never came home with that kind of money, especially on one job. I was elated."

Bobby took the money to his lawyer. Paul told him that he would need another two hundred dollars in two weeks for research costs. Unbelievably, just before the second payment was due, the owner of the laundry called Bobby in to readjust his machines' water levels back to normal. "Some of his regular customers had complained that their clothes were not getting as clean, and the laundry was losing business," Bobby says. "I earned the same amount of money to undo the job I had finished a couple of weeks earlier!"

A pretrial hearing was held on February 7, 1984. The dean of Bobby's Bible college, his only friend through this ordeal, already had agreed to test his children in advance and report on their exceptional scores in court. As the dean related these results, the assistant district attorney stood up and said, "We are not concerned with the test scores of these children, we're only concerned with the fact that this man is in violation of the compulsory school attendance statute." Bobby's lawyer answered, "Your Honor, the state's compelling interest is in the education of the children, not in the institution in which that is performed." Unfortunately, the judge sustained the objection. "This was a letter-of-the-law judge, and he decided to go forward with the trial," Bobby says. "I was very disappointed."

The court date was set for April 4, and in the meantime, life got even more complicated for the family. Nina felt so overwhelmed that Bobby decided not to work full days. So-called friends were urging Nina to leave her husband and stay with them. Even Bobby's mother once insisted on taking her daughter-in-law and grandchildren home with her, trying to help. "I said I didn't think that was a good idea," Bobby remembers. "I knew what Nina and I were walking through, and if we walked through it together, in the end we would benefit together. But if she left, I would never see her again."

A few weeks before the trial, the family received a subpoena for Rachel, age six, to appear in court. Bobby and Nina set up a mock courtroom in their home and rehearsed what would happen. "I asked Rachel all the questions I could think of," Bobby says, "and those turned out to be the very questions they asked in court. I couldn't believe it, my own daughter being asked to testify against me."

At the trial the district attorney stood and announced, "We received a call from So-and-So of Huntsville, Alabama, informing us that the children were not in school." This was how Bobby and Nina learned that her mother had turned in their family to the authorities. It was a shock. "I had not even considered her," Bobby says. "I thought we had been reported by someone in my church or community." Looking back, neither Nina nor Bobby consider the actions of Nina's mother to be malicious. "She, like so many parents, thought that public education was the superior option, that trained educators are the only ones qualified to teach," Bobby says. "She acted out of concern for Nina and her grandaughter."

The first witness Bobby's lawyer called for the defense was Rachel, a petite six-year-old girl with pigtails. Paul drew letters and asked her to identify them, and questioned her on basic math. He also wanted to know what kinds of things her parents were teaching her. When Rachel responded that family members learned verses and chapters of the Bible, he asked her to recite. Paul set up a chair in front of the jury for little Rachel to stand on. She began with the Psalms, chapter one: "Blessed is the man that walketh not in the counsel of the ungodly . . ." "At that point, the court recorder asked her to speak louder," Bobby laughs. "She bellowed it out, the entire chapter."

Rachel finished Psalm One and proceeded on to other verses. In the midst of her recitation, Paul had a sudden inspiration. The compulsory school statute was worded in such a way that if a parent was found to be in violation, the superintendent of schools was required to take over and move the case to the next level, that is, prosecution under the law. Paul asked to speak to the judge, and the jury was sent out of the room so he could point out this provision of the statute. The judge turned to the district attorney and asked if he could provide proof that the superintendent of schools was aware of the case and had orchestrated the steps. The district attorney said he was not able to do so. A recess was declared.

Bobby remembers the judge going in to his chamber to consider Paul's point. When he returned to the courtroom, he threw out the case. "Because the superintendent was not involved, it was a procedural violation," Bobby says. "This letter-of-the-law judge was our salvation, interpreting the law legalistically."

When the superintendent of schools discovered what the judge had done, he was furious. "I heard later that he and the judge had exchanged some serious words," Bobby says. "Finally the judge told him, 'If you bring a case like this to my courtroom again, I'll throw it out.' The superintendent was running for re-election that fall, and he didn't want negative publicity." This, plus the judge's warning, kept the school system from prosecuting the family further.

Only a few months earlier, Bobby and Nina had been alone and virtually friendless in their community. The positive outcome of the trial changed all that. "Interestingly enough, after this case was thrown out, homeschoolers came out of the woodwork," Bobby says. "I had come to the place where I realized I was a pioneer. Pioneers have to recognize that most people don't understand what they do." Now, there was more understanding.

That next year, homeschoolers in Florida organized to attempt to get a law passed that would protect them while satisfying the state's compelling interest in their children's education. In 1985, a favorable law slipped through the legislature in the wee hours of the morning, attached to another bill. In order to homeschool in Florida, parents were to first inform the superintendent of their intentions. They also were required to maintain a file of work products and a list of curricula used, and conduct an annual check of the child's progress through one of five choices of verification. "Now if the state wants to come in and verify your compliance, they are required to give a two-week notice," Bobby says. "If you fail to meet expectations, you have a year before you are forced to do anything. This Florida law is still one of the best homeschool laws in the nation."

Two months after the trial, Nina gave birth to twins and Bobby continued to work to pay the legal costs of his case, which totalled more than ten thousand dollars. Timothy was born in the summer of 1986, and the family moved back to Huntsville, Alabama, in December of that same year. But that's not the end of this story.

Much has changed since the trial. Today there are eleven children in the family. Bobby owns and operates two home-based businesses, MR. FIX-IT (MR for maintenance/repair) and MS. FIX-IT (MS for maintenance service), involving heating, air-conditioning, plumbing, and electrical work. Bobby John will soon be taking over the MS. FIX-IT business. All family members are actively involved in a music ministry, performing numerous concerts each year.

Little Virginia, one of the children involved in all the commotion in 1983, is now twenty-three. She has completed two years of college and plans to finish a four-year degree. She gained plenty of experience working for Bobby in the family businesses, and is a full-time secretary for a local defense contractor. She also plays piano and recorder.

Rachel, the six-year-old who testified at the trial, is twenty-two. She is enrolled in Bible college and plans to be involved in Christian ministry. She is also in charge of putting together the family's music programs, and is very instrumental in overseeing the younger children's music training. Rachel plays violin and piano.

Bobby John is twenty-one. He is enrolled in junior college, but primarily spends his days working on jobs through the MS. FIX-IT business. "He can do anything I do," Bobby says, and notes that his namesake especially enjoys short-term repairs and servicing. In the family's music team, Bobby John runs the sound and oversees the technical aspects of each performance. He plays piano, upright bass, and cello.

Lori Ann, nineteen, is taking two classes in Bible college. She plays saxophone and violin, and her career goal is to be a seamstress and designer.

At seventeen, Benjamin is the most natural fiddle player of the family, and also plays mandolin, drums, and sax. He is a senior in high school. He also works with the computer to complement the family ministry.

Billy and Bonnie are sixteen-year-old twins. Billy has a great talent for guitar, starting on ukelele when he was only four years old, and on guitar just a few months later. Every day, no matter how late he's home from helping in the business or other activities, he goes to the basement, turns on the amp, and plays. He is also very physical, and a hard worker.

Bonnie is an ardent reader, often curled up in her top bunk bed with a book. She plays violin, viola, and piano. She is known for her sweetness and willingness to always help.

Tim, fourteen, is very talented musically; if he can hear it, he can re-create it on the keyboard and piano. He also plays harmonica and had started on violin before taking up the keyboard. Because of his small stature (being shorter than his twelve-year-old sister) and cute smile, he easily wins the hearts of a crowd.

Red-haired Emily, twelve, plays recorder and flute, and with her beautiful voice, she sings many solos and duets during family ministry performances.

Nine-year-old Tommy plays violin and is learning to play drums and ukelele. He has a strong voice and a natural ear for harmony.

Katie, six, is known as Miss Personality. She never meets a stranger and loves to hug and kiss. Katie began to play violin when she was only three, and enjoys singing with Lori.

Nina is head teacher and facilitator of the family homeschool. She is in charge of the household. Bobby continues as main breadwinner and headmaster and chief planner for the homeschool. He and Nina work together, teaching academics as a team. "I have tried to always be involved," Bobby says. "I personally delivered my last three babies at home. I'm very much involved in raising them all. I can't relate to men who want to spend time with the guys, because my life-style is directed toward my family."

The children's lives are closely intertwined with their parents' lives as well. All eleven are required to share household chores, pitching in together to clean and organize on a regular basis. Each older child mentors and is personally responsible for one of the younger children, helping with homeschool, character development, and musical training.

The children also learn the trades involved in the family business. When they were younger, Bobby made it a point to include the children and take them along to repair jobs whenever possible. Once, he says, when Bobby John was two years old, he left him in a back room of a familiar McDonalds while he went to check the air conditioner on the roof. "Stay here sitting on Dad's toolbox," he told his son, and Bobby John did. When Bobby returned a few minutes later, the manager explained how he had tried to bribe the boy to leave the toolbox by offering him cookies, then a chance to sit in the manager's big chair. "I could not get that boy to budge," the manager said. "He told me, 'I'll have to check with Dad before I move from the toolbox.' "

Nina and Bobby hold firm convictions on child raising. "We believe you should put the emphasis not on doing, but on *being*," he says. "If you teach a child to be what he ought to be, he's motivated to do the right thing from inside, not outside. I do assert my will. I believe children need leadership and positive direction. But my objective is to equip each child to make his own decisions, and then Nina and I turn the responsibility of making decisions over to him or her. Because it's a developmental process, I wind up walking out my own dream as they move toward theirs."

Bobby thinks much can be learned from fathers and mothers spending daily, quality time with their children as they go about their work, and the story of Bobby John is one example of on-the-job character training. Bobby continues to take the younger children with him to as many jobs as possible. "Most days, on my way to work, at least four have lined up at the door asking me to take them along," Bobby says. The older children work with Dad side-by-side. At present they are constructing a large addition to their fourteen-hundred-square-foot house, with family members plumbing, wiring, and building.

All this fits into Bobby and Nina's philosophy of homeschooling. "Character comes first, then academics take care of themselves," Bobby explains. The family goal is "to produce children who will turn the world upside down for Jesus, productive citizens who will succeed in everything they do," Bobby says. "And my priority is to assist my children in discovering, developing, and living their dreams. Each child is unique, but each child wants to be connected to a common goal or purpose. Each identifies or connects differently, but they're always looking to find their part in what we're doing. My goal is to find their interest and plug them in."

Finding the children's interests, then plugging them in, has culminated in the family's music ministry. All thirteen perform together, from one to two commitments a week in "off-season" to four or more weekly concerts around Christmas and Easter. "The development of our present ministry actually happened in the last four to five years," Bobby says. "It was never my goal to do what we're doing professionally or even for that to be the central focus. We just wanted to create a memory for the children, develop our talents, and give God what we've got."

Bobby and Nina always believed in teaching their children musical instruments when they were young. Bobby chooses the first instrument, and the children help make choices after that. When Benjamin and Lori Ann were seven and nine, respectively, Bobby found a violin teacher for them who agreed to come to the house for their lessons. "All the children came in and watched her teach," Bobby says. "Before long, everyone wanted to play."

When the children were younger, the family also staged annual Christmas plays, with Bobby as the donkey. "We presented our play to neighbors and friends, whenever we went somewhere. Then we'd sing a song." Some of the first performances were held at the three McDonaldses in town where Bobby worked as maintenance supervisor. "We went in during off-hours, stood in front of the people eating there, performed, and walked out before they could do anything to us," Bobby grins.

The family offers a presentation that includes traditional and contemporary Christian music, bluegrass, country, classical, pa-triotic, Latino, and Christmas music. They also use puppets and share personal stories. In preparation for performances, each of the older, more accomplished children works with younger ones. Nina, who plays piano and harp, oversees the practicing and per-forming at churches, ladies' groups, musical societies, nursing homes, and civic organizations, primarily in Alabama, Louisiana, Tennessee, and Florida, but also as far away as California and Mexico.

During the week of Christmas, the family gives performances at many local businesses and public places, including banks, restaurants, the courthouse, and even a photocopy store.

Because their musical commitments can be very demanding, the family homeschools year round. The academic part of each day is a blend of book work from A Beka, Bob Jones, Rod and Staff, and other materials (some picked up at garage sales), plus educational videos. "The children have their assignments and they go with it," Bobby says. "Most homeschoolers superimpose the classroom on the home. I believe that children learn best by pursuing their inter-ests. I try to find those interests and not allow them to go dormant or be pushed to the side." If a child shows no interest in a particular subject, Nina and Bobby wait awhile. Rachel was not seriously mo-tivated to read until she was twelve, but now reads voraciously. The family has always been able to overcome academic obstacles. "I don't have a science lab or expertise in the more advanced math and science," Bobby says. "But I do have friends and resources where my children can get the same training."

There is no such thing as a typical day, Bobby says. "We know our ministry commitments, we know what vocal and instrumental music needs to be memorized and prepared, and we work accordingly. The children are required to work on music for fifteen to thirty minutes out of every hour for six to eight hours a day, although when we are not learning new material, the schedule relaxes." Daily plans also fluctuate according to the needs of the businesses.

Life is not all work and no play in this family, and fun times are an important part of life. The older children do not go out on dates per se, but they do host regular "date nights." Each teen is allowed to invite a boy or girl, plus both parents, to an outing. "I want my teens to learn how to build relationships with the opposite sex, and I want to know their intended friends and the parents," Bobby says. The last date night included pizza and card games at a local restaurant, then volleyball and table tennis at a nearby church fellowship hall.

The family spends much of their socializing time together when possible. They have taken a harmonica class together, and dance lessons, and church-related seminars. When Billy wanted to play baseball, Bobby made the difficult decision to deny the request because he thinks hobbies should be developed that will be most helpful to children in later life. "What is going to be of greater value to my children when they're older, knowing how to play soccer or a musical instrument?" he asks. There's also the problem of trying to schedule separate activities for eleven children. "I explained to Billy that if he were in baseball, I'd have to let his brothers and sisters choose activities, too," Bobby says. "We didn't want a life-style where we were always running in separate directions."

Even as it is, the family's demanding schedule can seem overwhelming at times. There are always financial pressures as well. Nina and Bobby both feel occasional discouragement and a sense of not being able to do it all. "In the course of life, discouragement is always something you have to deal with," Bobby says. "You have to have a certain plan ahead of time as to how to deal with it. What we do is to try and talk it out, get down to the real problem, pray, and face it head-on. I don't stay down long. I'm not a quitter."

It is obvious that neither Bobby nor Nina are quitters, but rather longtime homeschoolers who understand the meaning of perseverance. One of the family's greatest strengths is that in spite of all they've gone through together, they still love each other and have a common purpose and vision. "Despite our inadequacies, our children have succeeded," Bobby says. "We're amazed at what they can do." Best of all, Bobby and Nina see their children "discovering, developing, and living their dreams," Bobby says, "because by God's grace, we are living our dreams."

The family looks back at the arrest and trial of long ago as a valuable experience that helped them to grow. "The trial was part of our life," Bobby says, "not something we added to our agenda. Although the expense was beyond our resources, the court order seemed unnecessary, and the journey was so lonely at the time, we are grateful for the outcome. Because we live in America, we were able to defend our right to parental educational choice against those who saw our children as 'children of the state.' It was an adventure along the way."

Four

The Unschool Experience

Family:
Lori (43), Roy (48), Dylan (15), Jacob (9), Mira (6), Simon (4).

Location:
Columbus, Ohio, suburbs.

Best advice:
Borrow resources at first so that you don't waste money on that which you will never use.

Worst advice:
You have to have a homeschool support group and/or a teacher's certificate.

Favorite quote:
"We must be careful not to use every do-er's question as an excuse to turn life into School, to Teach a lesson, and then give a

Front row: Simon, Mira. Back row: Dylan, Lori, Roy.

little quiz to make sure the lesson was learned. There is the old story of the child who asked her mother about something, and, when the mother suggested that she ask her father, said, 'I don't want to know that much about it.' " (John Holt)

Favorite resources:

Home Education Magazine, www.home-ed-magazine.com, 509-486-1351.

The Complete Home Learning Sourcebook by Rebecca Rupp, Three Rivers Press.

The Teenage Liberation Handbook by Grace Llewellyn, Lowry House Publishing.

The Unschooling Handbook by Mary Griffith, Prima Publishing.

And the Skylark Sings with Me by David Albert, New Society Publishing.

Lori C. calls homeschooling "a wonderful, delightful, enlightening and magical" experience. She says her children love it, and she never gets discouraged. "I think homeschooling is a superior life-style," Lori adds, "and one that has brought all of us closer together."

What is Lori's secret? Perhaps some of it has to do with her view of education, sometimes called "unschooling" or child-led learning. "My philosophy is one of self-exploration, family-led and interest-based learning, and going with the flow of life. All life is learning, and so it should be exciting, stimulating, and participatory. My goals for my children are that they become happy, healthy, mentally well-adjusted, independent, and fully functioning adults who are connected to the world around them. All the rest is just icing on the cake."

Lori and her husband, Roy, made the break with public school when their eldest son was six years old. "Though Dylan spent the first grade in one of the most superior school systems in the state of Ohio," Lori says, "he was bored, understimulated, and wasted a great deal of time on administrative tasks like waiting in line." Lori and Roy were very concerned that their son was losing his zest for learning as well as his natural curiosity. "By being closed up in a school all day, he was missing out on so many life experiences—on real life in general," Lori says. "It was our conclusion that he could learn far more in a shorter period of time by being free to live life with the rest of the family."

When Dylan began homeschooling, Roy was—and continues as—an attorney who works in the affordable-housing field. He invests tax credit money in the construction and renovation of low-cost homes for the elderly and low-income people.

Formerly, Lori was an experimental psychologist in a large university. She was well on her way to earning a PhD, specializing in human learning and memory, when she decided to come home after giving birth to her second son. Now, one of Lori's primary roles is to oversee her children's life experiences, more as a facilitator than as a teacher. "As unschoolers, we pursue our passions together," she says. "We are all teachers and all learners."

Lori believes the best kind of learning takes place apart from a formal, packaged curriculum. "We use real books and magazines, real experiences, real conversations," Lori says. "We talk with our children at every possible opportunity. The optimal teaching moment occurs when a question is asked and answered. This phenomenon is observable at our house hundreds of times each day. All necessary subjects are woven into the fabrics of our lives, and each child reads, or has read to him or her, whatever sparks an interest."

When studying math, for example, the children cover basic concepts through everyday experiences such as cooking, building with wood, playing board games, and reading books such as *Mathematicians Are People, Too!* "The children once learned about angles—geometry—from hiking on the sand dunes at Lake Michigan," Lori notes. "They might figure mileage in the car, or the length of time to complete a journey. They sometimes count how many of each clothing item is needed for a weeklong trip, calculate the cost of items and change, tell time so they know when to be home, or deal with phone numbers and credit card purchases over the phone. The list is endless! They also work in workbooks that they have selected from a plethora of choices presented to them."

Self-teaching extends to all subjects. Dylan, Jacob, and Mira all taught themselves to ice-skate with no formal lessons. "I gave my children lots of time to experiment, and the opportunity to go skating weekly," Lori says, "and each one was helped by older ones. Mira was befriended by an elderly figure skater, and when she and Mira run into each other, the figure skater teaches her new moves." Little Simon has only been on skates three times and is already cruising around the rink.

The family has two computers that are used every waking hour when someone is home. All four children enjoy both fun and educational software, and Dylan is online. "The kids watch PBS videos and educational videos that are either purchased for them or checked out of the library," Lori says. "Sometimes, they see entertainment-type videos. We don't watch television." Instead, all four children keep busy with more productive pastimes.

Dylan, now fifteen, volunteers at the local science museum, with twelve hundred hours to his credit so far, and helps to train others. He also volunteers at the main library downtown, and frequently operates lights and runs crew (lights, props, etc.) for the local teen drama productions. Dylan learned to read and write because he was a cohost on a children's public radio show. "It was very important to him to do a good job," Lori says. "By the time he was ten-years-old, he was going to area bookstores and interviewing children's authors with tape equipment he brought with him from the radio station. He did this all alone while he had me sit in the van with the little ones."

Jacob, age nine, is a voracious reader. "When he was eight years old, he leaped from sounding out words to reading adult-level books within the period of one summer," Lori says. Jacob especially enjoys science fiction, *Animorphs*, and Harry Potter books, as well as reading about natural history, earth science, and historical fiction.

Six-year-old Mira is a dancer and a gymnast. "Since she isn't bound by a school schedule, she has ample time to engage in her skills," Lori says. Mira likes to sleep late, then listen to books on tape, write, look at books, and play with dolls. She works in math and reading workbooks that she's chosen herself.

Simon, age four, is never excluded from family learning. "We believe in cuddling and nursing and holding our young children, and including them in all that we do," Lori says. Simon keeps busy, on an ordinary day, in pretending with Playmobil figures, looking at books, riding his bike, playing hockey, and tagging along to his brothers' and sister's activities.

Much of the family's unschooling centers around outside-the-home activities. "We prefer a very active life and are all very athletic," Lori says, and their weekly schedule reflects it. Dylan works at the science museum on Mondays, and Lori and the other children may spend the day reading, doing science experiments or chores, visiting a museum or the zoo, and/or playing outside. The boys have ice hockey that night. On Tuesdays, Dylan volunteers at the library. Mira and Jacob have gymnastics classes and evening soccer practice.

Wednesdays, Dylan has a drama class and soccer practice, and the rest of the family reads, run errands, and swims in the free times between scheduled events. "Dylan and Jacob are home alone on Thursdays," Lori says, "working together on paperwork while I take Simon and Mira to story hour. Mira has a drama class, homeschool dance class, and a ballet class." On Fridays, Lori and the children often ice-skate, then play with friends in the afternoon before swimming lessons. The boys have ice hockey that night; Dylan is an assistant ice hockey coach.

Weekends are packed as well. Saturdays, Mira attends ballet classes and plays soccer, Dylan has soccer, and Jacob attends drama and magic classes and soccer. On top of this the family often sees a play or hikes in the woods. "Sundays are usually spent as a family," Lori says. "Sometimes we attend our Unitarian Universalist services, and sometimes we just stay at home with chores and large projects like building our new playground."

The family thoroughly enjoys all their interaction with others. "Socialization has been a problem in the past," says Lori, tongue in cheek, "but we have it under control now. The difficulty is in paring down, rather than adding to, the contents of the social plate." Lori thinks homeschoolers are far better socialized than those attending public school. "My children are peer independent and not peer dependent. They have lots of friends, some of whom attend school and some who do not. They have the gift of true socialization—they can relate to the full spectrum of humanity and not just those children who happen to be born in the same calendar year."

At one time, Lori was heavily involved with organizing homeschool support meetings, but decided to disband the groups. "I had a great time with the one I helped to run in our first few years of school-free living," she says. "But I came to see how participating in—let alone running—one eats up a lot of time that could be best spent on other endeavors. Also, many new homeschoolers are public school push-outs and are looking to their local support group to be their next institution from which to receive orders and services. I really disliked having that role. And I did *not* enjoy being exposed to all the behavior problems I saw in many of the kids who were coming to our events who had just been taken from schools. Often they were removed at the suggestion of the school, as if homeschooling were a thing to do when a kid was too much trouble for the teachers!"

Lori and Roy believe parents, not schools, should be in charge of their children's education. "I strongly feel that if one is to take responsibility for the education and direction of one's offspring, then it should not be partially handed back to the institutions," Lori says. "For that reason, we do not use public schools for any reason. We can find options that are more desirable, ones that address our children's desires. A blurring of the lines between home education and public schooling will ultimately lead to an erosion of our rights to home educate and our authority as parents."

The family puts a high priority on interacting with all kinds of people. "We don't choose to isolate ourselves within a community of other homeschoolers, only," Lori says. "We lead a full life within our greater community at large. I always tell new homeschoolers that there are many good activities in which one can participate and trips to be taken that are fun, but the trick to maintaining a manageable and rewarding schedule is to choose only the ones that are great and leave the rest behind. Without the development of this ability, you have the risk of running yourself ragged and deciding that you simply aren't up to the task of homeschooling. A frazzled family is not a benefit."

For Lori, mornings are almost always relaxed times spent at home. "I arise early and spend the next few hours alone on household tasks and aerobic exercise," Lori says. "I also work on my computer. I own several e-mail lists and participate on a dozen or so more. I write book reviews for several publications, work in my business, read news groups and the *New York Times*, and talk to my friends." Meanwhile, Roy leaves for work.

As Dylan, Jacob, Mira, and Simon awaken, they make their own breakfast, start an academic project, or help out with chores. The children are responsible for making their own beds, putting away their clean clothes, picking up their messes, and vacuuming. By his own choice, Dylan also does his own laundry. Even Simon helps with sorting laundry, cleaning up the playroom, and putting away toys. "We have a family rule," Lori says: "If you get it out, you put it away, and no one gets out a new thing until the last one is put away properly."

The children do not receive cash for chore work. "They are a part of the family," Lori says, "and as such, are entitled to their share of its benefits and are simultaneously responsible for their share in its upkeep. They've simply grown up with this philosophy, and it's natural to them."

Each family member chooses to handle certain household jobs. Roy cooks most of the evening meals and washes floors. Lori dusts, changes sheets, and cleans up bathrooms. She also does most of the laundry, hanging out clothes whenever possible. The family is very concerned about environmentally wise choices, and avoids using the dishwasher in favor of sharing the job of hand-washing dishes. "We feel strongly about living lightly on the land," Lori says. "We recycle and compost and buy items that have minimal packaging. We usually throw out only a half can of trash weekly, but we have a mountain of recycling."

Whether working, playing, or traveling to various activities, the family enjoys being together. "We eat dinner as a family virtually every night, and either take the children to sports activities or spend the evening at home," Lori says. "The hours before sleep are dedicated to reading aloud and being together." Some all-time favorite read-alouds have included *A History of the U.S.* by Joy Hakim, *Enchanted Forest Chronicles* by Patricia C. Wrede, and *The Little House on the Prairie* books by Laura Ingalls Wilder.

Lori is responsible for making sure that the children are in compliance with state regulations. Ohio homeschoolers must write a letter of notification. The state also stipulates that one parent have a high school diploma, that each child receive nine hundred hours of education, that certain subjects be covered, and that some form of assessment is provided each year.

Dylan, Jacob, Mira, and Simon have never been formally tested. "Having worked in the field of test construction in years past, I most emphatically do not support testing," Lori says. "My children have not and will not be tested. The tests do not measure what they are intended to measure and are still both culturally biased and sexist in nature." In addition, Lori and Roy believe that competition is best done with the self, "progressing over what you could do before and not how you measure up to someone else. That's why we submit a portfolio for assessment by a certified teacher of our choice, to ascertain educational progress."

Both parents work hard to ensure a good education for their children. Roy is very involved in homeschooling, especially in answering questions. "Occasionally I take the kids to work with me, or to meetings that expose them to another side of the real world," he says. "And we play games and sports together, helping to build their basic skills before they go into group sports." Roy also puts the younger children to bed. "We are both very well connected to our children," Lori says.

In spite of all good intentions, Lori admits that their family sometimes has bad days. "We chalk it up to being human," she says, "and not because we don't send our children to school." Roy agrees. "When it comes to things that go badly, we think these are issues or behaviors that would be a problem even if the kid went to school, so we deal with them as part of a parenting issue. Our homeschooling strategy flows directly out of a parenting strategy." A child who's having difficulty will be asked to find some "alone space" until "his or her feelings are centered."

Personally, Lori uses a number of strategies to keep herself centered. Friendships, both online and nearby, are helpful. "I'm learning and growing all the time, and that's how friends enrich my life, by increasing this growth," she says.

Lori also enjoys working in her part-time business, providing occasional consulting for homeschooling families and helping to run a transcript and diploma service for teen homeschoolers. "I assist families who are starting to homeschool in complying with state regulations, analyzing learning styles, choosing materials, being a sounding board when doubts are encountered, and sometimes offering family counseling," Lori says. In addition, she and a partner run the Institute of Alternate Learning. This organization assesses homeschooling teens in Ohio and West Virginia, and also provides transcripts and diplomas for them.

The family is productive and content. When asked why her children enjoy homeschool so much, Lori responds, "We don't school, we engage in living our lives," she says. "Our children are empowered to direct their own learning and their own lives by making decisions together with the rest of the family. It's been my experience that this way, nothing learned is ever forgotten, and acquired skills are always practiced." Dylan, Jacob, Mira, and Simon value their autonomy and independence, and, Lori notes, "We have never had a child who had the slightest interest in changing his or her current life-style."

Lori says she finds satisfaction in her children's attitudes, that they are happy, and that adults delight in interacting with them. When asked if she would like to go back and change anything in her life, Lori says she would have definitely unschooled, but with one qualification: "I would have started sooner."

David, Rodney, Naomi, and Mark

Five

Homeschooling with a Special Needs Teacher

Family:
Rodney (48), Naomi (44), David (14), Mark (12).

Location:
Sylvan Lake, Michigan (a small city).

Best advice:
The best curricula and the best schedules are the ones that best meet you and your family's needs.

Worst advice:
Put your children into public schools where they can be missionaries for God.

Favorite saying:
God will provide whatever you need, to do what He calls you to do.

Favorite resources:

World magazine website, www.worldmag.com

Answers in Genesis (creationist) website, www.answersingene-
    sis.org

Home School Legal Defense Association website, www.hslda.org

Crosswalk website, www.crosswalk.com

Second Harvest website, www.usedhomeschoolbooks.com

Naomi K. is wife to Rod and mother to David and Mark,
whom she homeschools. She works part-time for her husband in his electrical engineering business. She also baby-sits her
two-year-old niece, Stephanie. The difference between Naomi
and most homeschoolers, though, is that she accomplishes all
this in spite of being blind.

Although she manages her life very well, Naomi must deal
with certain daily frustrations. "Transportation is sometimes a
problem," she says, "and talking with people, especially in a large
group, can be difficult for me. It is hard for me to look directly at
the speaker. If you don't look at sighted people when they're
talking to you, they think you aren't interested." Reading printed
material can also pose a challenge. It is often several years before
printed books become available in braille or on cassette, if they
ever do.

Naomi was born sighted. When she was nearly two years old,
she lost both eyes to retinoblastoma, a form of cancer that devel-
ops on the retina. "I don't remember any of it," she says. "The
various attempts—chemotherapy and radiation, plus surgeries—
to save at least one eye were much harder on my mom than on
me, I'm certain." Both parents made sure that Naomi grew up
being treated as an equal to her two brothers and sister.

In 1962, Naomi was mainstreamed into public school. "That
was rather controversial at the time," she says. "I attended a public school with a resource room, where a special teacher and ten

to twelve kids with visual handicaps came during different times of the day. I learned braille, typing, and some other skills in the resource room. But most of the time, I was in a class with sighted children who were on my grade level."

When Naomi attended Ohio State University, the school provided a resource office, recorded books produced by Recording for the Blind, and readers for tests and other unrecorded materials. Naomi graduated with a degree in developmental psychology. She cared for children in her apartment while completing a few more postgraduate classes in elementary education. She met her future husband, Rod, at a singles group sponsored by her church.

Rod worked for General Electric as an electrical engineer for nineteen years, until January 1998, when he decided to go into business for himself as a consultant. Naomi now answers the phone for the business, finds information on the computer, and helps make financial decisions.

The couple has been married for eighteen years. Their son Rodney, called David, is fourteen, and has been homeschooled since second grade. He also works for his dad, filling in data on the computer, finding information Rod needs when he is working out of the office, and helping to load and unload tools. David likes homeschooling and has no desire to attend a formal school.

Mark, age twelve, is social and very interested in sports. He has always been homeschooled, "though he has asked to go to a 'real' school for a couple years." Naomi smiles. "We have told him we will consider it when he is ready for high school. Right now, he is too easily impressed by his peer group."

Naomi and Rod began homeschooling in part because it was difficult to arrange transportation for David to his Christian school kindergarten. "Then another problem arose," Naomi recalls. "David's first-grade teacher was a young, first-year teacher who loved doing all kinds of special projects with her students, but reading groups were held only two or three times a week. I guess she thought all her students were proficient readers already." David struggled with reading and consequently hated it, and Naomi found herself working with him several hours each night. "I thought to myself, If I'm going to spend so much time doing schoolwork with him anyway, why not homeschool him and avoid the transportation and schedule hassles?" she says. "Then I read a small article in one of my braille magazines about the Eyes of Faith Ministry, a library of braille Christian school curricula. That was my wake-up call. We began homeschooling David in the second grade and his younger brother, Mark, in kindergarten."

The family's homeschooling philosophy is derived from a passage in the Bible, Deuteronomy 6:4-9. "We feel that parents are directly responsible to God for their children's education, whether they see to it themselves or send the children to a formal school," Naomi says.

Naomi uses a packaged curriculum, A Beka, almost exclusively, though she did once try a Riverside spelling book. "Spelling is the most difficult subject for both my boys," she says. "I tease Rod and tell him it's genetic, since he also struggles with spelling." During Mark's fifth-grade year, the family purchased the new video classes offered by Bob Jones University and were disappointed by the lack of content. Since then, they have been part of the A Beka video homeschool program. "That, plus the braille curriculum, has worked wonderfully," Naomi says, "especially in the elementary grades. David, my reluctant reader, has turned into a bookworm and reads at college level now."

Since most A Beka material is in print form, Naomi has the teacher's books brailled. She can do this herself with the family's braille writer, a machine that looks like a modified typewriter with nine keys and dots in various configurations, but finds it takes a great deal of time. "When the boys were younger, I used the brailled teacher's books to read along with them, and did a lot of reading out loud," she says. "I also used them to go over the text questions with the boys. I don't use braille curriculum much now, just teachers' materials, which I braille myself or have brailled by a volunteer group here in Michigan."

In order to "read" a print book for herself, Naomi places it face down on her scanner, a machine that looks something like a desktop photocopier. The scanner transfers printed words from the book's pages into a computer. Naomi then accesses a program that reads aloud what has been transferred. "I have a choice of voices I can hear," Naomi says. "I like a male voice, one that's not too deep. When the computer reads back to me, it doesn't include punctuation, but I can go into an edit mode and find out where the commas and periods are." She can slow down and speed up the reading, a helpful option when skimming through a large volume of materials. Naomi is also able to key her own writing into the computer, use spell-check to correct mistakes, and have the final product read back to her.

A Beka's video school does much of the work for homeschool teachers. In the rented videos, students watch an actual classroom as teacher and students progress through the year, just as if they were physically present. "To my surprise, my boys identified with some of the students and liked or disliked some of the teachers, as they might in a regular classroom," Naomi notes. "A few times they have been very sad and even cried when saying good-bye at the end of the school year."

The curricula for A Beka's elementary grades consists of a video lesson for each day that contains all the subjects for the day: Bible, math, reading, language, spelling, history, and science or health. In the earlier grades, penmanship is also included. The package price of nine hundred dollars includes all student and teacher books and videos, including shipping costs both ways.

A Beka uses a different approach to junior and senior high grades in their video school. Each subject has its own video, and students are permitted to choose up to five different classes per year. David is enrolled in ninth-grade Bible, government, and world history from A Beka, plus a ninth-grade science class on CD-ROM from Switched-On Schoolhouse. Mark takes seventh-grade Bible on video and seventh-grade A Beka history using textbooks only. Both boys study Saxon Math through textbooks. Naomi paid extra for an A Beka video course in Spanish, and David, Mark, and their mother are learning the language together. The family has two "classrooms" set up, each with a desk, television, and VCR, one in the living room and one in the family room.

Overall, Rod and Naomi are pleased with the excellent treatment of phonics, language skills, and reading in the early grades of A Beka. "Now that the boys are good readers, these aren't so important to us," Naomi says. "But as a beginning homeschooler, I needed A Beka's thoroughness, especially in the basics. I didn't want to miss something important for my sons' education. I think the video school has given them a very good foundation, and now I feel we can branch out and try some different things."

Though Naomi and Rod generally have found A Beka to be a smoothly run company, there have been problems such as poorly recorded videos, missing test pages, and lost or delayed mailings. When Naomi sends back the first box of materials, the third one is supposed to be shipped while the family is working through the second box. Sometimes there are glitches, as when two of David's Bible videos were never sent last year. Instead, the family went ahead with the Bible classes using the teacher's guide only.

All of the video classes tend to be similar in format, but Naomi encourages her sons to respond to the teacher's questions and sometimes write on the marker board. If the teacher goes fast, a video can be set on pause to give David and Mark time to respond. Often Naomi and Mark discuss the text questions. "We are trying some variety to encourage both boys' interest," Naomi says.

David, Mark, Rod, and Naomi agree on a schedule at the beginning of each school year. "I want them to stick to a routine, pretty much," she says. "Otherwise they do their favorite classes first. That makes for a long afternoon." The daily schedule is flexible, and often flexed. "The plan is for each boy to be half done with schoolwork by lunch and finished with the rest between three and four o'clock. I allow short breaks in the morning and afternoon, and I urge the boys to go outside and play basketball, baseball, hockey, or some activity to energize them." Lunch lasts about an hour and a half, enough time to allow Mom to prepare a meal and finish some housework.

The weekly schedule varies with the seasons. On Sunday there's always church, and sometimes guests come over for dinner. Currently, David has driving classes three to four days a week, and debate class on Monday evening. Wednesday is church youth group meeting, and Thursday evening activities vary. Mark has roller-hockey practice late Friday afternoon and games Saturday morning. Naomi catches up on house cleaning, shopping, and other chores on Saturday.

The family begins formal schooling in mid-August and takes breaks as needed. If the boys are behind where Naomi thinks they should be, there are shorter than usual breaks at holidays such as Thanksgiving, Christmas, and Easter. Last year, David and Rod made a two-week mission trip to an orphanage in Moscow, Russia. Mark and Naomi continued school at home, but worked occasional half-days, so lessons were finished in mid-June that year instead of the end of May. Naomi and the boys agree that both teacher and students need a summer break.

Once school starts, there's a busy extracurricular schedule, and one of the keystone activities is David's debate group. The Home School Legal Defense Association (HSLDA) sponsors groups in each state, and participating students are given a topic and encouraged to research it while learning the basics of debate technique. Last year, David and his cousin Kathleen formed a group in Ann Arbor, a forty-five-minute one-way trip for Rod and David. They meet once a week. Last year's topic was "the Sixteenth Amendment and the income tax, both corporate and personal, should be repealed." Participants had to learn both sides of the issue and be prepared to argue two sides, pro and con. "Debating helps the kids learn to think and communicate more clearly," Naomi says. "It's done wonders for David, turning him from an introvert to an extrovert." David likes debate because it's an enjoyable social event as well as a kind of "scholastic sport."

Sports and music are also included in the family's schedule. Both boys took five years of piano lessons from a neighborhood teacher until she moved away. "David can pick up a hymn book, work for awhile, and then play the music," Naomi says. "Mark thinks he would like to switch to a baritone or tuba or trumpet in a year, when his braces come off. He's tending toward less involvement in music and more in sports like baseball, roller hockey, and basketball."

The boys and their dad have played community baseball for the last few summers. David is now umpiring the younger teams, and Mark plays every spring. Both boys have also taken advantage of swimming lessons and basketball classes offered through the local school's continuing education department.

One required "extracurricular activity" for both David and Mark is basic housekeeping, including cleaning, cooking, and laundry skills. "We think these are an important part of their education, too," Naomi says, "though they *are* still learning. They can cook fairly well, but need reminders from me." The first pan of brownies that David tried to bake himself were overly done on the top and still gooey on the bottom. "He assured me that he had set the oven at the right temperature and had not added any extra liquid," Naomi remembers. "Several hours later at dinnertime, I noticed the oven was set on 'broil' instead of 'bake.' The mystery of the brownies was solved, and I don't think David will forget to check the oven setting again."

Household and yard chores are assigned to each boy, and they trade each week, working them in when there's time. Both David and Mark help out by raking, mowing the yard, straightening their rooms, washing and drying clothes, and keeping things organized. "These chores get done right along with homeschooling," Naomi says. "Things are not as spick and span as I might like them to be, but with two boys and a dog, it probably wouldn't stay that way very long, anyway."

Naomi must do her own household chores "by feel." "I have to admit, since the boys are usually available, I am not as organized with my cans and packages as I used to be," Naomi says. "Things get moved around sometimes. It is safer to ask." Naomi recalls one occasion when she thawed a freezer container of what she thought was spaghetti sauce. "It turned out to be split pea and ham soup," she grins, "but I didn't find out until I set the bowl with pasta and sauce, already mixed, on the table. The boys cried out, 'Oo! It's green!' Rod and I tried it and it wasn't so bad. The boys wouldn't touch it, though."

The entire family has been involved in paid child care for the past two years. "We agreed to baby-sit so that my niece, Stephanie, would not need to go a day care facility," Naomi says. "The boys have learned to play with her, clean up, change her diapers, and feed her." Either Naomi, David, or Mark takes a turn caring for Stephanie while the other two do schoolwork. Naomi says this has been a great learning experience for both the boys, especially now that they're experiencing the rigors of keeping up with an active two-year-old. They also receive the rewards of splitting a two-dollar-an-hour baby-sitting check with their mom.

David and Mark have been given an allowance since they were in kindergarten. As the boys have grown older and more capable, they have earned extra money by raking leaves, mowing lawns, and shoveling snow. Both are required to save a certain percentage of their earnings as well as to donate 10 percent to the church. David and Mark pay at least half the cost of their own activities. David is saving most of his money, some in a Roth IRA and some in an account for buying his own truck. He works for his father several hours each week.

Rod has a home office but is often gone. "He installs, maintains, and tests equipment that brings in power from the electrical company to the big auto plants and steel mills," Naomi explains. "He works with the huge transformers that step up or step down the power to their machines." When a factory anticipates a "down time," Rod is often asked to come in while the power is being shut off. Though his schedule is flexible, and he has the freedom to turn down some jobs, he often works holidays and odd hours. This past Thanksgiving, the family arranged an evening celebration because Dad had worked from 2:00 to 8:00 A.M.

Rod's flexible schedule allows him to help out occasionally with homeschool, recording grades and filing papers. He also tutors David in algebra when needed.

Both Rod's and Naomi's extended family are fairly supportive of homeschooling. Rod has a brother and a sister who both teach their children at home. "My family lives in Ohio and are not much involved with us," Naomi says, "but they haven't said anything negative about our homeschooling our children."

David and Mark get most of their interaction with other children through the family's church. "From preschool on, they have both been involved in the AWANA clubs [church-related groups that teach the Bible to children] and all the activities associated with them," Naomi says, "including Grand Prix races with little wooden cars, and AWANA 'Olympic Games' competitions, with games ranging from beanbags to tug-of-war and foot races in a gym." David and Mark occasionally take field trips with other homeschoolers. Naomi, Rod, and the boys have attended several seminars—such as the creation science seminars given by Answers in Genesis—for homeschoolers. The family does not belong to a homeschool support group or co-op because of Naomi's inability to drive.

Each year David and Mark take the Iowa Basic Scholastic Achievement Test. David ranks above the ninety-ninth percentile, and Mark scores at the eightieth percentile in everything except spelling. "The tests have been helpful to us, giving indications of how well the boys are learning different subjects, and what subjects need special attention," Naomi says. "It also is good experience for the boys, I think, getting them used to these types of tests, which they will have to take in order to get into college."

The state of Michigan does not require testing for homeschoolers, but the law is rather complicated. "To my understanding, there are three types of homeschooling laws in our state," Naomi says. "One law is for parents who object on religious grounds to having state-certified teachers for their children. Another law, the Homeschooling Act, is for parents who wish to homeschool their children for other reasons. These two groups of homeschooling parents are only required, if questioned, to show evidence that their children have been learning appropriate subjects." A third law is in place for parents who want their children to be involved in some classes—such as music, art, or sports—with the local school system. These homeschooling parents are required to file a curriculum plan with their local school board.

The family has never had any trouble with authorities, but they tend to be careful. When Naomi began homeschooling several years earlier, Michigan's law was tough and home-schooling was not generally accepted. "Home School Legal Defense Association recommends homeschoolers 'lie low' and don't stir up trouble," Naomi says, "even though our present law is much more lenient."

Most of the time, Naomi enjoys homeschooling but fights discouragement now and then. "Sometimes the kids' attitudes get to me, when they're being uncooperative. Because we spend so much time together, the boys and I can rub each other the wrong way. And I never have enough time to get everything done." Naomi says it helps her to pray and talk with other homeschooling moms. Rod also has heart-to-heart talks with his sons as needed to improve attitudes and behavior.

Mark thinks homeschooling is all right, "but sometimes you have too much time after school, and you get bored." David is glad he's homeschooled. "I like homeschooling because I get to decide my own schedule for classes, except when my mom decides for me! I don't have to ride the bus to school or wait be-tween classes. I like being able to choose which classes I take and how I do the class, whether through video, computer, or from books." David says he sometimes misses the advantages of two chauffeurs instead of just one. "But having a mom who is blind doesn't affect my homeschooling much. I've always been homeschooled by her, so I wouldn't know the difference." Mark agrees.

Naomi is encouraged when she stops to look back on the family's homeschool journey. "Rod and I have definitely expe-rienced successes, such as watching our second-grader, who struggled with reading, reading at the fifth-grade level by the end of that school year," she says. "I have also been pleasantly surprised at how God provides the things we need when we need them to make our homeschooling successful. For me, that meant braille curricula when the boys were younger. Now that they are older and the braille curricula are not available, God has provided my talking computer-scanner. His daily provision of guidance and energy has also been humbling and amazing."

Sandy (holding Garrett), Kaitlin, Gil, Ryan, Charlie, and Chuck

Six

Life on a Pacific Island

Family:
Chuck (37), Sandy (34), Kaitlin (11), Ryan (7), Charlie (3), Gil (almost 2). Garrett was born a few months after this story was written.

Location:
Kwajalein Island, South Pacific Ocean.

Best advice:
Get rid of the textbooks! Don't "do school"; instead, educate, live, learn, and love.

Worst advice:
"Buy this book!" from people we don't know regarding books we haven't seen.

Favorite quote:
"I have no greater joy than to hear that my children walk in truth." (III John 1:4, the Bible).

Favorite resources:

Homeschool Digest magazine, P.O. Box 374, Covert, MI 49043.

To Train Up a Child by Michael and Debi Pearl, The Church at Cane Creek.

A Charlotte Mason Companion by Karen Andreola, Charlotte Mason Research and Supply Company.

Beyond Survival by Diana Waring, Emerald Books.

A Survivor's Guide to Home Schooling by Luanne Shackelford and Susan White, Crossway Books.

If you're one of those people who sometimes daydreams of escaping to a Pacific island getaway, meet a family who lives there year round. Chuck, Sandy, Kaitlin, Ryan, Charlie, and Gil G. are residents of the island of Kwajalein [KWAH-jah-lin], where Chuck is employed by a U.S. government contractor as a software engineer. Sandy, "keeper at home," homeschools their four children.

Although the family misses living in the States, they have had a pleasant experience as islanders. "Kwajalein is only three miles long and a half mile wide," Sandy says. "It's located in the Pacific Ocean between Hawaii and Australia, eight degrees north of the equator. It rains frequently, and in sheets, but it usually doesn't last long. A few times a year it rains for days. But the climate is beautiful! The temperatures are in the mideighties all year long, with nearly constant tradewinds."

Kwajalein Island is part of a ring of islands connected by a coral reef called Kwajalein Atoll, which forms the largest lagoon in the world. "The ocean is so blue that it looks like God added Tidy Bowl to the lagoon," says Sandy, smiling, "especially when the sun is high. I had seen photos before we moved here, but I thought they were color-enhanced." There are more atolls in the area that together comprise the country known as the Republic of Marshall Islands. Sandy describes Kwajalein as especially breathtaking, "with palm-lined streets, foliage, gorgeous flowers, white sand, and sparkling clear blue water."

U.S. citizens are not on Kwajalein for sightseeing, but instead, for national defense. Chuck works for Systems Engineering on a range safety project. "Kwajalein is right in the middle of all the controversy on the news over the new missile defense system," Sandy says. "They launch the 'kill vehicle,' which is visible to us as it goes up from another island in the atoll. We get to witness firsthand that light travels faster than sound." The missions cause major excitement on the island. "Missiles are launched from California, and they come streaking through the night sky like balls of light falling from a Roman candle," Sandy says. "Everybody who isn't working on the mission goes to the north shore to sit and wait for the light show." Radar tracks the missiles to make sure they stay on course, and many different kinds of sensors ensure they either land where they're supposed to land or are detonated before any damage is done.

The United States liberated the Marshall Islands in World War II from Japanese occupation, and then served as a protector of these islands as part of a United Nations plan. Since the 1950s, the American government has used the nearby vast expanses of ocean to test missiles. During early testing, the Bikini Atoll was accidentally contaminated by nuclear weapons, and the United States now pays steep retribution for the damage. The government also doles out rent to the Marshall Islands for the right to use some of the islands in the Kwajalein Atoll for housing radar-tracking equipment.

In addition to the Ebeye natives, there are twenty-five hundred American residents on Kwajalein. A small contingent are army personnel; a majority work for subcontractors. Most residents are on the island on "unaccompanied single status," though managers and engineers are allowed to bring along their families. Contracts usually run for two to five years. Out of the 2,500, there are about 350 children and 14 homeschooling families.

Home-schoolers on the island have a support group that organizes field trips. The little group has toured the military post office, the fire station, the hospital, and the police station to watch drug-sniffing dogs at work. "We have also visited air traffic controllers up in their tower, and several ships," Sandy says, "like *The Worthy*, which was originally commissioned as a spy ship for the navy. And we went on board an Indonesian 'tall ship' and met the Indonesian cadets. Different sailing vessels and planes visit the island periodically, and everyone runs down to the dock or airport to get a look." There are also nearby World War II memorials and battlefield artifacts worth seeing, both on Kwajalein and a nearby island. Star- and satellite-watching are a common pastime, given a night sky that's vast and very dark from a lack of city lights. "We can also rent boats for fishing and recreation," Sandy says. "Once when our family was riding through the ocean, a family of dolphins swam alongside our boat, playing and doing flips. It was magical and, coincidentally, it happened the day after we finished reading *Island of the Blue Dolphins*. We also rode to a deserted island with a jungle and spent the day imagining what it would be like to be stranded like the characters in *Swiss Family Robinson*, which we read last summer."

Unlike most Americans, homeschoolers on the island can't jump into their minivan when they're ready to sightsee or visit friends. "This is a bicycle community," Sandy says, "and the only vehicles on the island are government vehicles and the grocery store delivery van. I pull a Burley bike trailer behind my bike, and that's how I haul Gil and Charlie. Fortunately, the island is perfectly flat, but I do have to peddle against the wind."

Despite a limited choice of transportation, residence on Kwajalein does have its advantages. "In some ways, it's like living in the nineteen fifties here," Sandy says. "The children can ride their bikes to the store and run errands for us. It's very safe, and folks leave their doors unlocked. There is no crime or violence; our worst local crime is an occasional bicycle theft. Children play all over the streets." The island has one small grocery store, a convenience store, an eight-lane bowling alley, a post office, a free "fresh air" outdoor movie theater, a video-rental store, one sit-down restaurant, and a tiny department store called, ironically, Macy's.

Sandy's life-style on Kwajalein is dramatically different from the one she used to have. For the three and a half years after her first child, Kaitlin, was born, Sandy worked full-time as a software engineer for Intergraph Corporation in Huntsville, Alabama. "I was a cog in a very large organization," Sandy says, "working with a large government project to produce maps for defense purposes." Chuck produced aeronautical charting software for other countries' civil aviation authorities. "Chuck did the same kind of work as I did, and traveled frequently," Sandy says. "I had a hectic schedule and lots of overtime from meeting deadlines. Although the work was interesting, my heart was constantly being pulled toward home."

When Ryan was six months old, Sandy quit her job to become a full-time mom. "At that time, Chuck and I had only heard homeschooling mentioned in passing. Some distant relative was homeschooling, and another relative said, 'Can you believe what those crackpots are doing?' We had never actually met anyone who was homeschooling until the going-away luncheon my coworkers gave me. I realized my second-line manager and his wife homeschooled, and he was no crackpot!"

At home with Kaitlin and Ryan, Chuck and Sandy soon decided against preschool classes. "It seemed silly to send Kaitlin to school when I had just come home to be with her," Sandy says. "I went to the library and started to research early childhood education, and I accidentally bumped into the homeschooling books." Sandy and Chuck read several of Raymond and Dorothy Moore's books together, then *The Christian Home School* by Greg Harris. "This was an exciting idea, homeschooling," she remembers, "though maybe too idealistic. But God had already been leading my husband and me to forsake our career-oriented lifestyle, and it wasn't a coincidence that we stumbled onto homeschooling at this point in our lives."

In the beginning, Chuck and Sandy's goal was "to pull the family back together from the treadmill of life and establish some peace," Sandy says. "But during the first two years, as we read more and actually met homeschoolers, we started to see that this was a good way to develop godly character. We realized our children did not have to go the way of the world. Peer pressure and rebellion were not inevitable." Both parents began to look on homeschooling as a calling and a mission. "For us, homeschooling is the ideal situation for educating children and developing a close, loving, parent-child relationship," Sandy says. "We want to raise our children with a heart for loving and serving the Lord, to provide them with a good educational foundation, and to create a love for learning and study."

Sandy says their homeschool "started out very 'schooly.' I had loved school as a child, and those methods were all I knew. Dr. Moore's ideas didn't seem to apply to my oldest child, who was an early bloomer, and so we used regular curriculum at first." This changed when Sandy realized that "textbooks can take the joy out of learning, and don't always follow a natural pattern of learning. I love to research topics of interest, and I gravitate to really good books and hands-on learning experiences. It was very liberating to realize that we did not have to have textbooks for each appropriate grade level, with all their compartmentalized information."

Today, the family uses a very eclectic mix of books to teach. Their math program of choice is *Making Math Meaningful*. For language arts, Sandy started Kaitlin with levels two, three, and four of an older version of *Learning Language Arts Through Literature*, moving to *Simply Grammar* and *Editor-in-Chief*, a "fun reinforcement." She has also used *Alphaphonics*, *Spelling Power*, and *Explode the Code*. For history lessons, the children go through the Sonlight curriculum for third- and fourth-year American history and later, for learning about nonwestern cultures, plus Greenleaf Press books. "When I threw out our more structured curriculum, I mainly used the library and developed my own curriculum," Sandy says. "Then, I stopped doing most of my research when I found Sonlight."

As a guide for history and science lessons, Sandy is enthusiastic about Sonlight. This company features literature-based unit studies, "real books" (rather than textbooks), and hands-on science. "I discovered Sonlight when Kaitlin was halfway through third grade and I had just had Charlie. I had less time to hunt through the library, catalogs, and reviews for good books, and Sonlight's approach was very similar to mine," Sandy says. "I let them do the legwork for our history studies." The family follows Sonlight's schedule loosely. "I teach Kaitlin and Ryan together in all areas except math and language arts," Sandy says. "Sonlight history and science are very adaptable for multilevel teaching. As they tell you—and it's very good advice—don't become a slave to the schedule."

Sandy orders Sonlight materials in February or March, before the new school year begins each June. "You have the option of ordering some of the books or a complete package," Sandy says. "The complete package comes with all these great books, a lot of Usborne nonfiction, plus historical fiction for readers and read-alouds. You get a very detailed set of lesson plans, with notes, and the books and activities are scheduled out for an entire year. You can also order a very nice spiral-bound timeline for each child to keep forever, adding things as they're studied, and a laminated plain white map to draw on." Sandy also buys Sonlight's optional science kits that include all common items called for in experiments. "We have very limited shopping here," Sandy notes, "and our public library is almost smaller than my livingroom. In our situation of being in a very remote part of the world, Sonlight makes it possible to get the books and materials I need."

The family's homeschool schedule includes work on the Bible, reading, writing, arithmetic, and history every day. They also cover science experiments, *English From the Roots Up* (Latin and Greek root words), journal writing, composition, grammar, spelling, handwriting, math facts, *Alphabeterion* (the Greek alphabet), drills or games, art, and updating timelines on one or two days a week, alternating among these subjects. Saturdays are set aside for housework, review, listening to some classical music, and getting ready for the weekend. Because Kwajalein is across the international date line and Chuck's bosses want the island offices' schedules to overlap with workdays in the States, weekends are officially on Sundays and Mondays.

Besides basic language arts, history, science, math, and religion, Sandy and Chuck stress the importance of learning manners, sewing, woodworking, gardening, dish washing, laundry, infant care, bed making, cooking, mopping, and vacuuming, to name a few household chores. "Although I don't always practice what I preach, I believe in teaching the kids to work," Sandy says. "We get most of our chores finished in the morning, with Saturdays (Fridays in the States) set aside for heavier cleaning."

On weekdays, Chuck leaves very early for work, so Sandy leads a family Bible study around the breakfast table. The children go outside and play, if possible, sometime between 8:00 and 9:00 A.M. The older kids and Mom walk, with Charlie on his bike with training wheels and Gil in the stroller. Then the family stops at a playground to play with the toddlers. Back home, Kaitlin and Ryan start on their studies and try to accomplish as much as they can on their own, concentrating on math, phonics, or handwriting practice. "In the morning rush, I am usually fixing snacks and sippy cups, getting ready for lunch and supper, loading and unloading the washer and dryer, vacuuming up crumbs, and getting Charlie and Gil interested in playing with something," Sandy says.

To help handle her two- and three-year-old boys, Sandy keeps all the toys stored in tubs on shelves in the laundry room, behind gates and out of reach. "We have many different kinds of blocks and building toys, and I rotate them from day to day so Charlie and Gil don't get bored," Sandy says. "They can only have one toy tub at a time, and they have to pick up everything and put it back in the tub before I will go and get them another one. This has worked wonders, because they used to constantly pull out toys when I was busy with helping the older ones or working." Sandy has tubs for plastic animals, toy dishes and food, different kinds of blocks, musical instruments, train sets, lacing cards, puzzles, and more. "Sometimes I put the boys on the back patio, enclosed by a privacy fence, with homemade bubbles or Play Doh with all my cookie cutters," Sandy says. "I get ideas for activities for toddlers from *Slow and Steady, Get Me Ready* and other preschool play books."

Sandy tries to find time before lunch to work individually with Kaitlin and Ryan, checking math, introducing new concepts with math manipulatives, and/or teaching *Spelling Power* for fifteen minutes with each child. Sometime during the morning, Sandy often calls out passages of literature for Kaitlin to write down (dictation), assigns copying from a book for Ryan, and then checks the assignments. These techniques, plus narrating reading material (telling back, in a child's own words), are part of Charlotte Mason's philosophy of teaching, one that Sandy has found to be very effective.

Lunch break comes at 11:00 A.M. While the children run outside to play, Sandy prepares a meal and tries to handle all of her phone calls. "Right at noon, I put Gil down for a nap, and the house gets really quiet," Sandy says. "That gives me two to three hours of uninterrupted time to read to the kids and work with them on writing or projects." While Mom reads, Kaitlin and Ryan are usually sorting and folding laundry, then taking turns narrating, and Charlie often sits on Sandy's lap. Later, he plays independently, colors or paints, or completes a few pages in his "workbook."

Toddlers and babies are not a problem. "I just weaned little Gil, but nursing fits in with home educating," Sandy says. "When my babies were young and nursing more frequently, I just gathered the older kids around my comfortable chair and read or taught while I nursed. My older babies got too interested in what was going on to sit still and nurse, so I usually took breaks and went to a separate room with them. I would leave my oldest, Kaitlin, in charge when I spent time alone with the baby."

In the past, Sandy tried letting her younger ones watch public television or preschool videos during the times when she was working with the older children. "But I found this was not a good solution," she says. "It was a distraction to the older children when they were trying to work." TV viewing and video-game playing are limited to a few hours a week. And the family does occasionally watch quality videos, like those produced by Moody Science, or a movie once a month. "Chuck and I think TV wastes a lot of time and can do damage to children," Sandy says. "No one is allowed to sit and 'veg' in front of the TV or computer." The children use the computer mainly for *Mavis Beacon Typing*, *World Discover Geography*, the *World Book Encyclopedia*, and word processing.

Through the years, Sandy has learned the importance of plans and schedules. "But when unexpected things happen and plans change, I try to be calm and go with the flow," she says. "I now realize that I have to figure out my baby's schedule, and then figure out when I'm going to get everything else done. For two years I had been one of those people who fit all our studies between eight and eleven A.M. When baby number three came along, it nearly drove me crazy at first, until I learned to relax and work around Charlie's needs." Sandy also thinks it's important to turn on the answering machine, not picking up the phone or returning calls except during preappointed times of day.

Chuck is very involved in helping his wife, especially with homeschooling. "He fully participates in picking out our curriculum and books for us to read," Sandy says. "We always save our most exciting read-aloud book—one that goes along with our history studies—for Daddy to read to us at night. He leads worship and evening Bible reading, using the narration technique. The kids also narrate their day back to him, telling everything they've studied. This helps Chuck keep up with our history studies, and it helps me to see if the children were really listening and can relate the information in their own words."

Dad is in charge of P.E. "Chuck and the kids Rollerblade and swim for general fitness," Sandy says. "Kaitlin, Ryan, and their dad competed in a minitriathalon this year, with each of them taking a leg. I was supposed to do the walk/run with Ryan while I pushed Gil and Charlie in the stroller, but Gil woke up on the morning of the race with a 104-degree fever." Chuck also coaches or helps to coach the children's sports teams. He works with them on drills on nonpractice days, and attends golfing clinics with them.

On his days off, the children look forward to sharing other activities, like math, with their father. "He's also going to start working on the Keepers/Contenders of the Faith program on weekends," Sandy says. "That's a Christian scouting program where you earn badges for Bible memorization and various life skills. Keepers of the Faith is for girls, and Contenders for the

Faith is for boys. Also, as our sons mature, we plan to make them totally accountable to Chuck. He will leave a 'to-do' list for studies and chores, and I will be here mainly for reference for the boys."

Even with husband and wife cooperating, sometimes the family schedule can seem overwhelming. "Every year, when I start using the next year's material, I get very ambitious and make an overly idealistic schedule," Sandy says. "After a couple of weeks of driving myself crazy, we settle down to the reality of life." Sandy feels stretched at other times, too. "During the first couple of years, I experienced burnout at the end of the year," she says. "Now, homeschooling is such a part of our life that it is going on all the time, and there is never a sense of, 'I can't wait for the holiday!' We take breaks or half days for a few weeks to accommodate major household projects, traveling, sickness, or new babies."

Year-round schooling seems to work best for the family's "lifestyle of learning." "About every six weeks, we take a week off," Sandy says, "and that leaves us a one-month break sometime during the year, a week off at Thanksgiving, and a week off at Christmas. During our breaks, we're busy cleaning house, doing big messy projects, and taking extra trips to the beach." An ocean visit is a simple undertaking. "We just throw our beach toys, floats, and snorkel gear on the bikes and ride one minute to the beach, or walk," Sandy laughs. "During the public school year, we have the beach completely to ourselves during weekday mornings."

Kwajalein's homeschooling requirements are a little different from those of most states since the family is subject to whatever policy the base commander chooses to enact. Parents must sign an annual "release of liability" paper, stating that they will not hold local officials responsible for any injury or harm that may come to their children because they homeschool. They also turn in a mandatory yearly report to the superintendent, and the children are tested in grades three, six, eight and ten. "The tests are tedious," Sandy says, "and children are quizzed on the compartmentalized knowledge found in the scope and sequences and 'objectives' of public school. But our children have scored very well, and this keeps the grandparents and 'educrats' happy, since they think that good test scores are equivalent to a good education."

Island life has not interfered with the family's socialization in any way. "We don't do anything outside of normal everyday life to socialize our children," Sandy says. "If you live in a family with siblings, you have all the opportunities for socialization you need. If you can get along with family members, you can get along with anyone." Occasionally Sandy and some other homeschoolers collaborate for short-term teaching. "This year, I held a six-week, once-a-week class based on *Drawing With Children* by Mona Brooks while another mom, with two participating children and one toddler, watched our toddlers," Sandy says. "Next year, another mom and I will hold science experiment days. I love science, but since I've had more babies it has seemed like a chore to round up all the little doo-hickeys and make a mess. By having another family over, it will provide some accountability and keep me on track."

Back in the States, Kaitlin and Ryan were a part of music and choir classes for homeschoolers through the family's church, but that option is no longer available. They do enjoy being part of local, low-key, intramural sports teams on Kwajalein. Ryan has played basketball and baseball. Kaitlin has joined girls' baseball, basketball, and swim teams. Both have participated in junior golf clinics and tournaments.

Chuck and Sandy think of their current life-style as a modern-day *Little House on the Prairie*. "I have loved getting to know my children," Sandy says, "and I really do enjoy spending my days with them. I used to think all the fun ended when children stopped being babies and toddlers, but now I see that it's only the beginning." Both parents consider the high quality of family relationships as one of their successes.

But of course, no one's perfect. Sandy has at least one "hormonal" day a month when she feels discouraged. "I pray!" she says, "and talk to my husband. Chuck reminds me of all the reasons we do this." Sometimes she has regrets. "If I could do anything over, I would have spent more time learning real skills and studying the Bible, back before children, while I had time. I was prepared to be a feminist with a career. I wish I had been better prepared to become a better mother, household manager, and teacher." Sandy also wishes she had not been such a perfectionist when she started homeschooling. "Even though Kaitlin read early, I should have heeded a lot more of the Mooreses' advice and not been so hard on my oldest," she says.

Sandy likes to tell people, "Home-schooling is great for building character . . . in the *mother.*" She tries to remember this on days when she feels overwhelmed. "We're getting ready for vacation, and you ought to see what my house looks like this minute, with laundry, suitcases, and a floor that desperately needs vacuuming," she says with a sigh. "This is not always a good example of a well-organized homeschooling household." Sandy thinks "mothering is like the Peace Corps, the toughest job you'll ever love!' " Overall, she delights in being a mom and a homeschool teacher. "It's been a very good experience for us," she says. "We're praying that we get to help in our grandchildren's education some day."

Like their parents, Kaitlin and Ryan "really like homeschooling," Sandy says. (Charlie and toddler Gil are too young to comment.) "They like the fact that we can discuss God openly in our studies and enjoy good books written from a Christian perspective. They also enjoy the freedom and flexibility of our schedule and our family's togetherness. When people suggest that they might enjoy going to school, they protest loudly."

Perhaps Kaitlin, Ryan, Charlie, and even Gil appreciate homeschooling most when they're romping at the beach on a day while other island kids are at school. The three oldest especially love to snorkel in the lagoon. "There are lots of little fish near the beach," Sandy says, "especially the territorial triggerfish. When Chuck wanted to catch one for our tank, one of them swam up from behind and nipped him on the foot." Another time, when Chuck and Ryan went to another island to go snorkeling, Ryan was thrilled to glimpse a four-foot-long white-tip shark. "That's not my idea of fun," Sandy says. "I like to go walking on the coral when the tide is low, looking for interesting shells."

Chuck and Sandy don't think of their island life as always glamorous. "Getting to travel and live on a tropical island sounds idyllic," Sandy says. "However, as nice as the beach is, living here is not without hardships and a certain amount of unsettled feelings." The family realizes that they have a unique opportunity, Sandy says, "and we appreciate the experience the kids have had with a foreign culture and with a different life-style. But we look forward to settling down again in our own place in the States, out in the country, with critters and a big garden. I think the old saying is true: 'Go not abroad for happiness, for a rose blooms at your front door.' "

Randy, Emma, and Linda

Seven

A Life-style of Freedom and Holism

Family:
Linda (39), Randy (44), Emma (12).

Location:
Chaplin, Connecticut, a town of 1,200.

Best advice:
Relax! Everything always works out.

Worst advice:
Children regularly need to be in social groups of their peers.

Favorite quote:
"Imagination is more important than knowledge." (Albert Einstein)

Favorite books and resources:
Everyday Blessings by Myla and Jon Kabat Zinn, Hyperion.

The Teenage Liberation Handbook by Grace Llewellyn, Lowry
   House Publishing.
Family Matters by David Guterson, Harvest Books.
Thich Nhat Hanh's writings.
Anything by John Holt.

Linda, Randy, and Emma W. have made their own declaration of independence. "Freedom has always been very important to us," Linda says, "because both Randy and I had
parents who encouraged us to pursue our passions. We wanted to
continue living in this way, and it was natural to extend that freedom to parenting and unschooling."

   Holism is also an important part of the family's life-style.
Linda is licensed both as a registered nurse and a massage therapist, and is also a Reiki Master who teaches the ancient healing
art. "I spend my time studying holistic healing, spirituality,
sustainable living practices, organic gardening, and holistic
community-building," she says. "My dream is to create a holistic
living center for people to pursue sustainable living practices as
well as alternative holistic healing, a place for all ages. We would
hold workshops on alternative building, biodynamic gardening,
alternative healing, drumming circles, and community-building
events. Of course, there would be lots of celebrations, merry-
making, and music!"

   Randy holds a degree in sociology. He worked with at-risk
young people in youth services for several years, and has also developed outdoor challenge programs for youth and teens that have included twenty-one-day outdoor adventure programs. Currently he
is self-employed as a woodworker and carpenter with a special interest in the restoration of old houses. "Randy is considering pursuing violin making," Linda says, "and he plays guitar and sings, fixes
our cars, recycles everything, canoes, digs a mean double-dug garden bed, and would help you if you ever asked for it."

Linda, Randy, and their daughter together decided to un-school, "a continuation of a holistic life-style," Linda says. "Emma, chose unschooling as the best option, and we wanted to support her in that choice. Both Randy and I have learned important skills outside of a school setting, and we know that learning and the desire to learn does not have to take place inside a school building all day."

On a typical morning, Randy and Linda are up around 6:00 A.M. Randy does whatever needs to be done—including hauling in wood for the woodstove on winter days—and leaves for work. Linda logs on to the computer, catches up on mail, and does research on topics of interest. She is also involved with e-mail lists that provide support and information. And she spends time gardening, sewing, reading, playing recorder, cooking, driving Emma where needed, and studying.

Emma awakens around 7:30 A.M. Depending on the day, she may be leaving for one of a number of classes in painting, riding, pottery, violin, sailing, and/or ice-skating. She is also on a competitive youth gongfu (the correct way of saying kungfu) team at the Shaolin Wushu Center, taking seven classes a week. In between classes, Emma writes, studies, e-mails friends, keeps a journal, paints, reads, and plays. "We have the Saxon math books, and Randy does math with Emma," Linda says. "We also make use of lots of books, resources, the Internet, the library, and friends. Emma owns an Oak Meadow curriculum that she likes to use as a resource. We cover every subject, but not in a traditional way."

Instead of using reading workbooks or curricula, Emma taught herself to read. "We have always read to her," Linda says. "Language was something she's been interested in from the very beginning, the sounds of words, the music of words. As a younger child, she would tell ongoing stories for months and months. We have some beautiful wooden figures from Germany that have been one of her most treasured possessions. She has told stories with them since she was old enough to form sentences. I think these stories were very significant in her ability to decide to read on her own." Emma started to sound out words at an early age and was reading by the time she was six.

Emma also learned to spell in a very relaxed way, by reading and asking questions or looking up words in the dictionary. "We didn't spend endless hours on quizzing and drilling ways to learn how to spell," Linda says, "and one day, our daughter just knew how to spell, if you believe it. Of course, she is continuing to perfect her spelling, but has fewer and fewer mistakes and questions. Think of the time she's saved doing repetitive tasks by learning to spell on her own. What is perhaps more significant is that she knows she can learn and teach herself anything that she wants or needs to know."

Free to pursue what interests her, Emma enjoys immersing herself in certain subjects. When studying Africa, for example, she made both a kalabash and clay beads, read folk stories and wrote her own story, looked at maps, and researched whatever interested her. "Our days never seem to be typical, and involve a lot of different creative endeavors," Linda says.

Emma uses the Internet for research, writing, and staying in touch with friends and other unschoolers. The family didn't own a TV until Emma was ten years old, and only recently bought their own PC. "I think the imaginative life that Emma was allowed as a young child enables her to handle technology without it consuming her," Linda says. "I don't think it is physically healthy to sit in front of the TV or a computer all day. Your mind can't think for itself, and TV becomes an addiction." Instead, much "schooling" happens because of a very active schedule.

Dance has been a major activity since Emma was three years old. She took dance classes from a Belgium-born teacher for several years, then enrolled in the Hartford School of Ballet's pre-

professional program. "All that intense training in ballet, character, pointe, and creative movement shaped Emma in a way that I
believe will always be with her," Linda says. "She was eight when
she began classes at the Hartford School of Ballet and left just
one year ago after a final performance of *The Nutcracker.* Her
training was excellent and she excelled as a ballet dancer."

The family came to realize that the ballet world is not exactly
a nurturing and holistic place, though there were many benefits.
"Emma *did* learn commitment, discipline, working through pain,
and coming to class and rehearsal even if she didn't feel like it.
She learned to work with great masters of ballet from Russia to
Italy, but she had to forgo many events with other friends due to
the time commitment."

The last semester Emma was at the Hartford School of Ballet,
she enrolled in a gongfu class for homeschoolers. Linda, Randy,
and Emma were all taken with the teacher, Master Hu Jian
Qiang, a Chinese national champion and gongfu film star from
China. "Emma was so impressed with Master Hu's character as
well as his skill, she decided to leave the ballet school and pursue
martial arts," Linda says. "She is now on the youth competitive
wushu team that trains for performance and competitions. Last
year in Baltimore, Maryland, at the International Kungfu Wushu
Competition, Emma won two gold medals, one for a group form
and one for a solo eagle form." She also has traveled twice to
China with the school on a cultural exchange and tour of the
country. "Right now, gongfu takes up a large portion of her life,"
Linda says.

When investigating classes for their daughter, Linda and
Randy look for teachers who do more than teach. Emma's violin
instructor of six years, for example, is a classical violinist who also
plays in a rock-and-roll band. Pottery classes are taken with a
woman who is a professional potter, right in her studio, where
students can watch the entire process taking place. Emma's wa-

tercolor painting teacher is also an artist, making her living by painting. "The opportunity to work with artists teaches Emma about the realities of the world," Linda says. "It is not something removed to a classroom."

In addition to arts-oriented courses, Emma currently takes horseback riding lessons and innovative sailing classes at Mystic Seaport. She also has been involved, through the years, in a staggering number of activities: museum education classes at Old Sturbridge Village, drumming circles, theater, library events, contra dancing, folk festivals, performances of theater, dance, and music, museum visits, canoeing, hiking, homeschool gatherings, and specific lectures on interesting topics. For now, her main interest is in archaeology. "We are in touch with someone nearby who is involved in an archaeological dig with the Mohegan Tribe," Linda says, "and it is a possibility for Emma to participate on the dig as a volunteer."

Even a very casual observer can see that there's no problem with socialization here. "We are out in the world all day long, in classes as well as having friends over," Linda says. "To the mainstream culture, socialized means 'fitting in,' being the same, hanging out with the same age mates all day long. We 'socialize' wherever we go."

Instead, Randy and Linda try to expose their daughter to people from all walks of life. "It is important for Emma to be learning that everyone is valuable: the local farmer, the old man down the road who sits and waves as we go by, the professor, the artist, the master, the little child . . . whatever that person chooses as a life path," Linda says. "We live in an area where there are two major universities with a pretty large population of college students and professors. We also live in a rather poor town. So we see both sides of the spectrum. We drive to the local food co-op in an economically depressed area. 'Why do we get to buy organic food and there are people walking down the street without coats on?' Tough questions, but being out in the world we can talk about them, and maybe decide what we can do to help or participate to improve things."

"Our daughter is with many different ages of people all day long, and she gets along with them," Linda continues. "It wouldn't occur to her to leave someone out because they are younger or different. I see school-socialized kids do that all the time. I would ask these people who are worried about socialization, 'How kind is a child? Can he speak with adults, does he include others, is he interested in all sorts of people and situations?' If people can answer yes to these questions, then perhaps the child is well socialized. But I would bet it had to do with his or her parents and not the fact of being in a school all day long."

Emma has close contacts with her parents as well as with teachers and friends. Randy is not home as often as Linda is. But since he is self-employed, he is often available to bring Emma to outside classes and take a day off to be with the family. "When Emma was younger, Randy took her to work with him a few days a week," Linda says. "Because of this, they have an incredibly close bond." Randy reads to Emma every night and has done so since babyhood. He's given his daughter guitar lessons, gone to rallies with her for homeschooling and home-birth advocacy, talked about all sorts of important issues, built a tree house with her, done gardening, gone for hikes, and ridden his bike with her.

Since Randy and Linda are involved in politics, Emma grew up with it, too. "Randy always took Emma to meetings of the little town where we live," Linda recalls. Emma attended inland wetland meetings and conservation commission meetings with her dad, and when wetland site walks were scheduled, father and daughter would go, too. "Emma thought it was fun to sit and color, or look at books, while a meeting was going on," Linda says. "Then one day, she'd ask some question about what she heard at a meeting, even though she'd looked as though she wasn't paying any attention. The questions became more detailed and inquisitive as she got older."

Connecticut, where Randy, Linda, and Emma live, suggests each homeschooling family file a letter of intent with the superintendent's office, which may in turn request a portfolio. "We don't file the letter of intent," Linda says. "What we provide for Emma in the way of education cannot be matched by our local school district, so therefore we feel that we don't need to go through the formality of filing and presenting a portfolio."

The family is also opposed to testing. "A standardized test only tests material that a school has covered," Linda notes. "Let's face it, all schools teach to the test. What a waste of time for these children. If schools want to do that, they should just send kids home with the information, then have them come back and take the test once they've memorized it." Linda thinks testing doesn't measure whether or not a person can think. "It measures whether or not one can take a test," she says. "Plus, what does a test tell you? That the teacher taught the child the right material. This whole testing mentality needs to be reevaluated. Do students know how to build a house, sew their own clothes, grow a garden, care for another person?"

Testing also implies that a set curriculum must be taught. "There is so much to learn, I don't see how any school can pick a curriculum and say 'This is what you need to know.' That standardization drives me crazy. Why must we all fit into little boxes where everyone has to know the same things? If this were the case, where would the writers, poets, artists, musicians, storytellers, dancers, naturalists fit?" Instead, Linda and Randy think one's life should be devoted to areas in which one excels. "If everyone did this, can you imagine the joy and happiness that would radiate from this planet?" Linda asks.

Linda is well aware of how different their life choices are from others. "I would say that the difficult part of unschooling comes from the fact that most of the rest of the world is in school," Linda says. "People everywhere are following the same general plan of nursery school, school, college, jobs. It is always surprising to me, that they don't believe that they have any other choices. I would like for Emma to have grown up with many more unschooled children, because when you choose to unschool your outlook is very different from the rest of the population. It's tough to find families who share a similar philosophy of life and child-rearing who also have kids the same age."

Since the family has only one income, finances can be a challenge. "I sometimes question whether we're doing the right thing, with me not working for pay," Linda says. "I deal with it by talking with other homeschool friends and my husband. They always remind me that we're doing a great job and this will all work out. Still, I would like to be able to share in bringing in more money."

There's also the problem of finding time to do household chores. "This isn't always the easiest thing for me," Linda says. "Our day is broken up a lot with going to outside activities, so it's easy to get sidetracked. Emma is more diligent about getting house stuff done than I am."

Every September, Linda finds it challenging to avoid being caught up in the frenzy of school preparations. "I sometimes envy the fact that people have their lives tied up in neat little packages in regard to education for their children. But when autumn leaves start to change here in New England, and we go to the pond and marvel at the beauty, I realize all the children inside those brick buildings are missing this. I am grateful to be able to live this unschooled choice along with my daughter. It's a chance for me to share in something unimaginable to always schooled people. It's like having another chance at a childhood, yet living this one with your eyes wide open."

Randy and Linda are fortunate to have two sets of extended

family members who wholeheartedly endorse their unschooling decision. In addition, "most of our close friends homeschool," Linda says, "so naturally they support what we're doing. I think when you choose to do something different from the mainstream, it's helpful to have a good support system. I feel that we have that. I need it, because when we began unschooling, I didn't anticipate Randy being away from home as much as he is. In an ideal life he would be home and share more, both work and play."

Both parents are dedicated to helping their daughter continue to have a keen interest in life. "One of our goals is to help Emma be true to herself," Linda says, "not to follow the herd. The gift we're giving our daughter is to be able to take eighteen years of her life, at the beginning, and really discover who she is, what she's good at, and what it means to be a good person. We're giving Emma the space to pursue many interests, and to reflect on who she is and where she wants to go in her life."

This doesn't mean Emma is allowed to slack off. "Freedom is a simple concept, but an everyday challenge," Linda says. "Choosing freedom means making difficult choices. You can decide to pursue personal interests, but how do you structure your time, your day? A path of freedom requires a great amount of responsibility." Linda believes that freedom does *not* mean that you do whatever you feel like doing at a given moment. "Perhaps you're in a competition or a performance. This requires hard work, rehearsals, time, and commitment," she says. "You make a decision to participate, and then you give it your very best. It is an internal motivation. It isn't imposed from the outside by external rewards. We take the things we're involved in very seriously. If Emma is in a class, she is prepared, gets there on time, and works hard."

Achieving a life-style of holism and freedom has been an ongoing journey for the entire family, Linda observes. "You never arrive!" she says. "When you decide to unschool you are in many ways making a very radical political statement and choice. You are choosing to ignore what most people claim to value and uphold and saying, 'It doesn't matter what you are doing. I am over here following this path, one of freedom.' It takes a lot of courage to unschool, to dance to the music in your heart. I think the real value in unschooling is providing a space for viewing the world that is unique to the individual. If more people who claim the value of holism had the courage to unschool, perhaps many more people could claim their talents and gifts and offer them up to the world, for all to share and find inspiration."

Front row: Rachel, Angie, Josiah. Back row: Jonathan, Lauren, Olivia, Michael.

Eight

Christian Americans of African Descent

Family:
Michael (35), Angie (36), Lauren (10), Jonathan (8), Olivia (6), Josiah (4), Rachel (2).

Location:
Florissant, Missouri (St. Louis suburb).

Best advice:
You have to find what works for your family, because you can't live off the strength of other people's convictions.

Worst advice:
Set up one room of your house as a schoolroom, and put all your kids' desks and materials in there, and the rest of your house will stay clean.

Favorite saying:
"Wear the old coat; buy the new book."

Favorite resources:

For the Children's Sake by Susan Schaeffer MacAulay, Crossway
    Books.

Veritas Press Books (a classical program), 1-800-922-5082.

Genevieve Foster's books; all of them.

World magazine, 1-800-951-6397.

Usborne books (representatives advertise in the yellow pages).

"I see myself as a Christian American of African descent, in
that order," Angie Y. says, "and I tend to look for those
qualities in others in that order, as well." Angie and her husband,
Michael, live with their five children in a north St. Louis suburb.
They have homeschooled for six years. "The homeschool movement is full of what I would call faithful Christians who love their
country, but to say the African-American population is underrep-
resented would be a serious understatement," Angie notes. "In
our previous homeschool group, we were almost always the only
African Americans at any activity. Where we live now, we may be
one of two or three."

Fortunately, Angie is used to interacting with people of different races, as she grew up in a nearly all-white school system before St. Louis's infamous desegregation program. Both Michael
and Angie also attended St. Louis's Washington University, a
prestigious school that's listed as one of *USA Today*'s top twenty
colleges and universities in the country. "I graduated from Wash
U. with a degree in business and a minor in French," she says. "I
formed some of my opinions about home education because of
my experiences there. It was very intense, and many students
could hardly keep up with the day-to-day course work. It seemed
like a race to the finish rather than an institution for higher
learning. But I did learn to manage my time! And I graduated
with a confidence that I could do anything."

Following graduation, Michael and Angie were married. She

worked full-time, first as a salesperson, then as an undergraduate recruiter and admissions counselor at Washington University. For several years, her job took her all over the country promoting the university to the nation's best students, and later evaluating their applications for admission.

Angie's eighth year of employment at Wash. U. was a difficult one. "I was pregnant with our third child, Olivia," Angie says. "And the Lord was making it clear to me that I needed to be home to raise my children. I remember asking a dear friend why God would place such a conviction upon my heart with no apparent means of carrying it out." At the time, Angie was making about 60 percent of the family's income, and with another baby coming, the couple needed the additional room of a new house. "To make a long story short, after much spiritual ranting and raving, we moved into St. Louis with all the stereotypical problems that plague life in the city: poverty, illiteracy, drug use, gangs, et cetera. It was the only place where we could afford a larger house. I quit my job, had a new baby, and started homeschooling in the same month."

At first it was an aversion to city schools that convinced Angie and Michael to homeschool. But as Angie studied more about educational methods and philosophies, it became obvious to her that the public school system at large was seriously flawed. "Those flaws were very apparent in my twenty-five-thousand-dollar-a-year university education, which left so little time for real learning," Angie says. "To find out more about my options, I spoke to friends at church, whose home-educated children I greatly admired. I read volumes on home-education, and familiarized myself with the homeschool networks in St. Louis. It became clear to me that this was a part of God's calling for our family."

Because of this sense of calling, Angie takes her role as a homeschool educator very seriously. "As an admissions counselor, I evaluated applications from students who attended high schools that were publicly lauded as being the best of the best," Angie recalls. "And I was all too frequently disappointed to find these students unable to write coherently, reason logically, or argue persuasively. Many had been so indoctrinated by their secondary institutions and their 'politically correct' curricula, they had no idea how to use primary sources in research or to form opinions apart from those of the herd."

As devout Christians, Angie and Michael have set three priorities for their own family's education. Their first and primary goal is to show their children, through every means possible, that God is at the center of all things. "We should live our lives to His glory," Angie says. "He has made us and all that we know: science, mathematics, art, music, and language. He has specifically guided the course of human history for His purposes and men do well to learn His Word and His ways . . . most importantly through a personal relationship with His Son, Jesus Christ." Angie and Michael are disturbed by "a sad dualism in much of even 'Christian' society today that teaches us that religion is for Sunday and the rest of the week really has nothing to do with God. As children of an awesome God, we cannot help but see His hand in every aspect of our lives. To ignore that presence is a dangerous denial of who we are and what life is about. That's why we focus on developing godly character and seeking God's will for each of our children."

Second, Angie and Michael hope, in their homeschool, "to feed the love for learning we believe God instills in every child," Angie says. "Typically this is squelched by too early and too tedious institutional schooling, and by methods that ignore individual gifts and needs. Learning is not something we do in a particular room at particular times. We do it all the time in both conventional and nonconventional ways, times, and places." For these reasons, Angie tries to pay close attention to learning styles and readiness. "Our first child, Lauren, was reading fifth-grade material in first grade. Our second, Jonathan, is reading second-grade material in first grade. If one comes along who is not ready for first-grade material until second grade, we will adjust accordingly."

The family's third goal for homeschooling is "to encourage the academic and personal excellence we see lacking even in many of our best academic institutions in this country," Angie says. "This means, for example, that the academic assignment is not done until the correct answers are deduced and understood. It means we acknowledge that there are many questions that have more than one answer. It means we read every book keeping in mind the author's background and perspective. It means there are no out-of-bounds questions. It also means Mom and Dad spend a lot of time in the encyclopedia and in prayer." Personal excellence is defined by the family, in part, by dressing modestly, speaking correctly, acting politely, and working diligently. "At least the children know those are our expectations." Angie grins. "We've got a lot of training yet to do."

When Angie began teaching at home, she was most focused on producing academic excellence. Testing was an important means of measuring that excellence. Lauren took her first Iowa Test of Basic Skills in 2000, scoring in the ninety-seventh percentile overall. "What a relief!" Angie says. "The children will take exams every year, once we're sure their reading skills are well developed, so they can become familiar with the requirements of standardized testing."

Angie has set up what she calls "a natural learning environment" in the family's home. "We have shelves filled with books in almost every room," she says, "and magazines and newspapers available, and lots of comfortable places to read. Susan Schaeffer Macaulay's book *For the Children's Sake* shaped much of my thinking on home-education. Hence, creating the 'natural learning environment,' encouraging observation and thinking skills, and tending the spiritual person will always be at the core of what we do."

Angie and Michael make it a point to carefully observe their children to determine what interests they have. "Lauren is linguistically oriented, like me," Angie notes. "She reads well and fast and likes to write. Last year she started a novel, a saga about *Animorphs*. She has also written three or four short stories, so I sometimes let her write one for credit instead of giving her the usual assignments."

Jonathan is the mechanical type, one who enjoys putting things together and taking them apart, so he's been provided with a tool set and plenty of hands-on activities with bugs and animals. Olivia is an actress and an artist. She keeps busy with supplies from a seven-foot cabinet in the basement filled with paper, paints, paper towel rolls, yarn, and other art materials. "While Josiah may be my timid little boy, it is clear that he has an uncanny appreciation for order and structure," Angie says. "Maybe he'll be a future architect . . . or a drill sergeant. And two-year-old Rachel makes trouble for everybody. When we discover the younger children's special interests, we will build upon them, as well."

Angie is not afraid to make adjustments if her approach or method isn't working. "We change curricula every year, adding or subtracting where appropriate," she says. "Usually we wait until the school year is completed, although a friend once loaned us *Hooked on Phonics* and we gave it back after the first tape." Lauren's personality and learning style make her a good prototype for the other children. "She's a great student, typically working hard and being cooperative and responsible," Angie says. "Once she's done something, I can then determine how it will work for Jonathan et al. These poor eldest children, always the experimental rats!"

A typical school day begins with Lauren checking her schedule and folder for the day's work. Since Lauren is a self-starter, she only consults Angie if she has a problem or needs additional resources. Around 9:00 A.M., Jonathan and Olivia begin Saxon Math while Angie gets the youngest children dressed and busy. At about 10:00, Lauren works on violin practice and language arts. Olivia is in charge of pick-up and clean-up while Jonathan practices penmanship; then Jonathan sweeps and Olivia works on penmanship. "Around eleven, I read with Jonathan while Olivia plays with Josiah and Rachel," Angie says. "Then I read with Olivia while Jonathan acts as baby-sitter. Lauren is usually working on science or history during this time. I try to have all the academics finished by lunch."

Afternoons include a time for the children's naps and resting, and Angie grades papers and makes phone calls. "I think it's important for the children to have a lot of free time in the afternoon," Angie says, "though Lauren does have to make corrections on anything she's missed before the nap time is over. I fix dinner and we all do some cleaning, like scrubbing stains out of the carpet, laundry, or emergency cleaning. Today I had to go outside in the rain and pull trash out of the gutters because water was pouring over the top of them." On many days, Angie and the children also run errands in late afternoon.

When Dad comes home, there's much cause for excitement. "My husband always seems to have jobs that keep him on long hours and odd schedules," Angie says. "Home-schooling allows us to sometimes stay up late to greet Daddy and still get our rest by sleeping in the next morning." At present, Michael is director of a start-up program called Cyber Community Center. He is in charge of encouraging disadvantaged people to learn how to use technology like computers, then partnering them with companies who need employees. In the past, he has worked not only with the United Way, but also the St. Louis Association for Retarded Citizens and the American Red Cross. "The kids all run to Michael the minute he's at the door," Angie says with a smile. "They have to show him new books, or the latest sewing project, or something else they've been doing. Chaos reigns, at least momentarily."

Though Michael doesn't usually teach, he plays an important part in their homeschool. "Dad's role largely consists of review, pop quizzes, rewards, special honors, and lectures on how lucky the kids are to be learning the things he was never taught," Angie says.

Dinner is a family affair, as Angie and Michael make it a high priority to eat together. Afterward there are a variety of activities, depending on the night of the week. Lauren, Jonathan, and Olivia play soccer through a homeschool co-op on Monday nights. Tuesday nights are reserved for cleaning and major laundry duties, when all clean clothes are taken out of baskets and put into drawers. Wednesday nights the family attends church Bible study, where there's a play and discussion time for children. Thursdays there's Pioneer Club at a different church, a co-op where parents help guide children of all ages through various projects, similar to scouting programs.

The weekends are also full. "Friday nights are our play nights," Angie says. "We occasionally hang around the house and watch TV, go out to eat, or socialize in some way. There's also a fellowship at our church, and we usually go to that." On Saturdays, the family may share a special activity, go someplace with Dad, catch up on yard work, or simply prepare for church services the next day. Some Sundays, the family spends the entire day at church, or they may stay for the morning only. Much of their life centers around their church. "We are very active," says Angie. "My husband is a deacon and I am church librarian and an alternate Sunday school teacher."

On Monday mornings, academic study begins anew. Angie has chosen her curriculum carefully. In language arts, for example, "We learn reading through phonics, mostly Phyllis Schlafly's *First Reader* and *Bob Books*, with a little Dr. Seuss sprinkled in," Angie says. For grammar lessons, Angie likes *Shurley Grammar*, beginning in second grade and used intermittently. "We start the book a year late and skip every other year," she says. "The repetition needed in the classroom only bores us." Rather than using traditional handwriting workbooks, Angie assigns copy work related to current Bible study or other schoolwork.

Science lessons center around Usborne books, experiments, frequent nature walks, gardening, and trips to the zoo. "My daughter Lauren, who does not like science, enjoyed the expeditious treatment of topics and the format in *LifePacs*," Angie says. "These are individual books, fifty pages each, on topics like the solar system, the human body, or electricity, where a student reads and answers questions, moving at her own pace. Jonathan would never tolerate just *reading* about bugs." To accommodate her hands-on boy, Angie checks out activity boxes from a nearby nature center or the St. Louis public library. "Inside one activity box on trees was a poster, a game called Into the Forest, cross sections of real tree rings, activity books, and samples of leaves, twigs, nuts, and cones," she says. "Jonathan likes all that kind of stuff. This year we're going to keep journals on trees and flowers and learn to press and preserve specimens."

Toward the end of each week, the children work on foreign language study and art together. "Even though I had a French minor in college," Angie says, "we're all learning *Power-Glide Spanish* together. We're also going through *Drawing with Children* by Mona Brooks. My husband was a history major and my forte is in business marketing, so art does not come naturally to either one of us, nor to some of our children. We have learned that artistic endeavors are enough to bring a perfectionist like Lauren to tears."

Music instruction is handled through a Thursday morning homeschool cooperative. "The musically talented moms teach, and the rest of us watch the babies, sew costumes, provide snacks, and do whatever else is needed," Angie says. Lauren, Jonathan, Olivia, and Josiah are all part of various choirs, joining over 150 other children. In addition, Lauren plays violin in a string ensemble, Jonathan plays recorder, and Olivia participates in an elementary music-theory class. Handbells, guitar, and orchestra are also available through the co-op.

To learn social studies, the younger children listen to history read-alouds or dramatizations or watch videos. "With Lauren, we have settled upon a classical history program from Greenleaf Press, a sequential study of the Old Testament, Egypt, Greece, Rome, and the Middle Ages," Angie says. "We begin the Renaissance and Reformation time periods next year." So far the family has taken a year to cover each major civilization. "When we studied Greece, we acted out Greek mythology with role playing: I was Hera and Michael was Zeus," Angie laughs. Study of Egypt involved reading *The Golden Goblet* and other historical fiction, making a model of the Nile River out of sand and salt, and constructing a pharoah's double crown, crook, and flail. "But mainly we read, read, read," Angie says. "We also talk to our kids more than we know most parents do. We discuss *everything.*"

To supplement schoolwork, the children watch relevant videos, "mostly on subjects like community helpers, fire and bike safety, and so on," Angie says. "And we also enjoy *National Geographic* programs." Lauren uses the computer for research and practical skills using the "Encarta Encyclopedia" and the Internet, and e-mails family and friends. Angie makes it a point to sit right beside her while she's online. The younger children are allowed to play some educational games on the computer.

The family homeschools year round, from July through June. "We take breaks for holidays, birthdays, and other special events as we need them," Angie says. "We can do a road trip this Wednesday and schoolwork on Saturday. We can go visit Nanna and Grandaddy in April and continue on with school through June. The long calendar is what allows us to finish the formal work by noon most school days."

With afternoons and evenings free of structured academics, there is plenty of time for socialization. "Our children interact with adults respectfully and easily," Angie notes. "Sometimes a little too easily. I had to have a talk with Jonathan once when he approached a man who appeared to be homeless in a south city park. He asked the man, 'What are you doing, fishing there? Can we fish, too? Do you know you're not supposed to be fishing here? What's in your bag?' "

On another occasion, the family had an interesting experience on a city bus ride. "I was struggling with the stroller," Angie says, "and I told the older children to sit where they could see enough seats together. Before I could stop them, they went straight to the back of bus. The local high school had just let out and there was a strong smell of pot. Lauren asked, loudly, 'What is that smell?' and subsequently leaned over to a guy who looked like a real thug. She asked him, 'Do you think you could open a window? There's a really bad smell in here.' My children know no strangers."

The children make contact with their extended family whenever they can, but both Michael's and Angie's parents live out of state. All four grandparents appreciate homeschooling now, but "my family and friends were wary of homeschooling at first, having no experience with it," Angie says. "Michael's parents are very laid-back. They told us, 'Just don't end up in jail and embarrass us all.' My parents were pretty vocal. But when they saw the 'proof in the puddin',' so to speak, they became very supportive."

From social skills to academic excellence, homeschooling has been a wonderful experience for the family "in every way except one," says Angie. "I am tired all the time! Also, my house is always messy, even though the children do have chores." Lauren washes dishes and cleans the counter and the table after meals, Jonathan sweeps, Olivia picks up the house, and Josiah acts as Mom's go-fer. Dad helps out, too. "But if our resources were unlimited, I'd get a housekeeper and an au pair," Angie says. "I love *teaching*."

Learning together, working together, and playing together has encouraged family friendships. "One pleasant surprise for me has been the experience of seeing us all become so close," Angie observes. "Unfortunately, the way my children value my company and my opinion is something rather foreign to many families these days. We live as a team, with each member making contributions appropriate to his or her age and gifts. So we have a true sense of needing each other." This is one of many reasons why Angie and Michael intend to homeschool "until we feel like we are holding the children back due to limited knowledge or resources."

Lauren, Jonathan, Olivia, Josiah, and Rachel enjoy homeschooling. "Our children like the fact that when we go to the zoo or art museum, there are no lines," Angie says. "They like taking off class for that one eighty-degree day in February or for their personal birthdays. After this past year of public school violence in the media, they seem to be less curious about schools. But they're still lobbying for parent/teacher conference days."

Wherever they go, whatever they do, Angie and Michael make it a point to teach the children about their African heritage and expose them to the culture. "Our church, a fairly traditional black church, plus our school, family, and neighbors are all an intricate part of our lives, and we rely upon them for things culturally unique," Angie says. "Every now and then, it's good to retreat to the music, foods, and family we grew up with. We want to be sure to pass on to our children a high regard for the unique traditions of African Americans and the worthy individuals who helped to forge those traditions."

Like any black person in America, Angie has experienced both racial discrimination and acceptance. "I notice when someone snubs me at a particular event, and that has happened. But it has also happened that people have said to me that they are glad they know us, because they don't want their white children to grow up with only white friends." Angie and Michael share a similar conviction. "We work to expose our children to various races, religions, and points of view, and since we won't find much of that diversity in our homeschool group, we go elsewhere. We attend cultural events around the city, we listen to National Public Radio, we talk to people in the park and at the store and at the library and at the zoo. We talk ad nauseum."

Angie strongly encourages other African-American families to consider homeschooling. "I want *everyone* to know: You *can* do this," Angie says, emphatically. "You *probably should* do this." The couple views homeschooling as a very positive life-style for African-American parents. "It saddens me to recognize that even though our black children are least served in public schools, we are less inclined to take charge of that schooling ourselves," she says. "I think that has a lot to do with a general reliance upon 'the system,' as well as a lack of confidence in our own abilities. Let's face it, my academic accomplishments have, in part, given me the confidence to choose this course. I can imagine the mental hurdle many parents who have little confidence in their own schooling have to overcome. Also, others who have spent years trying to get into the 'right schools' aren't easily led to see that the object of their desire is not working in their best interest. For years we have heard, 'Education is the key to success. Do well in school and you'll go far.' And that slogan didn't include homeschooling. Home-schooling is what many black people did before they let us into 'real' schools."

Michael and Angie believe it's critical that this generation of American children are raised and taught well. "Home-schooling is an effective way to undo a significant amount of damage that's happened to our culture in the last hundred years," she says, "to knit our families together again, to reestablish learning as a life-long exercise, and to steep children in the Word and ways of God. For the nation, this change is critical. For African Americans, it is imperative!"

Clockwise from top: Susan, Daniel, Linda, Scott.

Nine

Accelerated Learning

Family:
Steve (41), Janice (40), Susan (16), Daniel (12), Linda (9), Scott (5).

Location:
Columbia, South Carolina.

Best advice:
You don't have to do every single problem in the books. Tailor schoolwork to your child, based on your knowledge of your child.

Worst advice:
Your children need *more* socialization and activities.

Favorite quote:
"He gives strength to the weary and increases the power of the weak. Even youths grow tired and weary, and young men stumble and fall; but those who hope in the Lord will renew their strength. They will soar on wings like eagles; they will run and not grow weary; they will walk and not be faint." (Isaiah 40:29-31, the Bible).

Favorite resources:

A Survivor's Guide to Homeschooling by Luanne Shackelford and Susan White, Crossway Books.

More Hours in My Day by Emilie Barnes, Harvest House Publishers.

Crowned With Silver magazine, P.O. Box 6338, Longmont, CO 80501.

No Greater Joy (bimonthly) newsletter by Michael and Debi Pearl, the Church at Cane Creek, 1000 Pearl Rd., Pleasantville, TN 37033.

To Train Up a Child by Michael and Debi Pearl, ibid.

Janice and Steve S. never planned to homeschool any of their children. And they certainly couldn't have imagined, several years ago, that their oldest daughter, Susan, would graduate from high school at the age of fifteen and enroll in college at sixteen.

The adventure began during Susan's first year of public school, shortly after her fifth birthday. "She was enrolled in an all-day kindergarten, and I wasn't pleased with that," Janice recalls. "Susan got on the bus at seven-thirty A.M. and didn't get home until four P.M. By that time she couldn't seem to remember what she had done during the school day." Janice was also concerned about Susan being held back; though her daughter knew the alphabet thoroughly and was anxious to start reading, the teacher spent three months on the letters A through J.

Janice spoke with a mother who was homeschooling and became convinced that she wanted to try, too. Steve was not as sure, having hoped that Susan could have a positive influence in her school. Still, the decision was made to homeschool, and Susan left her kindergarten class at the beginning of Christmas break. A friend loaned the family A Beka phonics reading material. "Susan caught on very quickly," Janice says. "She had no trouble learning to read or to solve math problems."

At the time, the family was living in Charlottesville, Virginia. Daniel was a baby. "Right from the start, I believed that educating my children was one of my responsibilities as a mother," Janice says. "One of my top priorities was always to teach them to enjoy reading. Once a child can read well, he can learn just about anything he wants to or needs to from books." Steve and Janice also place a high priority on character training. "In our home-school situation, there's an opportunity to learn self-discipline, patience, obedience, kindness, and putting others first," Janice says. "These are some of the character traits we've worked on through the years."

At first Janice intended to homeschool for just one year. But as a devout Christian, "more and more I realized how important it was for Susan to be well grounded in her faith before she was under someone else's influence for eight hours a day," Janice says. "Now the reason I homeschool is so I can control how and what my children are taught, because it's my God-given responsibility to do so."

Home-schooling Susan in the elementary years went very well. "She was always willing to do her work," Janice remembers. "She seemed to enjoy it, and she sat down and did it, even when she was very young. She has always had an almost-photographic memory and memorizes things very easily." Janice used A Beka materials for most of her daughter's early course work.

When Susan was twelve years old and in sixth grade, she and her mother attended an A Beka book fair. Susan had the opportunity to watch a promotional video about Pensacola Christian College, the publisher of A Beka materials. "Susan was so impressed with the school that she decided then and there that that's where she wanted to go to college," Janice says. "And she decided she wanted to start when she was sixteen."

Janice had reservations about this idea, but took Susan seriously and agreed to help her accelerate through high school.

"My daughter has always been driven to succeed," Janice says. "She always liked to be the best speller, the fastest at math. She likes competition. We were close, but she still wanted her independence."

Mother and daughter began to map out a plan to attain the goal of a high school graduation at the age of fifteen. Since Susan was an avid reader, she was very skilled in English and grammar and seemed to naturally absorb what she needed to know. "She basically skipped seventh grade," Janice says, "including grammar, spelling, and seventh-grade math. When she took a standardized achievement test at the end of eighth grade, she scored in the ninety-seventh percentile and above."

To stay on schedule, Susan needed to get another year ahead and complete high school in three years instead of four. Janice checked with Pensacola Christian College to learn more about their admissions requirements. For a major in speech communications, Susan's interest at the time, she needed four years of English, two years of math, two years of foreign language, two years of science, and two years of history as the minimum requirements.

Susan found the English requirements easy to fulfill, as she had read all the classics and still enjoys perusing weighty literature, such as Shakespeare's plays, just for fun. For science, she completed a ninth-grade Bob Jones general science book and a tenth-grade A Beka biology course, complete with an intense six-week lab taught by a local teacher. *Power-Glide French* helped her meet the foreign language requirement. Susan's history courses included geography, government, American history, and world history.

One main concern was math. "We left A Beka math, and that was the biggest mistake I ever made," Janice says. "I had heard Saxon had the best algebra book, but Susan had a hard time with it. I hate math and I imparted that attitude to my daughter! She didn't try very hard, and even with a tutor for algebra, she barely got through it." Susan finished geometry in the *Key To* series. The only C on her transcript was from a math course, Algebra I.

In the spring of 2000, Susan graduated from homeschool high school and moved that summer to PCC in Pensacola, Florida. The entire family had moved the summer before from Virginia to a suburb of Columbia, South Carolina. "By the time Susan left for college, we were living in a metro area of a half million," Janice says, "in a medium-sized house with a small yard. We miss our old home in a rural area with four and a half acres of land."

Steve is now a computer programmer at Columbia International University, a Bible college and seminary. Steve takes one post-graduate course each semester "in order to help me understand and apply the Bible," he says, "and to be prepared for future Christian service."

In homeschool work, Steve sometimes conducts science experiments with the children and tutors math. "He helps in many ways," Janice says. "One way is, if I say, 'This just isn't working,' he'll ask, 'Why don't you do it this way?' He's a real problem-solver." In his rare free time, Steve loves to golf. He makes his own clubs and has even built equipment to help him analyze and adjust them.

Daniel is is an avid computer player, not only a game master but also skilled in installing and configuring programs. He produces a small newspaper that he sends to friends in Virginia. He enjoys sports, especially a game of basketball with Dad, skateboarding, and reading. Daniel, like his older sister, finds memorizing easy and learns well in school.

Two other children, Linda and Scott, have joined the family since Susan began kindergarten many years earlier. "Although Linda is a very bright child, it has been a challenge to figure out what books and teaching methods work best for her," Janice notes. Linda plays violin and piano and enjoys reading, gymnastics, and craft projects. "I started teaching Scott a few months ago and he is already reading," Janice says.

"He seems to be a lot like Susan, picking things up very, very quickly." Scott likes to sing and does so whenever and wherever he can.

While Susan is busy at college, 550 miles away, Janice, Daniel, Linda, and Scott are occupied at home with school. On Sunday nights, Janice plans the lessons for the week and writes them down in each child's assignment book.

Most school days, Daniel gets up at 7:00 A.M. and starts his work. He has his own Bible study and prayer time, and then tackles Saxon math, which takes about an hour.

Linda sometimes gets up early, too, and completes an easy assignment such as spelling or penmanship. If Scott is awake at that time, he watches a video from a series such as *Veggie Tales* or *Adventures in Odyssey*. Janice sleeps in until around 8:00 A.M. as she often stays up until midnight the night before; she begins her day with personal devotions. Breakfast is scheduled for 8:30, with morning cleanup finished by 9:30.

The official school day begins with group prayer and a Bible study from *Character Builders* by Ron and Rebecca Coriell. Then comes daily science class: Janice reads from a sixth-grade textbook, often followed by experiments. Daniel is expected to do more than Linda, something appropriate for his grade level. Scott usually chooses to stay and listen.

The next subject on the roster is English. Linda is working through *Easy Grammar* (and Janice thinks it's *too* easy, though it has worked well for Linda). Daniel is in an A Beka English book, which includes composition assignments. Both Daniel and Linda also have assignments in A Beka spelling books and the *A Reason for Writing* penmanship course.

While Daniel and Linda are completing their English lessons, Mom spends time with Scott. Janice is teaching kindergarten skills with an A Beka preschool numbers/phonics book, preschool workbooks (available at stores like Wal-Mart), *Teach Your*

Child to Read in 100 Easy Lessons by Engelmann, Haddox, and Bruner, and A Beka's kindergarten reading program.

If school has gone smoothly, around 11:00 A.M. Daniel plays with Scott while Janice works with Linda in Saxon 54. "We tried A Beka math, but the workbook is very colorful, laid out in such a way that it's hard for Linda to focus on one thing at a time," Janice says. "To help her concentrate, I had to tape paper over sections she wasn't doing. Saxon is boring, black and white, and that works well." If Daniel needs math help after Janice finishes with her daughter, Linda takes a turn playing with Scott.

Lunch is scheduled around noon regardless of how many subjects have been covered that morning. Daniel washes the breakfast dishes every day, usually right before lunch. Everyone helps to set the table, and Linda and Daniel make their own sandwiches.

When time allows, history and geography lessons are covered before lunch, and if not, afterward. "Last year I did something like unit studies with history and science," Janice says. "We picked topics that interested us, then went to the library and got books on those topics for each child's grade level. We spent a long time on the human body, at least two months. We traced Scott's body onto a big piece of paper and drew and labeled body parts as we went." Janice uses A Beka's third-grade textbook, *Our American Heritage*, as a starting point for history lessons, and supplements with library books and *Geography Songs* cassette tapes.

In addition to cassettes, the family also enjoys videos such as those produced by Bill Nye and Eye Witness, and educational computer games such as "Where in the World Is Carmen Sandiego?", "GeoSafari," and "Math Blaster." They often use the computer for research on the Internet.

Janice likes to finish schoolwork by 1:30 P.M. at the latest. "If the kids have played around and not done their work, they may have homework," she says. "Whenever they dillydally they have to do extra work." Janice admits that she started out "rigid" in her school schedule but is now more relaxed. "I would love to go by a schedule, but it doesn't seem to work in real life."

Just because daily school ends, that doesn't mean other activities do. On Monday of each week, Daniel, Linda, and Scott are enrolled in three separate gymnastics classes. "Tuesday is the day I do housework, go grocery shopping, and run errands," Janice says. "I also make time to stay home and do things needed there. I have to have the time to clean the bathroom and catch up on laundry."

On Wednesday, Linda has violin lessons, and all three children are involved in AWANA, a club at their church, in the evening. Thursday night, Linda has orchestra rehearsal with the University of South Carolina's "The String Project," where graduate students are teachers and charge only fifty-dollars a semester for weekly lessons and orchestra rehearsals. "This is part of a nationwide program, and it's very good," Janice says. "The only bad part is that we have to drive fifteen to sixteen miles downtown in rush hour traffic."

Every other Friday, a local homeschool group of fifteen to thirty families sponsors roller-skating at a nearby rink. Compared to public school children, "you can see the difference in the way homeschoolers act," Janice observes. "The older kids watch out for the younger ones. Mothers of three-year-olds can sit and talk while their children are skating, because they're safe on the rink."

Once a month, also on a Friday, Janice and the children rendezvous with the homeschool group and participate in the Presidential Physical Fitness Award Program. "We meet as a big group to actually run the events and be timed," Janice says, "and that includes pull-ups, sit-ups, a mile run, a shuttle run, and more. We also work on these events at home, two or three times a week, just to practice." Twenty-four laps around the family's yard totals a mile. "I walk it, but I can't run a whole mile," Janice says, laughing.

Each weekday has a designated chore. "On Mondays, I scrub the kitchen floor, clean the counters, stove, and other surfaces," Janice says. "Tuesday is bathroom cleaning day. On Wednesday I clean the bedrooms and change the sheets. Thursday is 'minimal cleaning' day, and on Friday I vaccuum."

On Friday nights and Saturday afternoons and evenings, Janice works as a waitress at a "country cooking" restaurant. "I would rather not work," she says. "I don't like giving up my weekends. I'm a real homebody, and I want our family to be together." Janice started working away from home because the family needed a little more income due to Susan's college expenses. "I chose waitressing because I can make a lot of money, ten to twelve dollars an hour including tips, without working too many hours," she says.

While Janice is at the restaurant on Saturday, Steve often takes the kids places, such as to the high school track, or occasionally to a $1.50 movie theater, followed by dinner at McDonalds. On Sundays the entire family attends Sunday school and church.

Janice and the children homeschool from mid-August through the end of May each year. "We stop even if books aren't done," Janice says, "and then start the next year with a review. We also take a two-week break at Christmas and one week in spring." One hundred and eighty school days are required by South Carolina law.

In addition to a number of mandatory days, the state also specifies what subjects must be taught in homeschool, including reading, writing, math, social studies and science for elementary school; in seventh grade and up, literature and composition are also required. South Carolina offers parents the choice of registering through the local school district, with required testing; joining the South Carolina Association of Independent Home Schools, which stipulates parents must have a high school diploma or GED, also with required testing and meeting the above requirements; or belonging to an umbrella group, again, with the above requirements but minus the mandatory testing. The family has opted for this third choice. Going by the rules, they maintain a plan book, attendance records, and a portfolio of samples. Janice also fills out semiannual progress reports and makes sure she documents the children's academic progress.

After living in South Carolina for a while, Janice misses her home state of Virginia. "In Virginia I had a big support group, most of my and Steve's extended family, and lots of friends," she says with a sigh. "I haven't made as many friends here, and my children don't have many friends at present. Homeschoolers here seem to be self-sufficient. They have their own friends or church and don't need others." Fortunately, relatives on both sides have encouraged Janice and Steve in their decision to homeschool, and this has helped in balancing a lack of local support.

For Janice, homeschooling has been harder than expected. "I had a good experience with homeschooling until this last year," she says. "If all I had to do was to homeschool, and someone else handled the housework, then it wouldn't be as hard. Trying to be a good wife, mother, and homemaker . . . everything can seem overwhelming at times."

Faced with this feeling of being overwhelmed, plus a certain amount of isolation, Janice seriously considered putting the three younger children in school. "In my heart, I really wanted to continue homeschooling," Janice says, "but given our situation, I wondered if Christian school would be better for the children." Steve and Janice talked things through and agreed to make some positive changes. "Steve has agreed to help Daniel with algebra, and that is a huge relief," Janice says. "I just ordered my A Beka books for next year, and we are definitely planning to homeschool."

When asked if she would homeschool again, given the choice,

Janice answers affirmatively. "I'm not so sure about the accelerating part, though," she muses. "I don't want to hold Daniel back, but hopefully he won't want to leave home so early."

Susan, on the other hand, "would recommend accelerating for others, though I don't know that everyone would want to do it. My classmates here at Pensacola Christian College tell me they wouldn't have wanted to leave home so young."

If the family had stayed in Virginia, Susan says she might have decided to attend community college classes there rather than go away to a four-year institution. "After we moved to South Carolina, there wasn't anything for me there," she says, "so I put all my efforts into finishing high school early. Because there was nothing else to do, I spent many days doing schoolwork for eight solid hours. That's how I started early in August of my last year and finished in March." Susan adds that she has always been determined when she decides to do things. "I pushed myself," she adds, "especially my last year of homeschool."

Though Susan is very close to her family, for several years she has had ambitious plans for her life and has been anxious to get on with them. "At the rate I'm going, I'll graduate from college when I'm nineteen with a double major in speech communications and prelaw," she says. "I want to go to the University of Virginia law school and study international law. It's my goal to do something useful that will have a lasting effect." Susan says she's not interested in getting married or having children. Instead, "I want to go into politics someday," she says. "I've always been interested in it. I guess I'd like to go to the Senate or maybe even higher than that if it's possible."

From junior high years on, Pensacola Christian College has seemed the perfect place for Susan to pursue her goals. "I was excited about coming to college, and the thought of being around a lot of Christians was very appealing to me," she says. "It's very safe here, the people are really nice, and I'm getting a good education." (Janice adds that she would have never let her sixteen-year-old daughter attend an away-from-home college unless the institution was very strict.) "The campus is beautiful," says Susan, "with palm trees and lovely buildings, just like it was in the video I saw when I was in sixth grade."

Janice and Steve miss Susan but think they made the right decision. "Susan is very quiet and reserved, but she has many friends at school and feels comfortable there," Janice says. "We don't see her very often. She was home for Christmas when she had a five-week break, and we hope to see her for a week in June."

Susan finds it difficult to come home to visit because she is extremely busy. Last semester she took twenty hours of course work, with classes in criminal justice, English, French, New Testament survey, Old Testament survey, speech, astronomy, and introduction to computer. She also works in the school library, shelving books and helping patrons. "I like my work a lot," Susan says. "That's why I'm staying on campus this summer. I'll work in the library for $7.50 an hour, 40 hours a week, and I receive free room and board." In addition to school and work, Susan is involved in weekly Christian service, passing out pamphlets door-to-door. She enjoys swimming in the college pool. She is also an accomplished musician, rising at 6:00 A.M. each morning to practice piano for an hour and a half.

Both Susan and her siblings have enjoyed the flexibility that homeschooling has offered them. Daniel, Linda, and Scott appreciate the fact that on most days they can finish their work by noon. They relish their freedom to take off days from school and visit family in Virginia or take a field trip to the zoo. And Susan is glad she had the opportunity and the freedom to accelerate her high school years.

For Janice, Susan's finishing high school and succeeding in college has been one of her greatest successes so far. "Steve and I can look back and say, 'Wow, we did it. We helped her graduate.' Though sometimes I wonder if I did the right thing, because I gave up two years of having her at home with us." As a mother, Janice wishes her daughter was closer and more accessible. But as a homeschool teacher, she says, "I'm proud of Susan. We all worked together to help her realize her dreams."

Front row: Aren, Joan, Nathan. Back row: Eli, Simon, Miriam.

Ten

The Jewish Home-
school Experience

Family:
Joan (48), Aren (46), Miriam (18), Simon (15), Eli (12), Nathan (10).

Location:
Sharon, Massachusetts (suburb of Boston).

Best advice:
Trust your kids, trust your mother's heart and gut feelings about your kids. Listen to your kids, what they are saying as well as what they are not saying.

Worst advice:
The school personnel know your child better than you do.

Favorite quote:
"Never doubt that a small group of thoughtful, committed people can change the world. Indeed, it is the only thing that ever has." (Margaret Mead)

Favorite resources:

Complete Home Learning Source Book by Rebecca Rupp, Three Rivers Press.

The Teenage Liberation Handbook by Grace Llewellyn, Lowry House Publishers.

Growing Without Schooling magazine, www.holtgws.com

Home Education Magazine, www.home-ed-magazine.com

The Kaleidoscapes Support Forum for Home Educators, www.kaleidoscapes.com

Joan and Aren H. are observant Jews, and it's important to them to raise their four children as Jews. To that end, Miriam, Simon, and Eli, their three oldest children, were enrolled in a nearby Jewish school. Then . . . "I first started looking into homeschooling when our youngest son, Nathan, was in nursery school," Joan says. Aren and Joan had planned to enroll Nathan in the same Jewish day school that his older siblings attended, and brought him to the kindergarten screening. Joan explains, "The screener said to him, 'Stand up, turn around, and clap your hands.' Nathan asked, 'Why?' The screener repeated, 'Just do what I say. Stand up, turn around, and clap your hands.' And Nathan again asked, 'Why?' After several minutes of this, the screener wrote down that Nathan couldn't follow three-part instructions."

So began the family's homeschool adventure. "My original intent was to homeschool kindergarten, but Nathan and I ended up just doing stuff together," Joan says. "We went shopping, we read books, we spent time at the school doing activities and going on trips with his siblings' classes. We got very involved with a school theater production, played games, and went to the playground. And we talked all the time."

After a wonderful year at home with his mother, Nathan entered kindergarten at the Jewish school where Miriam was then in eighth grade, Simon in fourth, and Eli in second. Joan began to actively volunteer in one or another of the children's classes throughout the year. "We had been involved with this school from its inception," she says, "and I knew all of the teachers and most of the students very well. But being there virtually every day, I began to see things about the school itself and my children's interactions there that I had never seen before." Joan learned, for example, that Miriam did not really fit in well with the rest of her class. Simon was placed in a class away from his three best buddies, and he found it hard to make new friends; the school was not cooperative in moving him, making for a very difficult year. And Eli's class for the following year was slated to be held in a space Joan and Aren thought unsuitable.

Joan was fed up with the school's lack of attention to certain areas and other changes that she saw as negative. She also had difficulty picturing six-year-old, active Nathan in a classroom, even under the best of circumstances. "I knew that being in that school and that classroom would squelch every bit of the drive and energy that make Nathan such a terrific kid," she says. Public school enrollment was not an appealing option. "At the day school, Jewish teaching was seamlessly integrated into our children's day," Joan says. "We were reluctant to lose this flavor of learning in their lives and felt that we could provide it better at home than would be the case in the public school/afterschool religious program so many Jewish children encounter." So one by one, Joan and Aren made the decisions to homeschool all three of the boys.

Meanwhile, Miriam attended public high school and did well for some time. Then she began to experience prolonged, intense harassment from a fellow student. "On the day I told her point blank that she never had to go into the high school again unless she wanted to," Joan says, "it was like an enormous weight was lifted from her." Miriam stayed at the school long enough to perform in the fall musical play, then came home to learn with the rest of the family.

Joan says she homeschools "because I want my children to be passionate about something, and to have the time and opportunity to pursue their passions." On the practical side, Joan and Aren have listed three essentials. One is literacy: the ability to read, write, and express oneself orally. Another is life skills: everything one needs to know to get through life, like driving, computer literacy, basic nutrition and health, hobbies, and math. The third essential is Jewish studies: learning the Hebrew language, various prayer services and other synagogue skills, and customs of laws and holidays. "I want my children to be Jews who find both joy and awe in studying Torah, celebrating holidays, and following mitzvot (commandments)," Joan says.

Jewish studies are an essential part of the family's curriculum. All four children are learning Hebrew. Miriam and Simon take classes through a high school program at Hebrew College in Boston, and Eli will begin there soon. Miriam also works with Nathan on prayers and reading Hebrew using some materials from a Jewish educational supplier. Eli studies with the synagogue's cantor in preparation for being bar mitzvahed; at that time, he will accept personal responsibility for performing God's commandments.

In addition, the family tries to cover and discuss a reading from the Torah each week, cycling through the five books of Moses each year. "As we go through the Jewish year and observe each holiday," Joan says, "we do some reading, online research, and a lot of talking about how and why we observe. Much of our holiday learning comes from *doing.*" At Pesach (Passover), for example, the children are involved with the physical work of preparation, like cleaning, changing the dishes in the kitchen, and cooking special foods. They also prepare spiritually by reading through the Haggadah, a special book used for the seder (a service-with-meal that defines Pesach). Miriam led her first seder this year.

Each holiday is celebrated together as a family, and usually with other families as well. Seven weeks after Pesach comes Shavuot, where an all-night study session ends with morning prayers at daybreak. During the summer, the family mourns the loss of the Temple on Tisha B'Av. "Every fall, we turn to one another and ask forgiveness in preparation for Rosh Hashanah and Yom Kippur," Joan says. "Soon afterward, we come to Sukkot and together we build a *sukkah*, a temporary dwelling in which we eat (and sometimes sleep) for eight days. Building and decorating the *sukkah* is probably everyone's favorite part of all the holidays."

Hannukah is a time for lighting the candles each night and singing. "Last year, we exchanged no gifts as part of our savings plan, so that we could all go to New Mexico to be with my grandmother on her one-hundredth birthday last December," Joan says. For Purim the family enjoys baking and making gifts of food for their friends. It's also a challenge to come up with a family costume to wear to the synagogue's *megillah* (reading of the scroll of Esther). "Last year, in keeping with our commitment to science fiction, we were 'aliens in black,'" Joan says grinning, "making the universe safe from the scum of the Earth." After Purim the yearly cycle of holidays is nearly complete. "Then it's time to start thinking about Passover again," Joan says.

Every week the family is commited to *shabbat* (Sabbath), joining together on Friday evening to celebrate, being a part of the community during services on *shabbat* morning, and making Saturdays "an island in time," Joan says, "separate and different from the rest of the week, a day of true rest." Even when the family is traveling, they make it a point to observe *shabbat*—complete with the lighting of the candles, blessing the children, and sharing challah (egg bread), and wine—and to connect with other Jewish families.

Judaism is constantly interwoven into every aspect of the family's life, from holidays to daily routines. "We have a *mezuzah* (a decorative case attached to the door frame that displays a piece of parchment with the words of the *shema*, a central Jewish prayer) on every door of the house, and we touch one as we enter and leave," Joan says. "We thank God for our food before and after meals, and because we keep the laws of *kashruth* (kosher), we are aware of this Jewish choice every time we buy, prepare, or eat food." Aren attends prayer services at the synagogue each morning and occasionally in the evenings. Sometimes one or more of the family joins him, or they may have a morning prayer service at home.

Joan tries to find ways to incorporate Jewish teachings into ordinary experiences. "When we work at the nearby cat shelter or perform animal rescues, we talk about the *mitzvah* (commandment) of kindness to animals," she says. "If a friend is sick, as one of Eli's friends has been this past year, we perform the *mitzvah* of *bikur cholim*, visiting the sick. Always, always, we look for ways to perform *tzedakah*, not just charity, but acts that are righteous."

"Religious" time can also mesh with "school" time. When planning gift baskets of food for Purim, for example, Joan and the children make a list, estimate amounts to be prepared, and determine the cost of it all. "That's organization skills and math," Joan says, "and the baking itself involves science and math. Putting the plates together is creative arts. And planning the delivery route around town uses map skills."

This doesn't mean that the family unschools. Joan is currently utilizing Clonlara, an umbrella school that offers support, advice, and record-keeping, though it doesn't provide a set curriculum. In the past, she has used a number of complete curricula packages, including Oak Meadow and Calvert.

Joan has not been completely pleased with any of the packages. "We have tried virtually everything from the very structured, like Calvert, to totally child-led learning," Joan muses.

"We are still working at finding a balance between the two extremes. I think that all of the packaged curricula we have seen are too structured for us. But the days go by more easily if we have some projects in hand. We are starting to think of our educational approach as 'unit studies.' "

Joan and Aren do not test their children, though Miriam will be taking the SAT and ACT tests.

The family members all read well, though some started later than others and most learned between the ages of eight and ten. "I talk to them fairly frequently about what they are interested in and try to steer them to nonfiction and biographies that complement their interests," Joan says. "We look at the papers together and talk about what's going on in the world. We have maps and globes so we can find out where things are happening. I figure this covers most of the literature and social studies they'd be getting in school." The children do math work, though not from a formal program. Joan is reviewing some Saxon math texts with the younger boys. "They are also asked to write in a journal every day," Joan says, "but since they're not required to show me what they've written, I'm not always sure if they are writing. Every now and then, when I'm feeling paranoid, I pull out a workbook and do some grammar or punctuation activities with the younger boys; these spurts rarely last long."

Science is very experiential. Recently, for example, Nathan and Joan traveled with other homeschoolers to The Butterfly Place, where they observed—and watched films and exhibits about—butterflies. They returned home with two caterpillars to "hatch." "Both cocooned and emerged on schedule," Joan says, "but one's wings never fully opened. We did some reading about butterflies and what happens to butterflies with 'disabilities' like this. We released the healthy one, but Nathan decided to keep the other one instead of turning him loose to be some other animal's lunch." Joan sees this science lesson as an illustration of her role as a homeschool educator. "I am here to play with the children, help them find resources, drive them to the library or wherever else their interests lead them, help them find explanations and answers for their questions, and make suggestions when they can't think up anything on their own," she says.

A typical day for the family starts with a 5:30 A.M. alarm. Aren is out the door early, for morning prayers at the synagogue are at 6:15. He takes a train into the city or rides with a friend to his work at a computer company, where he designs and codes software for business applications, manages a group of programmers, and mentors new programmers, in the company. "High-tech in the Boston area pays very well, so we are able to live easily on one income," Joan says, "though we did sell our big house in an inner suburb and buy a smaller house in a farther out suburb when I quit working." Joan's former job involved technical writing and training with another computer company.

By the time Aren leaves for work, Joan is usually out of bed. She likes to begin her day with a cup of tea and an e-mail session, since she administers one mailing list and subscribes to several others. Miriam gets up early to work on her American School lessons while it's quiet. "She had a rather long hiatus after leaving the public high school, but is now zooming through her units at the rate of one or two a day," Joan says. By 7:30, Joan has finished her e-mail, Miriam has completed her American School course work for the day, Simon is up and dressed, and the younger boys are beginning to stir.

Joan tries to "start school" by 8:30 or 9:00. "On the days when we do formal schoolwork, we'll all sit down at desks in our newly organized school room," Joan says. Miriam might be doing research on the history of theater, a project for the synagogue youth group, creative writing, or e-mail correspondence. Simon reads or looks through his assignments. Joan goes back and forth between the younger boys, depending on which one has the more urgent question.

Much of the time, Eli and Nathan are working together or on similar projects. "Yesterday they did fractions using Hershey's chocolate bars and an accompanying book," Joan says. "Then they did Internet research on chocolate. For one activity, I gave the boys a big bag of M&M's and had them sort by color, estimate, count, and prepare a pie chart showing the distribution of colors within a bag. My plan is that they will also make a poster, write a report or story, or put together some materials . . . something that looks like a final project when we're done with the chocolate study." Joan adds that she often has plans like this, though they're not always carried out.

On any given day, each of the children works independently. Eli is reading through a book on codes, one of his favorite interests, and sometimes Joan gives him an assignment in code. Nathan often works on his website. Meanwhile, Simon may want to show his mother what he's done or share insights. Miriam might also be in and out of the room, discussing something she's read.

Sometime every morning, the boys need a break for some active play like basketball or baseball. Miriam and Joan may join them, or take a walk. Then comes more sedentary schooling. "Right now I am reading aloud *Black Ships Before Troy* by Rosemary Sutcliff," Joan says. "The boys are having great fun finding the sources for many literary allusions."

The family eats lunch around noon. Afterward comes a special project, piano practice, bar mitzvah practice for Eli, Hebrew study for Nathan, continued reading aloud, and/or individual assigned reading.

In the evenings, Aren gets home at approximately 6:15. While some of the family members begin fixing supper, the others may do chores. After supper, chores are finished and there's read-aloud time for Nathan and whoever else happens to listen. The younger boys are in bed by 9:00 P.M., 10:00 at the latest, Miriam between 10:00 and 11:00, and Simon, close to midnight.

Evenings—and for that matter, most days—include widely varying activities. Sundays are busiest, with Eli's bar mitzvah classes, Miriam's Talmud classes, karate lessons for all three boys, Cub Scout den and pack meetings for Nathan, Boy Scout meetings for Eli, and synagogue youth group meetings. Miriam occasionally baby-sits.

Monday mornings, the younger boys are involved in a homeschooling theater group that takes much of the day. Miriam, Eli, and Nathan take piano lessons at home. Monday nights are one of the rare evenings when everyone is home, though this changes during baseball season.

Tuesdays, Wednesdays, and Thursdays the family has "school" in the mornings and some free time in the afternoons. Miriam takes the train to her Talmud class again on Tuesday. Wednesday evenings are karate classes for all the children, and Aren often has evening meetings for Cub Scouts or the synagogue. Thursdays, the two older children go to Hebrew classes in a nearby town and Joan sings with the community chorus. Aren, Miriam, and Simon shop for groceries on the way home.

Fridays are different from most other days. "We will do some school activities," Joan says, "but we also spend a fair amount of time getting ready for *shabbat*, cleaning, cooking, and making sure everyone has clean clothes to wear to services." Aren always comes home before sundown on Fridays, as *shabbat* begins at sundown. "We light the candles, bless the children, have challah and wine, and eat a leisurely meal together," Joan explains. "After the meal, we have our only dessert of the week, and then we sing the grace after the meals together. Everyone goes to bed earlier on Friday; by Friday we are tired and need our rest."

Saturday is, of course, very special. After a relaxed wake-up time, "we all walk to the synagogue in waves," Joan says. "Jewish

services are a little more free-flowing than most Christian services, and people tend to wander in and out and may pray on their
own while other things are going on." At this synagogue, services
last for more than three hours. Joan and the younger children
often arrive later than Aren and the teenagers, around 10:00
A.M., in time to hear the Torah reading and *d'var* (teaching,
something like a sermon). "This is one of our big social events of
the week," Joan says. "After services, we stand or sit around and
schmooze with other members of our community. Sometimes we
will go to a friend's for lunch or they'll come back to our house."
Saturday afternoons are lazy, and may include a walk, reading,
naps, swimming, or a late-evening video.

The family homeschools year round, "more or less," Joan
says. "We are not very structured about our homeschooling, and
we take breaks when necessary. Last year, I needed to be with my
mother in New Mexico for an extended period. Simon came with
me, and Miriam, then seventeen, stayed home with her younger
brothers. At first I sent Eli and Nathan some things to do every
day, but it didn't take long for that idea to lose its appeal. So their
summer vacation started a little early."

Joan schedules field trips whenever she senses the need for a
break. "We love going to the Boston Museum of Science," she
says, "and Washington, D.C., though that obviously takes a little
more time and planning." Day-to-day, the family members wind
down by surfing the Internet and watching videos. "Shakespeare
is a perennial favorite," Joan says. "We rarely watch TV, but we
have enjoyed Masterpiece Theater productions like *David Cop-
perfield*, *I, Claudius*, and Ken Burns's *Baseball* series, plus PBS
shows like *Bill Nye the Science Guy* and *Krafts' Creatures.*" The
family also has a hobby of comparing books to movies and stage
and film versions of musicals. "We watch a lot of musicals on
video, both taped stage productions and filmed ones," Joan says.
"And if we learn all the songs, that counts as music, right?"

Joan seldom gets a chance to relax and indulge her own personal interests, but she does manage to fit in some pro bono graphic design work for several organizations. Ideally, she says, she'd like to do more handcrafts, sewing, web page design, singing, and playing the piano, and have a little time for exercise. She'd also enjoy learning more about gardening and weaving, and engage in serious Jewish study. Practically speaking, there simply aren't enough hours in the day. "I feel very personal-time challenged," is the way she puts it.

Joan is not required to spend much time complying with state regulations on homeschooling. Her first responsibility in her particular district, initially, was to compile information about her qualifications. She also had to write a brief description of the proposed education plan, provide access to the kind of home-schooled materials used, and come to an agreement on one kind of periodic reporting or evaluation. The local superintendent and school district (who, by law, decide on exactly what is required) are open to—and accepting of—homeschooling, making Joan's job easier.

Still, she has her hands full. Besides the responsibilities of homeschooling, there are other duties, like household chores. "We divide the daily and weekly chores into four categories and rotate them among the four kids," Joan says. The categories include kitchen, cats, floors/surfaces, and bathrooms, and each involves several responsibilities. The children are in charge of most of their own laundry, cleaning their rooms, and fixing their own breakfasts and lunches. Evening meal preparation is shared equally by kids and adults. At least twice a year, usually coinciding with Passover and Rosh Hashanah, there is a major drive to clean the entire house.

"We are never 'caught up,'" Joan observes, "and I'm beginning to believe that this is a normal condition for homeschoolers. In the absence of paid outside help with cleaning and laundry, how can you pursue your interests and learning opportunities and still have clean floors (when the kids are in and out of the house fifty times a day), immaculate surfaces (when projects-in-progress are spread out everywhere and books are in constant use), clean laundry (when there's never time to do it), and so on. Plus the simple fact that so many of us are at home so much of the day, even when we're running all over the place, puts much more wear-and-tear on our house and possessions than those of families whose kids go to school and whose parents are at work all day."

Though Aren works away from home, he is an active participant in family life. He is pack master of Nathan's Cub Scout group, a former chairman of the youth committee at the synagogue, and has coached Miriam in volleyball and Eli and Nathan in baseball. Aren also acts as both Joan's and the children's consultant. "The kids call him several times a day to let him know what's going on or to ask questions," Joan says.

In spite of family togetherness and plenty of outside socialization, Joan and the children feel isolated at times. "Because we started with older children and a larger family, it has often been hard to find other families to mesh with," she says. "There are teenagers in the area who homeschool, but it is difficult and time-consuming to get together with them." Joan and the children sometimes miss the warm and caring school community they left behind. "Despite our best efforts, we have not managed to retain many of the friendships we had formed while a part of that community," Joan says.

Fortunately, both of Aren's parents and Joan's mother support the family in their homeschooling. Joan also has two very good friends, both Jewish homeschoolers with larger families and children of similar ages, to whom she can "talk" via e-mail and on-line chats. "Together, the three of us formed an e-mail list for Jewish homeschoolers nearly two years ago," Joan says. "This group has been another major source of support."

Support is important to Joan, since she expects to continue homeschooling until her youngest goes off to college. All four have been offered the opportunity to return to school, public or private, but each of them has decided against it. Miriam, Simon, Eli, and Nathan show varying degrees of enthusiasm for their studies, but all agree that they want them to be at home, at least for now. "Like all else, we have good days and bad days," Joan says. "On the good days we have some really neat stuff going on, no one gets mad at anyone else, the dishes are washed, the chores are done, and everyone has clean laundry. While those days are few and far between, on balance I think we've had fun and we've learned some amazing things together."

Joan has been surprised to discover how very different her children are. "I expected my children to love having the freedom that I wish I had been given, to pursue their own interests in their own way. Instead, some of them have consistently asked for more structure, for schedules, for assignments," she says. "We're a work-in-progress. We are constantly finding things that work for us and things that don't work for us."

Because of this transition, Joan says she felt at a tremendous disadvantage for some time, "like I didn't know how to teach. It must be all my fault, I thought, that my kids were lazing around the house reading and building things with Legos. I kept checking out—or buying—every book on education and homeschooling that I could find, hoping that I would find the magic answer that would make everything fall into place for us." Recently Joan was reading yet another book that promised "successful teaching strategies," when she suddenly realized, "Is *this* all it is? I do *that!*" she says. "It was a kind of epiphany to learn that 'teaching' wasn't this vast unexplored territory that I was ill-prepared for and poorly equipped to do."

Aren and Joan recognize that homeschooling has been good for their family. "Miriam left public school in a state of anxiety and depression and spent a long time recovering," Joan says. "Today we have a happy young woman who is facing the future with confidence and vision. If we had forced her to stay in school, I believe we would be dealing with a very different person today." Joan imagines she might still have placed all her children in school, if she had the chance to relive her life, "but I think I would have taken them out sooner."

The flexibility of both educational choice and of homeschooling in general has been a real plus. "Being free from a school schedule made it possible for me to spend an extended period of time with my mother last summer when she needed some assistance," Joan notes, "and to do spur of the moment things that keep the kids up late, like accepting tickets to watch the Celtics play. Or staying up to finish reading a riveting book."

Joan notes that all in all she and Aren have been pleased with their homeschooling experience. "It has taken us a while to really understand the amount of pressure to conform and to perform that the children were under while at school," she says. "Now our children are happier and more confident in their ability to deal with new situations, and they are finding out for themselves what their passions in life are."

Aren and Joan agree that it is not easy to be an observant Jewish family while homeschooling. "Judaism is very centered on community," Joan says. "Education is an important value for most Jews, and choosing an alternative type of education, like homeschooling, is sometimes regarded with suspicion. Home-schooling has put us at odds with our Jewish community in some ways."

Joan and Aren work hard to provide their children with the kinds of Jewish education and experiences that they would participate in effortlessly if they were still in a day school or after-school religious program. Still, "despite the difficulties," Joan says, "we believe that homeschooling is the right thing for our children and our family."

Front row: McKenzie, Duncan. Back row: Connor, Ian, Rian.

Eleven

Homeschooling with ADHD Children

Family:
Susie (39), Mark (40), Connor (11), Ian (10), Rian (pronounced like Ryan, 9), Duncan (6), McKenzie (4).

Location:
Clearfield, Utah (a small town close to Salt Lake City).

Best advice:
Don't take mothering so seriously that you don't enjoy your children.
Make your school like a home, not your home like a school.

Worst advice:
Homeschooling will work if you get the right curriculum.

Favorite quote:
"What is most important and valuable about the home as a base for children's growth into the world is not that it is a better

school than the schools, but that it isn't a school at all." (John Holt)

Favorite resources:

Wild Days: Creating Discovery Journals by Karen Skidmore Rackliffe, SunRise Publishing, http://members.aol.com/Wilddays nature/

Learning All the Time by John Holt, Perseus Press.

The Successful Homeschool Family Handbook by Raymond and Dorothy Moore, Thomas Nelson.

The Joyful Homeschool by Mary Hood, Ambleside Educational Press.

Homeschooling on a Shoestring by Judith Allee and Melissa Morgan, Harold Shaw Publishing.

Although their son Connor was officially diagnosed with attention deficit hyperactive disorder (ADHD) when he was nine years old, Mark and Susie C. knew from the time their firstborn was very young that he would never make it in a public school environment. "Even in the church's nursery, his excitement and activity were treated as if he needed to be disciplined rather than educated differently," Susie says. "We realized, from this experience and many others, that Connor would do much better in homeschool."

The family now has five children, including a second ADHD son, Duncan. "Being home, my ADHD kids have a safe haven for learning academically and learning to handle their emotions," Susie says. "Children with ADHD are often 'bully bait.' Bullies like to get a reaction, and with ADHD kids, they get a real show. The bully steps back, watches the fireworks, and the ADHD child, who has a hard time with his emotions and stress, reaps the wrath of the teacher and gets in trouble." Susie has seen this happen too many times—at Scouts or the swimming pool, in the neighborhood—to put her children in public school, where it would happen daily.

Having two ADHD sons has been a real challenge, Susie says. "It's hard when you have children whose problems are invisible. If they had Down's syndrome or another physically recognizable condition, people would have a clue that the child was different and would expect different behavior. But when your ADHD eleven-year-old throws a toy across the room, he just looks like a brat."

Home-schooling gives Mark and Susie a chance to deal with behavior problems. "Anyone who thinks that children need to go to public school to learn to deal with conflict has never spent much time with her own children," Susie says. "Learning to share possessions, as well as share Mom's attention, creates some incredible learning moments. When children have someone there who truly loves them, rather than someone who is willing to go on strike for more money, their confidence increases as they master their emotions and learn that they *can* be in control of themselves."

One difficulty with having ADHD children is that not everyone agrees on a method of teaching control. "I've been snubbed by many homeschool moms who feel that I'm damaging my children because of my decisions," Susie says. "But we've tried many things, and for us, behavioral modification and medications work best."

When she first began homeschooling, Susie was more "schoolish" in her approach. "Connor rebelled and hated school," she says. "Can't say I blame him." Susie realized that by using a variety of interesting materials rather than a set curriculum, she could better accommodate her children's academic needs. "I read some books by the Moores, and this really helped me relax. I realized that I was doing exactly what I wanted to avoid by keeping my son out of public school. I was forcing him to learn in a way that wasn't right for him."

Susie adjusted both her homeschool teaching style and the curriculum to fit her ADHD sons'—as well as her the other children's—needs. "Connor was an early reader and very good at math," she says. "Duncan was right on track with his learning, but it seemed slower to us because his older siblings had learned at such a young age. Being at home, we were able to meet the needs of both boys without a special class. We just allowed them to learn at their own pace and in their own way."

Connor and Duncan responded very well to the Miquon Math program. "I started my three oldest children with Miquon, and I absolutely love it," Susie says. "My son Ian is a very visual learner, and using Cuisenaire rods (colored measuring rods, an essential part of the Miquon program) with math really helped him grasp certain concepts. My daughter Rian is an independent learner and could correct her own mistakes with the manipulatives. Connor and Duncan, my ADHD children, were able to 'handle' the math and not just see equations on paper." Now Connor, Ian, and Rian have graduated to *Key To* workbooks and Saxon Math.

With the exception of math books, "we use some texts, but only as a starting point," Susie says. "In addition, the kids read library books of their choosing. We make use of lots of projects, unschooling, field trips, etc. We try not to draw too many lines separating life from learning." In the summer, for example, the children's science lessons center around what's happening in the backyard. "We watch the insects, we learn about the plants," Susie says. "Or our science might be following the space shuttle's mission and launch. We try to use those wonderful teaching moments to reinforce what we've learned or to introduce new concepts."

Susie's philosophy of education leaves little room for a teacher lecturing and students taking notes. "I don't do detailed lesson plans, just a brief outline of what we wish to learn from our study," she explains. "We don't use a lot of curricula. That doesn't mean we don't read, because we read a great deal, together as well as individually. Besides a daily quiet reading time for the kids, they also read in their rooms before bed." Family reading includes plenty of interesting books, like historical fiction and titles published by Dorling Kindersley, that tie into particular themes.

Susie uses books as well as hands-on activities for history unit studies. "Everyone gets to participate," she says. "Right now we're learning about the ancient meso-Americans. I copied several coloring book pages on this subject, and McKenzie, my four-year-old, colors these. Six-year-old Duncan has made a step pyramid temple with duplo blocks. My older children find information on the Internet about these people. We watch TV programs and videos which support the topic."

All five children also participate in both the local support group's field trips and family field trips, often tying them in with a unit. "Yesterday we visited a Mexican restaurant called Mayan, and attended an IMAX film called *The Mysteries of the Maya*," Susie says. "While the older children focused on the architecture and customs, my husband and I were interested in the impact of the Spanish on the natives and their advanced knowledge of math and astronomy. McKenzie was fascinated with the animals of Mexico, and Duncan loved the weapons," Susie reports. "Everyone gets something from a lesson when it's fun!"

Since the family learns in a relaxed fashion, and often together, babies and toddlers are not a problem. Susie describes a typical math session: "Each child has his or her own materials. While I work with my six-year-old son in either Miquon or grocery-store math workbooks, his older brothers and sister work in their *Key To* books or Saxon, and they come to me with questions and to help them check their work. My four-year-old daughter plays with the Cuisenaire rods that her six-year-old brother uses and gets to see firsthand how she'll use them one day. In the meantime, she's learning about 'greater than' and 'less than' by comparing the sizes of the rods."

Susie finds that most of the time the younger children want to be involved with "schoolwork" like the big kids. "When my youngests were babies, they'd be right there with us during the school day," Susie says. "I'd nurse the baby while reading with the children." Toddlers always have been allowed to come and go as they please.

Like the rest of the family, Dad also operates on a free-flowing schedule. Mark, a home-based computer programmer, has his own consulting business designing flight and submarine simulators for civilian and military contracts worldwide. Mark and his partner, who also works from his home, set their own hours. "If I need to take off, my husband takes care of the kids," Susie says. "If he meets with a client and the client doesn't mind, he takes the older kids with him and they get to fly on the simulations."

Mark doesn't participate in school in the traditional sense, but does take the children golfing or to play racquetball or to a matinee, enlists their help in projects like remodeling the basement, works on the computer with them, and helps with math and other homework. "He's excited by our children's accomplishments and supports me completely in my efforts," Susie says.

The family follows a loose schedule that varies from day to day. Susie and the children usually sleep until 8:30 or 9:00, with breakfast—something like waffles—soon afterward. While the kids practice piano, draw, or read, Susie works on the computer. She edits and writes a free online newsletter called *I Love Homeschool*. "I always wanted to do something like this," Susie says, "and I figured with it being online, I wouldn't have to have cash to get it going."

In the late morning, everyone starts on chores. Susie helps the children with laundry and cleaning, dusts, handles the heavy cleaning, and, later, makes dinner. "The kids like to cook so they often make lunch," Susie says, "and I'm there to make sure the kitchen doesn't burn down." Chores such as laundry, bathroom cleaning, and vacuuming are rotated monthly. The family also takes breaks during the day to do chores as the need arises. "A few minutes away from a lesson is a great help," Susie notes.

Mark and Susie use allowances and earnings just as an employer would. "The children get allowances based on their performance, attitude, responsibility, and whatever other factors come to light," Susie says. "If they don't keep their rooms tidy, they don't get allowances. If they don't do their extra work and schoolwork with a good attitude or don't give it their best shot, they lose money. If they performed poorly at a 'real job,' they'd either lose money or get fired. For us, this system feels like 'the real world.' "

Chores complete, each child receives a list of what needs to be accomplished academically. The family might do one of several projects. Rian recently constructed a homeschool science fair project on the life cycle of the monarch butterfly, complete with a four-foot-long papier-mâché caterpillar model. Susie and the kids once made a pizza with each topping representing different parts of a cell.

Some days a field trip is planned. Other days the family might "do car school" while running errands. "We listen to language tapes, multiplication songs, geography songs," Susie says. "We quiz each other on which laws of physics apply as we drive. We play state capital games when we see out-of-state license plates. The kids take turns reading out loud, and we discuss what's read."

Occasionally the family spends a morning at the family recreation center. "We wanted to help our children find activities that they can do for a lifetime," Susie says. "When Mark and I were in public school, we spent a great deal of time on track-and-field, gymnastics, soccer, and other team sports. But since I've left school I've never jumped a hurdle nor hurled a discus. We wanted our children to learn activities that they could use for most of their lives. They love swimming and racquetball."

At some point in the day, lunch is served. Then comes more learning, mostly child-led. One afternoon last week found Duncan playing computer games: "Reader Rabbit 1," "Math Blaster" (first-grade level), "My Amazing Human Body" (DK), "A Castle Adventure" (Fisher Price), and "Jump Start Spanish." "I could hear Duncan and McKenzie upstairs jumping around and singing along with the songs in Spanish," Susie smiles. Duncan also worked in *Alphaphonics* with his mother and found the Blues Clues website, where he played more games.

The same day, Rian completed several pages in the blue Miquon book, read a couple of chapters in her *Little House in the Big Woods* book, e-mailed a friend, found a website that offered good deals on Beanie Babies, and painted a watercolor of the fruit on the dining room table. She also worked on "butterfly wings" for her science fair display, cardboard pieces cut into the shape of wings and painted intricately.

Ian cleaned the gerbil cage and read up on gerbil and guinea pig behavior, typed a letter to his cousin, worked in a McGraw-Hill math workbook, read about stars and sharks, and surfed the 'net to find the best buy on a Dreamcast controller.

Connor e-mailed his pen pal, completed some math in his *Key To* book, read about aircraft carriers and did some experiments on buoyancy, and measured the street to compare its length to the length of an aircraft carrier. Connor, who's interested in *Star Wars*, enjoyed working on a *Star Wars* mission kit he received from Scholastic Books. He practiced his drawing skills by copying *Star Wars* ships from a book.

Susie also "did school." She practiced flute, read a children's story in French, worked out on the treadmill, and wrote a couple of articles for the newsletter.

Traditional school subjects may be covered in the morning, afternoon, or evening, depending on the day. Susie's list of essentials include math and computer, language arts (reading, spelling, writing, penmanship), foreign languages, history/social studies, science, home economics, life skills, and physical education. "We use life to teach many of these subjects," Susie says. "For instance, we read the newspaper and watch TV news for social studies. Home economics is chores, baking, cleaning, managing one's allowance, learning about bill paying, etc. My kids practice their spelling by writing pen pals and working on science projects like posters. And science and history is watching documentaries on the Learning Channel or Discovery Channel."

Susie often starts with a traditional textbook and then improvises from there. "I purchased *English From the Roots Up*," she says. "Using that and whatever we can find on the Internet and CD-ROMs, we're approaching foreign languages by starting with the Latin/Greek roots and then adding French, Spanish, and Italian words, even some Japanese for Connor. We're assembling a notebook as we go, taking our time so we'll remember the words and not just skim over them." In addition, the children practice speaking foreign languages at breakfast. "One morning I noticed conversations in a mixture of English, French, Spanish, and Italian," Susie says.

A friend of Susie's once called her way of homeschooling "eclectic." "I used to think I was an unschooler," she says. "Then an unschooler railed on me because we used a math curriculum. I didn't know what to call myself! I knew we weren't curriculum-based. We didn't use all of the Charlotte Mason method, just a few things. We didn't do all our learning via unit studies. The term 'eclectic' seemed to fit."

Susie thinks "being eclectic" has been the best thing for her family. "I've seen many people completely burn out and send their precious children back to public school because they couldn't make a particular curriculum work in their home. They felt like failures. It was as if they were trying to force a square peg in a round hole." Susie says she's tried using materials that didn't fit her family, and finally put them up for sale on the Internet. "I like being able to pick and choose from the many incredible resources out there," she says. "I love being able to use the library for much of our materials. I love being able to change when we need change. I love that there are no wrongs to what we do. The only wrong in being eclectic is using what is wrong for your family. 'Whatever it takes' is our motto."

What it doesn't take is testing. "I monitor the children daily, so I already know their strengths and weaknesses," Susie says. "We've seen from our own educational experiences that when you test, you generally teach to pass the test, and study with the same intention. Our goal is to have independent children who love the adventure of life, love to serve others, and love learning."

Learning takes place year round. The family usually take two weeks off in December, still reading and working on crafts, and a couple of weeks off in the summer. "We still do activities in the summer," Susie says, "but we do it at the pool or in the park or on vacation." Last spring, Mom and the children accompanied Dad to Europe on business. "I found it interesting that some people asked if we'd make up for the school time missed after we returned," Susie says, smiling. "As if visiting a foreign country wasn't educational!"

Now the family has a goal of living together in France sometime in the next few years. "We've visited Europe a few times as a couple, once as a family, and my husband has been to Europe on business countless times," Susie notes. "My husband and I each lived in Europe individually years ago. This has sparked our family's passion for foreign languages, other cultures, geography, and world events."

These are certainly not the only passions in the family. Each child is involved in outside activities. Susie takes flute lessons on Monday evenings. Ian and Rian have piano lessons on Thursdays. Susie is currently on the lookout for a class for Ian that will help develop his interest in Japanese cartooning, as well as a karate class for Connor.

All five children are involved in scouting programs, which Mark and Susie see as an extension of their homeschool. Connor has Cub Scouts on Tuesday evenings and Ian, on Wednesday evenings. Two Fridays a month, Rian participates in a home-school junior troop, with Susie leading the homeschool Brownie troop. Even Duncan and McKenzie are part of a preschool scouting group that Girl Scout leaders have set up for siblings of the older girls.

The family actively participates in a Latter Days Saints (Mormon) church. "Our church takes no stand on homeschool or public school, but teaches that the parents are responsible for their children's welfare in all areas," Susie says. "We exercise our faith to receive answers to prayers and insights as we home-school, but I don't use religious curricula. When we learn science, for example, we teach what we feel to be true as well as other theories, so that when our children are faced with oppos-ing views, they'll be able to handle them on a sure foundation."

Considering the family's involvement with Scouts, music les-sons, and church, Susie's response to the question "What about socialization?" is to roll her eyes. "Our children interact with each other daily," she says. "There are people of different ages, different personalities, different temperaments under one roof. They play with people in our neighborhood. They participate in a variety of activities of their choosing."

Susie has learned that most people define socialization as "in-teraction with other children." "I tell them that for us, socializa-tion means much more," she says. "We're teaching our children to be productive members of our family so they can be produc-tive in our neighborhood. Then when they're older, productive members of our community and, later, the world."

Mark and Susie think of socialization as behaving well in a so-cial situation, and they work hard to develop this in their children. "We set standards of behavior and set the example for them to follow, especially for our ADHD boys," Susie says. "I don't think the public school system teaches true socialization. They teach a child to conform to the group around him. I don't want my kids conforming to a group of children who make fun of those who are different. I don't want my teens conforming to a group where doing their assignments means they're inferior and weird, and where they have to smoke, drink, and have sex to fit in."

When some friends pulled their children from public school, they told Susie that the kids didn't want to listen to them. "I kept assuring them that as they worked on family dynamics, their children would learn to respect them," she says. "When a child is in school, the teacher slowly replaces the parents as the authority figure of a son or daughter's life. It takes some time to switch it back to the way it should be."

The family's homeschool is close to "the way it should be," Susie thinks. "I love homeschooling," she says, "and the kids love it, too. We live a homeschooling life-style. We don't try to mimic the public school's schedule or time blocks. Our children like being able to sleep late if they're tired. They love going to the movies in the middle of the day. Learning is fun and exciting for my children, because they don't have to worry if it is going to be on a test. They can read for enjoyment, because they won't have to write a book report consisting of five paragraphs, with five sentences in each paragraph. And they love being able to express their ideas without being mocked by their peers."

As homeschooling parents, Mark and Susie appreciate a life-style that doesn't revolve around report cards and PTA meetings. "We don't have to meet in the principal's office when the school bully threatens our ADHD children," Susie says. "School and all its entrapments don't exist for us."

The children tell Susie she's the best teacher in the world, a role she thoroughly enjoys. "It's wonderful to be with your child as he takes his first step and says his first word," she says. "With homeschooling, I get to be there as they reach other milestones as well. I was able to hear my children read their first words and spell their names for the first time. When they make one of their many realizations and discoveries, it is my husband and I who get to share that celebration with them." Even more, Susie has discovered new personal interests while helping her children learn. "In addition to taking flute lessons and learning to speak French, I'm reading more than I've ever read before, and getting more organized as the years roll on," she says.

This is not to say that life is always perfect. "There certainly are unique challenges in homeschooling," Susie says. "Perhaps some see these as problems with homeschooling. But I see them as family challenges. Normal family problems may be magnified when families are together for longer periods of time, such as kids arguing, kids not wanting to listen to their mother or father, and a mom with burnout."

Susie has experienced burnout firsthand. "When I was pregnant with my fourth child, I was so tired and sick and grouchy, I found I was overreacting to everything," she says. "A child would spell a word wrong and I'd cry, feeling that they'd never learn. I was so rigid in my expectations. When my oldest, Connor, told me he hated schooling I cried even more." Then Susie decided to step back and unschool for several months. The transition was difficult for her, but wonderful for the children. "This is when the kids discovered they loved cartooning," she says. "They filled sketch pads with their favorite characters and made up their own. They gathered snails, put them in a 'keeper' and watched them, wrote stories about them and read library books about them. They also saved coins, counted them, and figured out how much money they'd need to eat at McDonalds."

Discouragement still comes occasionally. "I find that most of my fear and discouragement comes when I try to take on more than I can handle," Susie says, "you know, the 'super mom' thing.

We do a lot as a family, and sometimes this gets to me. I find that I need to take some time for myself, to have quiet and just 'be.' "

For the most part, Susie and Mark's families have been very supportive of homeschooling. "I've never received any negative comments from family over our decision to homeschool," Susie says. "I could tell some were concerned because of their questions at times, but to my face, I've never received negative comments. The negative comments have usually come from strangers or acquaintances who overstepped their bounds and tried to force their unsolicited and unqualified views on me. Most friends have been positive and helpful."

The local school has also been supportive. "Our district is very helpful and not manipulative, as I know some can be," Susie says. "They allow us to borrow texts if we wish, and they distribute the phone number for the state's homeschool organization so that homeschoolers can find support." Utah requires four to six daily hours of schooling for elementary school children, and more for older students. "I never have a problem with the time," Susie says, "since we usually do activities or projects at all hours of the day."

Susie has been pleasantly surprised by several aspects of her homeschooling experience. "I've been amazed, watching the way children learn," she says. "Holt and others have written and lectured about it, but I don't think it becomes real until you see it for yourself. Unschooling is one example. We don't unschool exclusively, but there have been times when my kids unschooled completely. I could hardly believe how well they learned and the projects they voluntarily undertook. Once, Connor and Ian, then seven and six, used one of our human body CD-ROMs as a reference and made a small book about the systems of the body."

Mark and Susie intend to continue homeschooling through high school. "I see no reason to stop," Susie says. "The children's educational opportunities are far greater at home. Beyond academics, there are also the very real benefits of mentoring, apprenticeships, the chance to attend college early, and working in a real job for real money."

For this family, the benefits of homeschooling also include tangible help for their ADHD children. "I'm glad Connor and Duncan can learn at their own pace and in their own way without being labeled," Susie says. "Labels in the public school system can be damaging, because kids learn to think that they're stupid or inferior if they have a learning disability label stuck on them. Teachers and other kids treat the labeled children differently as well."

Through homeschooling, Mark and Susie try to give all their children—and especially Connor and Duncan—the opportunity to pursue their own interests in their own time. "If Connor were in public school, I doubt he'd have the drive to learn algebra or Japanese, and he's dabbled in both under his own leadership," Susie says. "I would also be concerned about his enthusiasm being crushed by tests and homework in public school." Duncan, like Connor, has a real zest for life and learning. He prefers to do his homeschooling at various times of the day. "That way, when his attention runs short, he can work and play when it is most natural for him," Susie says.

Home-schooling is often a difficult task, and some of us might imagine teaching two ADHD children at home to be even harder. "I don't think so," Susie says. "It certainly requires patience, organization, time, and lots of love. These virtues develop with practice, and I guess I get lots of practice. But I'm a mother. I need those qualities anyway."

Timothy, Linda, Jonathan, and Rachel.

Twelve

Homeschooling Single

Family:
Linda (48), Timothy (18), Rachel (16), Jonathan (13).

Location:
Richfield, Minnesota (a suburb of Minneapolis/St. Paul).

Best advice:
Make a decision about homeschooling for one year at a time, and if you can homeschool only one child, homeschool the oldest.

Worst advice:
Your children will get a better education if they are in public school.

Favorite quote:
"Education is not the filling of a bucket but the lighting of a fire." (William Butler Yeats)

Favorite resources:

Homegrown Kids by Raymond and Dorothy Moore (currently out-of-print but still widely available).

The Five Love Languages of Teens by Gary Chapman, Northfield Publishing.

Homeschooling the High Schooler by Diana McAlister and Candice Oneschak, Family Academy Publishing, 23420 Jordan Road, Arlington, WA 98223.

How to Really Love Your Teenager by Ross Campbell, Chariot Victor Books.

I Kissed Dating Goodbye by Joshua Harris, Multnomah Publishers.

L inda H. first became interested in homeschooling when she heard Dr. Raymond Moore discussing the issue on a radio program in the 1980s. "My oldest was only a toddler," she says, "but after studying Moore's books *Better Late Than Early* and *Homegrown Kids*, I knew I wanted to follow this course of homeschooling."

Prior to the birth of her children, Linda had worked as director of Christian education in a church for six and a half years, overseeing all the educational and youth ministry programs. With Timothy's arrival she became a full-time mom. "I have always had a deep underlying commitment to raise my own children," she says. "My husband and I had mutually agreed that I would stay home with them and not put them in ongoing day care to be raised by others. We believed strongly that parents are the best people to raise their own children." Rachel was born in 1984 and Jonathan in 1986.

When Linda was pregnant with Jonathan, the family faced serious financial and personal struggles. "This was an unstable time for me," Linda remembers. "I didn't have the emotional energy for homeschooling and put it on hold indefinitely. Timothy started kindergarten at the public school. I focused on my marriage."

The couple spent six months in marriage counseling, but to

no avail. Linda's husband moved out in 1988, when the children were one, three, and six years old. "I had only a few dollars," she remembers. "I faced an immediate decision: find a job quickly or apply for welfare. Because of my deep convictions about raising my own children, I made the choice to apply for welfare, $621 a month. I felt my children had already lost one parent; they weren't going to lose the other."

A month later, a woman from the church called and asked if Linda would be willing to provide day care for her children during the summer months. A county official told Linda that any cash she received would reduce the amount of her already minimal welfare check, but suggested an alternative: bartering. Linda went back to her friend who needed child care and explained the way the system worked. The friend suggested opening a separate checking account and depositing the money she would have given Linda into that account, then paying her bills out of it. A relative found a dependable car for the family and arranged to cosign a loan. Linda's child care job paid for the car, other necessities, and part of the tuition for a correspondence writing course.

In 1989, eighteen months after their separation, Linda and her husband divorced. "I grieved the loss of all my hopes and dreams for homeschooling," Linda says. "I never spoke to my children about homeschooling, nor did I talk about it with any families who homeschooled. I believed it was impossible for a single parent to homeschool."

To supplement her meager income, Linda began speaking at women's retreats, teaching classes at various churches, and writing magazine articles and youth ministry curricula. "Each provided some additional income, yet allowed me to nurture and invest in my children," she says. In 1990, Linda worked for the U.S. census and was allowed to keep her entire paycheck without penalty. Several church members helped by taking care of the children while Linda worked.

When Jonathan, her youngest, started kindergarten in 1992, Linda attended a small Bible college part-time to earn a two-year degree in ministerial training in addition to her degrees in teaching and Christian education. She began to take advantage of more opportunities to speak at area churches. In turn, these churches wrote checks directly to the Bible college to pay for Linda's books and tuition; this was another form of bartering allowed by the welfare system. After graduating, Linda was invited to intern at a church two days a week. She planned to begin in September of 1995.

It was not until the summer of 1995 that the subject of homeschooling surfaced again. When Timothy was ready to start eighth grade, Rachel, fifth grade and Jonathan, third grade, they each began asking if their mother would teach them at home. "I was evasive," Linda says. "I didn't want to discourage my children, but I didn't want to give them hope, either. I was worried about paperwork, regulations, procedures to follow—overwhelmed by unknowns, because I had never checked into any specific information or even spoken to anyone about homeschooling. I told the kids that I'd love to have them home, but I didn't see how it could work."

Linda had an about-face after having a conversation with a single mom who was going to start homeschooling. "She gave me lots of current information I didn't have and explained basic procedures," Linda says, "but most of all, she was another single mom. That opened the window of possibility for me. And then suddenly something changed. God ignited the desire that had been deep in my heart all those years." Linda never again spoke with the woman who gave her such inspiration. "That was a great example of a divine appointment," she says, smiling.

Timothy and Rachel came home for school that year, though Jonathan stayed in public school. "As a single parent, I knew I couldn't suddenly start homeschooling all three of them," she says. "Single moms must have a strong support system to be able to homeschool successfully. I was fortunate to find much practical support from homeschooling families in my community and church." Still, Linda rightly anticipated the challenges ahead.

When Linda started an internship at the church in September, the family's homeschooling began as well. Sometimes Timothy and Rachel came to work with their mother and did schoolwork in another room of the church. Sometimes they studied at home. "Home-schooling was really a natural expansion of the kinds of learning we had been doing all along, discussing issues, exploring new things, and reading fascinating books together," Linda says. "I had already instilled in my children a love of learning that blossomed even more as we officially homeschooled."

The next school year, Linda homeschooled Jonathan and Rachel and enrolled Timothy in ninth-grade of public school. Halfway through the year, Timothy began asking his mother if she would homeschool him again. Linda was completely taken by surprise by this request, as she had thought of Tim's past homeschooling as a one-year venture. "When he kept asking, I knew I needed to pray about it and seriously consider his request," she says.

Two weeks before school started that fall, "God spoke clearly," Linda says, "that this was a special window of opportunity in Timothy's life and I should do whatever it took to have him home full-time that year." Linda homeschooled Tim for tenth grade. "I watched him grow and mature," she says. "He had the unique opportunity that year to apprentice one day a week with a man who had a home repair business. Timothy not only expanded his skills, but spent valuable time with an adult male he admired. I had been praying for adult role models for him, and this was a definite answer to prayer." Rachel stayed at home, and Jonathan went back to public school.

While coordinating homeschool, Linda was also dealing with money problems and the demands of work. Her church job proved to be much more involved than she expected. Though her salary helped her get off welfare, the number of hours she worked, plus speaking engagements, exhausted her and created great stress for the entire family. Timothy offered this advice: "Mom, anyone can do the things you do at your job, but no one else can homeschool us." Soon afterward, Linda asked her employer to reduce her hours. A month later, at Jonathan's request, he came home for school. "So within the 1997–98 school year I made two major changes I never expected to make: homeschooling a high school student and homeschooling all three of my children at the same time," Linda says. "I have never regretted either decision."

Linda took a financial leap of faith by deciding not to reapply for welfare payments. Her ex-husband, who lives ten miles away and sees the children every other Sunday, was sending regular child support payments. With this small amount plus a tiny income, the family became self-supporting.

Linda thinks the rewards of homeschooling are worth the financial sacrifices she's made. "Dr. Moore's research shows that children developing naturally in a nonpressured environment have rapid growth in learning," she says, "while those pressured to learn before they are physically ready are discouraged with learning. That's why we all like the freedom to learn in the ways we choose, according to interest and learning style."

Decisions on homeschooling are made one year at a time. "As a single parent, many circumstances influence my ability to homeschool," Linda says. "By prayerfully making a decision each year about whether to homeschool and who is to be at home, I am released from pressure to make a long-term commitment I might not be able to keep." Linda thinks this "one year at a time" philosophy encourages each family member to treasure the time they have together. "It also helps me to stay focused and ask, 'If this is the only year I can homeschool, how do I want to invest in the lives of my children?' "

Sometimes the difficult decisions have produced unexpected opportunities. "When I cut back the hours at my job," Linda says, "I was not only able to have the time to bring Jonathan home, but also time to start writing a book." Presently, she works as a bookstore salesperson one to two days a week to help her learn about the retail side of the book business. She continues to speak on topics related to Christian growth. She also teaches occasional for-pay, four- to six-week classes on worldviews, American history, and other topics to junior and senior high homeschoolers. "Over the years I have turned down several jobs that would have suited me," she says, "but would have sacrificed my children."

A flexible working schedule enables Linda to meet the academic challenges of homeschooling. "Minnesota requires that math, English, social studies, science, health, and physical education are taught through the eighth grade," she notes. "Our family's homeschool high school graduation requirements include practical living skills, money management, preparation for marriage, specific subjects my children choose, and Bible study."

One of Linda's priorities is to help Tim, Rachel, and Jonathan develop a Christian worldview. "I want my children to have a growing relationship with God and a firm foundation in God's Word [the Bible] that will equip them to face the complexities of life," Linda says. "This is the foundation of our homeschool. It influences how we study our subjects and the activities we pursue."

The family uses a group unit study approach for Bible study, history, and reading, and often discusses books together. "We recently did a Bible study on compassion, what it is, and how it is demonstrated," Linda says. "Then I noticed a book in a store about Mother Teresa, so we started reading it together. We watched a movie, read another book, and our reading blossomed into an extensive month-long unit study about Mother Teresa's life and ministry to the poor, the aged, orphans, and lepers, and then on to the geography, history, culture, and religions of India. The unit study ended with us gathering supplies for a homeless shelter nearby."

Another unit study began when Linda and the children read a novel, *Guilt by Association* by Michael Farris, about a prolife group accused of burning down an abortion clinic. "The story involved several court scenes and appeals up to the Supreme Court, and taught us much about the U.S. legal system," Linda says. "We had many discussions about the Bill of Rights, the court system, abortion, and a comparison of recent court decisions with the Bible." As a follow-up, Jonathan decided to write a play in the form of a trial. He wrote, directed, and acted in the play, *Homeschool on Trial: Do Homeschoolers Really Learn?* It was presented at the annual area homeschool awards night.

Linda and her children plan the lessons, but sometimes school takes a different direction than expected. "I have learned to trust God as the ultimate teacher in our homeschool," Linda says. "Time and again as we study together, we all see how God weaves a particular theme throughout all our subjects, and I know I didn't plan it that way."

Homeschooling allows the family the freedom to follow a subject of interest or to rearrange their schedule. "I believe that homeschooling adapts to the ebb and flow of life more easily than traditional schooling," Linda says. "If someone needs help remodeling their house, we adjust our schedule so we can help. If someone needs child care, we try to be available. We look for practical ways that we as individuals and as a family can demonstrate God's love to others, and homeschooling gives us the flexibility to do so."

Such flexibility is a real plus in the midst of crises. When Linda had emergency gallbladder surgery a few years ago, her children stayed with various homeschooling families for a full week. "They continued their learning and joined in some subjects with the families they were with while I recovered at home from surgery," she says. "Homeschooling made it much easier."

Homeschooling also makes it simpler to take advantage of unusual opportunities. A couple of years ago, a personal friend of the family's walked the length and breadth of the United States, praying for America and encouraging others to do the same. "Rachel had gone with the youth group to walk with John for five days in Nebraska," Linda says. "At the end of the summer, Rachel, Jonathan, and I drove down to walk with him in Iowa for two days. We ended up staying with him and his family for eleven days, prayer-walking daily, staying in their RVs, sleeping in a homeless shelter, eating at a soup kitchen, leading worship at a church we visited, taking part in a city prayer rally, being on TV on the news, and witnessing many answers to prayer. It was an unexpected change of plans, but clearly a good start to the school year."

During at-home school times, the family uses a variety of experiences, tools, and resources to help them complete their assignments. The computer is available primarily for writing reports. Videos teach geometry, world history, worldviews, and more. They visit the library frequently. With Linda's help, her children map out their own plans and methodology for finishing their annual schoolwork. "School is not a separate compartment of our lives, but an integral part of our corporate life," Linda notes. "We all teach each other new things as we learn them."

Linda encourages an atmosphere of appreciation and encouragement in the family. "I have found out a lot about learning styles and try to honor the uniqueness in each of my children," she says. "Timothy is highly skilled at fixing things, Rachel is the ace speller, and Jonathan loves to cook. Rachel helps Jonathan with math, and Timothy helps Rachel and Jonathan with science."

Timothy's natural ability to understand how things work and repair them has been a real asset, and he learned much during his apprenticeship. Timothy is attending a discipleship training school of Youth With a Mission (YWAM). "His team spent a week in Mexico building a house for a single mom and her three children," Linda says. "They also helped with clothing distribution and played with children in an orphanage." Timothy's team also went to Japan for two months.

Rachel has a deep love for babies and little children. When a friend of Linda's had a baby, Rachel volunteered to spend one morning each week helping the mom care for the baby and her sister. "Rachel has been doing this for two years and loves it," Linda says. "We all recognize this gift, and it is part of her schooling." Rachel also went on a mission trip to an orphanage in the Ukraine to care for very young children. "She loves to serve people, whether it's working with children, older people, or volunteering at the library," Linda says.

In addition to cooking, Jonathan likes drama, computers, drawing, and writing. An original poem he entered in a contest will be published in a national anthology, and one of his drawings is featured in a book of original artwork. He also writes adventure/mystery stories. "Jonathan tends to learn in spurts," Linda says. "He'll study a subject intensely, and then it's on to another topic. Sometimes he likes to have math days, when he completes six to eight math lessons for fun, or reading days. Our homeschooling environment welcomes his unique preferences." When Jonathan decided he wanted to learn German, he not only studied a Power-Glide German course, but also checked out all the books on German from the local library.

There is no typical day, though the overall format is schoolwork and books in the morning, and projects, individual study, work, and volunteer activities in the afternoon. Monday and Wednesday mornings are "together school" times, when Linda lays out the plan for the week, provides instruction in group subjects, and gives assignments to be completed. Tuesday and Thursday mornings are study days. Thursday afternoons Linda meets with the children individually to discuss their assignments and subjects. Friday is set aside for library visits and special activities.

Everyone meets daily for lunch and discussion. Afterward, Linda's jobs vary from household work to writing and preparing to speak. Three days a week, Rachel serves dinner at a senior-living dining room. On Tuesdays and Wednesdays, Jonathan delivers five hundred newspapers by walking or biking. Evenings are reserved for church youth activities and sports. "But no matter what we're doing, our family and our home is the central base for our learning," Linda says. "This produces a sense of belonging and well-being, and keeps the family as the primary influence in my children's lives."

September through May, Linda and the children focus on academics. "We all need a change of pace to learn in different ways in the summer, including camping and vacations," Linda says. "I schedule two to three weeks off at Christmas and one week at Easter. No one has regular school on his or her birthday. They get to pick whatever they want to learn about, in whatever way they choose, on that day."

Linda believes it's important for her children to concentrate on more than at-home book learning. All three have been involved in both extracurricular activities and classes outside the home, including music and drawing lessons, city softball, baseball and soccer teams, a church basketball league, biology and chemistry labs for homeschool high school students at a local college, drama camp, basketball, church youth camp, and youth retreats and conferences. "Homeschooling provides many opportunities for socialization with a wide range of ages," Linda says. "Variety in kinds of people and environments is very important to us. And by not being strongly influenced daily by peers, my children learn to recognize and appreciate their uniqueness without being pressured by others to conform."

Linda considers herself privileged to live in an area where there's an excellent relationship between the school district and homeschoolers. In addition, the state offers postsecondary education options (PSEO), where high school students can attend college during their junior and senior years. Timothy took classes at a community college during his senior year for both high school and college credit, as well as completing some subjects at home.

Minnesota requires the teaching of basic subjects plus yearly testing. "Our homeschool support group takes the test, usually the Iowa Basic, together as a group," Linda says. "My children have always scored very, very well. They did well in public school, and they've improved each year since they've been home."

Timothy, Rachel, and Jonathan are expected to excel at more than academics. Laundry, cooking, and cleaning the kitchen and bathroom are all part of their training in life skills. Everyone has specific jobs on certain days, and jobs are rotated every few months.

Paid work always has been an integral part of the family homeschool. Timothy started a once-a-week paper route at age eleven, delivering eighty papers in the neighborhood. Rachel and Jonathan assisted him, then got their own routes. For more than seven years the children delivered this weekly newspaper, which is now Jonathan's responsibility. "Delivering five hundred newspapers each week has been a wonderful teaching tool in organization, punctuality, servanthood, time management, communication skills, cooperation, and perseverance," Linda says. "Minnesota winters can be extremely cold."

Tim held a part-time job at a garden center for two years. This past year, he worked at Taystee Bakery Outlet, where he unloaded shipments of bread, stocked shelves, and helped customers. "We had a good discount and lots of bread," Linda recalls with a smile.

Linda thinks working provides "a different way to learn, including the opportunity to manage money. As a single parent, I carefully manage my own money and have spent much time teaching my children God's view on money, that everything we have comes from and belongs to Him, that we are stewards." Each of her children willingly contributes 10 percent of his or her income toward worthy causes, saves some money in an "after high school" savings account, and budgets the rest. "From their work earnings, they pay for youth events, sports activities, and summer camp," Linda says. "They buy most of their clothes and contribute ten percent toward household expenses. They have had to learn the realities of living within their means, and it has built character and wise money management skills." The family has been debt-free for seven years.

In spite of Linda's accomplishments, homeschooling as a single parent has been a tremendous challenge. Because her relatives live out-of-state and are generally unfamiliar with homeschooling, Linda cannot go to family members for support. Instead, she relies on many friends, both homeschoolers and others who live nearby, for encouragement. She is part of a statewide homeschooling association called Minnesota Association of Christian Home Educators (MACHE) that holds an annual conference and offers support. Linda has led a discussion with other single parent homeschoolers at a MACHE conference.

During stressful times, "I have learned to pour out my heart to God and tell him my concerns and frustrations," Linda says. "Sometimes we've been pushing too hard and we all need a break for a day. Sometimes I need to take time off to fulfill other pressing responsibilities while my children keep learning on their own. Sometimes we all need to go to the park or spend time with friends. It helps to ask, 'Why am I homeschooling?' and recall the reasons and goals I had when I began, to help keep everything in perspective."

"I have tried not to copy or compare," Linda continues, "but instead, to recognize that God has given me as a gift to my children. I try not to measure up to some impossible standard of what my homeschool should be like. I realize that I will never have as great an opportunity to influence a person's life as I have with my own children. I cherish them as gifts from God, and I invest my life into them."

Timothy, Rachel, and Jonathan appreciate their mother's commitment. Having attended public schools for several years, all three are keenly aware of the advantages of homeschool.

Jonathan says he likes homeschooling "because it's really fun, I get to go at my pace, and I'm together with my family. The only disadvantage to homeschool is, you don't know as many people because you're not in a class, and you don't get some of the good school lunches like Italian dunkers and Charlie Brown pie." Rachel enjoys homeschooling because she can spend more time together with her family, even if they're all doing different things. "I can learn more about my special interests and I can learn more about God," she says. "I thought about going back to public school but didn't because it's too loud. It gives me a headache, it's too long, it starts too early, and you don't get one-on-one teaching like you do at home."

Linda expected to enjoy homeschooling, "but it's even more enjoyable and fulfilling than I thought it would be," she says, "with many surprising benefits." Teaching Timothy at home, for example, helped his mother to really get to know and understand her son. "It radically changed our relationship," she says. "I am convinced that during the junior high years, our children need the additional love, acceptance, support, and encouragement that the homeschool environment can offer. I am glad I had the opportunity to be available at that point in Timothy's life."

Timothy graduated on May 27, 2000, with a private service he planned himself. "It was a wonderful ceremony," Linda says, "and a privilege to give him his diploma." The service included times of worship, reading of scripture, and prayer. Tim's youth pastor delivered the main address. Speeches were given by both Tim and Linda, and Rachel and Linda sang a duet. Linda's parents were present and found it an eye-opening experience. "They were impressed because Tim designed everything himself, with my help," Linda says. "They had never seen any homeschooler's graduation." Tim's father also attended and gave a speech. "He has been quietly supportive of my homeschooling," Linda says. "He knows me and my education background, and it's not been a question."

Years have passed since Linda went to court for a divorce she didn't want. "I was extremely angry with God," she remembers. "I had thought if I stayed close to God and prayed and tried to reconcile, He would fix my marriage. I asked Him, 'Where are you in the middle of this?' " As Linda wept bitterly over her situation, she felt God saying to her, "Don't look around you, at the people or circumstances. Look at Me. I am your Abiding Hope. I am the one you can depend on, I'll see you through this, I'll meet your needs. Put your hope in Me." That moment was a turning point in Linda's life. "I have learned to trust God more and keep my eyes on Him," she says, "and I have discovered his faithfulness to my family."

Linda's ongoing passion to raise her children to be "godly adults" gives her the strength to continue. "I'm committed to homeschooling my children during the high school years," she says. "It provides such an amazing opportunity to significantly influence their thinking, attitudes, and behavior." Some consider Linda irresponsible, questioning why she refuses to get a full-time job and put her children in public school. "There are those who think I border on being crazy," she says. "However, I know that God has called me to mother my children and has unfolded homeschooling as part of that plan."

In 1995, when Linda was filling out the paperwork needed to begin homeschooling, she discovered that every Minnesota homeschool must have a name. "I was praying about this and the words 'Abiding Hope' flashed through my mind," she says. "Six years earlier, when I was facing an unwanted divorce, God had told me clearly that He was my Abiding Hope and I needed to keep my focus on Him. Now, I realized that in this new venture of homeschooling, He was again promising to be my Abiding Hope." Linda named the family school Abiding Hope Academy. "The name recognizes that God is the teacher of this homeschool," she says. "He is the one who restored the hopes and dreams for homeschooling He had put in my heart long ago."

Brian with little sister Heidi.

Thirteen

A Homeschooler Goes to College

Family:
Tim (47), Kathy (40), Brian (20), Christie (17), James (15), Scott (13), Bonnie (10), Peter (9), Timmy (7), Isaac (5), Benjamin (3), Heidi (2), Justin (newborn).

Location:
Newark, Delaware (home base); Purcellville, Virginia (college base).

Best advice:
Listen to your heart. If you want something, even if you're not sure it's good that you want it, listen and trust God to answer.

Worst advice:
Make sure you're prepared so you can get into college. Being prepared is more important than living and enjoying today.

Favorite quote:
"You are my beloved son, in whom I am well pleased." Mark 1:11, the Bible.

Favorite resources:
Wild at Heart by John Eldredge, Thomas Nelson.
The Subtle Power of Spiritual Abuse by David Johnson and Jeff VanVonderen, Bethany House.
Sacred Romance by Brent Curtis and John Eldredge, Thomas Nelson.
Tales of the Kingdom by David and Karen Mains, Lamplighter Publishing.
The Healing Path by Dan Allender, Waterbrook Press.

B rian V. is a lifelong homeschooler. For sixteen years he learned at home. Now he is homeschooling in college.

The oldest of eleven children, Brian was the first to leave his home in Newark, Delaware. He is a freshman majoring in political science at Patrick Henry College, a brand-new school that is geared especially toward homeschoolers. In its first year of operation, Patrick Henry consists of only one large building in Purcellville, Virginia, that houses everything but the students, including the offices of the Home School Legal Defense Association (HSLDA). A dorm is under construction and nearly complete.

Brian spends most of his weekends at school, but occasionally commutes three hours home to Newark. He loves his family and misses them. "One of the things that has been fun about being the oldest of so many kids is I've learned how to enjoy people in the midst of inconvenience," he says. "That's been valuable for my character and helpful in learning how to relate to others. Little kids can easily be a *big* inconvenience," he says, laughing.

When at home, Brian joins many "little kids," his ten siblings from infancy to age seventeen. "I remember watching the movie *Cheaper By the Dozen* and I couldn't figure out what was so funny about it," Brian says. "That was how I lived. I grew up in a house with two refrigerators. I learned to cook meat forty pounds at a time and to negotiate a huge pile of laundry." At one point there were six boys sleeping in Brian's bedroom: a bunk bed was set up with two on the top, two on the bottom, and two on the floor on mattresses.

Kathy, Brian's mother, is the children's primary educator and a part-time writer on homeschool subjects. For many years she was the editor of *KONOS Helps* newsletter. Husband Tim runs the family business, Tim's Great Stuff, a curriculum-bagging service that provides sacks filled with literature for conventions.

The family has homeschooled since 1984. Brian had just finished a year of Christian school kindergarten when his parents gave him the option of returning for first grade or being taught at home. He chose the latter. "Initially, our extended families were very skeptical about the idea of homeschooling," Kathy says. "During the first years of homeschooling, when there was a question of its legality, I was afraid to let my children outside before three P.M. My mother was a social worker, and I lived in fear of her hotlining us, turning us in to the authorities. This wasn't unfounded, because my brother told me, after she died a few years ago, that she *had* considered suing us for custody of the children." Tim's mother thought it was a shame when Brian was taken out of school. "Now she asks us how we were so smart to homeschool, and notes how great the kids are," Kathy says. All eleven have been taught at home for almost their entire lives.

Brian has been exclusively homeschooled since first grade. "It was a good experience for me," he says, "very, very good. I discovered learning as something to be excited about." Kathy taught Brian through the early days of the homeschooling movement, when critics were carefully watching test scores as proof of homeschoolers' academic success. In spite of this, Kathy and Tim decided early on to abandon traditional textbooks and teach primarily using KONOS Character Curriculum (www.konos.com).

KONOS organizes learning into unit studies built around particular character traits of God: orderliness, trust, patience, and wisdom. Subjects such as language arts, history, science, art, music, and Bible study are explored through the reading of great literature and an extensive list of suggested hands-on activities. Children of all ages can be included in the same unit as they learn the basics together, and older children can be given extra assignments to cover a topic in more depth.

Brian vividly recalls the family's long ago study of medieval times, KONOS-style. Kathy helped the children create costumes of troubadors, jesters, knights, and ladies-in-waiting. Together they looked through books on coats of arms and then each designed his or her own, painting them on banners or shields to be hung on the wall. Brian memorized the story of William Tell and recited it to "the king," his father. He and his best friend staged a sword fight. The children learned the words and music to *Greensleeves*. "We planned a huge medieval feast," Brian remembers. "Very few people had heard of homeschooling at that time, so we invited all our friends and family from church and shared the event to show them what it was all about." As a direct result of this experience, several parents in their area decided to begin homeschooling.

When Brian was growing up, his family was usually involved in a cooperative with other families who taught KONOS. "Those are some of my best memories, having co-op with friends, dressing up as Indians, making a huge model of the human ear," he says. "My school time memories were the same as play time memories. This is where I gained a lot of my interest in history, government, literature, science, everything." Kathy was recently making crafts with some of the children, using a glue gun, when Brian walked in. "That smells so good!" he said. "Just like a co-op day!"

During the years Brian was at home, Kathy, new to home-schooling and lacking confidence, often changed curriculum. One constant in her teaching was use of the Montessori method. "I tried to incorporate the ideas of creating a prepared environ-ment and respecting a child's work and interests within the choices I set up for him or her," Kathy says. "When I read the Michael Olaf catalog about the various stages of childhood, I saw how homeschooling had allowed us to support each stage, and that allowed me to sharpen and focus everything I did."

The family always has stayed committed to unit studies. "My mom didn't realize that by making Indian pudding, reading sto-ries about Native Americans, and camping out in teepees, I was learning and succeeding in school," Brian says. "I discovered his-tory through people's lives. I got to experience what it was like to discover a scientific principle without knowing it ahead of time. All of this fit in the context of learning."

Because of the particular way in which Brian learns, KONOS was an excellent choice of curriculum. "I like to come at a subject from every angle, build as many relationships to it as possible, taste, touch, and bounce it around," he says. "I pick up loads of facts and transfer them to other bodies of knowledge. KONOS helped me to do this." In high school, Brian went on to the more advanced KONOS History of the World (H.O.W.) study plans and liked them very much.

As a pre-teen, Brian asked for special privileges and got them. "When I was twelve and we were considering high school, I told my parents I wanted to go straight from algebra I into physics," Brian says. "My dad said, 'OK, let him do it!' I created my own unit studies for physics." Brian completed a six-CD physics text-book, read Einstein's and Steven Hawkings's books, watched a movie on physicists, and talked to Madeline L'Engel, author of *A Wrinkle in Time*, by phone. "My parents allowing me to study physics on my own was a pivotal point for me," Brian says. "Ultimately, they let me make my own decisions about what I needed to do to graduate."

The same year he studied physics, Brian started his own lawn-mowing business by passing out flyers around the neighborhood. As a teenager, he designed board games and computer software. "I had a consulting company called HeartDrive," Brian says. "I worked with the author of a children's handwriting program, and basically, I listened to her ideas and then tried to make the computer carry them out. She did the artwork and I did animations, interface, and sound, plus most of the design work. We refined it together, and then took it all to a professional to encode everything." The handwriting program, the Barchowsky Fluenthand, is available now on CD-ROM (www.bfhhandwriting.com).

Brian helped his father in Tim's Great Stuff for six years, supervising, stuffing bags, doing secretarial work, and designing new projects. He also built the company's business system, organizing all the hard files on the computer so information could be accessed quickly to create form letters, packets, and labels as well as analyzing company data. He learned a great deal about running a business and building relationships with clientele.

Brian also learned the fine points of household chores. "In our house, unpaid work—'family duty'—included cleaning up after oneself and helping with housework," Brian says. "I didn't really learn to sew, but I could do almost everything else, including a little cooking." For years he was the breakfast chef in charge of fixing pancakes, oatmeal, and other delicacies. "I also learned a lot about housekeeping, and that's been a big help at school," Brian says. "I know what to do to clean a room and do it fast. I learned about thoroughness and how to make the decisions to get a job done well."

Throughout Brian's teen years, it wasn't always easy for Tim and Kathy to give their son the freedom to choose. Kathy allowed Brian room to explore, educationally, until state-mandated high school requirements began to press in on her. At that point she tried to help Brian meet the requirements as quickly as possible. "Mom thought I should get As *and* learn," he says. "When I was fifteen I was prepared to graduate from high school. I wanted to write a book and do some other things. Mom felt I should concentrate on earning credits for college. What happened was that I lost both. I was stressed out about these things I was trying to achieve, and torn because I couldn't pursue what I loved."

Brian officially completed high school work at sixteen but wasn't yet ready to make a decision on college. He spent the next four years pursuing a number of interests, taking music courses, practicing violin for several hours a day, completing computer programming for pay, studying Greek and Roman classics online, creating business proposals and web pages, and participating in ministries. "All the while I had this nagging feeling he should be 'getting on with his life,' " Kathy says. "I missed the point; he *was* doing real life."

"High schoolers have way too much pressure on them," Brian comments. "I think teens are most productive if they take a more relaxed pace." He also believes high schoolers should be given a great deal of freedom to help them gain a sense of what it's like in the world outside the home. "How do parents empower a young adult to go into life?" he asks. "Train him how to live, help him find what he desires, and give him the courage to pursue that. He can always learn algebra or correct bad spelling later."

Brian's philosophy of learning has remained essentially the same in college as in high school. Most of the professors at PHC take a textbook approach to teaching, encouraging the students to meet requirements by doing homework every week and passing tests. "I take what I have to do and redirect it," Brian says. "I've decided to basically transform my college education into unit studies. If I'm studying something I love, then I'll learn. Today I've made the choice I'm going to do what I love now. I listen to my heart."

Brian recalls his past experiences with KONOS activities as an aid in completing his schoolwork. "In western civ this year, I absorbed in two minutes what I needed to know about the Middle Ages," he says. "Charlemagne, Pippin the Third, and others meant something to me and were tied to my memory as real persons. What could have been a boring class was fun because I remembered all the stuff I used to do in KONOS."

If he were to add up all the study hours required for his courses, Brian says he'd have no time to eat or sleep. "I'm not getting As here; that would be a mark of insanity," he says with a chuckle. "If I need to do something, I just do it. My study time is very focused. I don't worry about academics; I just live my life."

A typical day begins with weight training and running, Bible reading, "and getting in touch with God," then breakfast. Brian plays guitar in the folk band that performs for PHC's daily chapel services, and practices every morning. Chapel is at 9:00.

On Mondays, Wednesdays, and Fridays, classes include U.S. history, English composition, and Old Testament survey. Lunch is served in a first-floor dining hall. Brian works from 2:00 to 4:00 for the Home School Legal Defense Association as a database assistant to the administrator, where he upgrades projects and implements software. At 4:00 on Mondays and Wednesdays he enjoys an hour and a half choir practice.

Tuesdays and Thursdays are more relaxed. After the normal morning routine and chapel, Brian takes western civilization and rhetoric (public speaking) classes. He works for HSLDA from 4:00 to 6:00 for a total of eight to ten hours a week, a job that pays for part of his tuition.

Every evening includes dinner in the dining room, studying until 8:00, a second practice for chapel, and then more studying. Friday nights, Brian goes swing dancing with a group of students. He spends most Saturdays hitting the books, with an occasional break for a favorite sport like football. Students hold their own worship services Sunday night.

Although Brian is officially a political science major, "I am a Christian, and that is an educational program in itself," he quips. "I'm very interested in human rights across the world, and I might like to get into international politics. Ambassadorial work possibly, or missions work. For me, it's important that I'm open to people's pain before I try to help them in their pain. If I go into missions, I would want to live with the people I'm trying to help."

Brian is actively involved in a church of three hundred who meet regularly in one of many smaller "house churches." "It's safer than an institutionalized church," he says, "down-to-earth, and with little need to establish authority. It begins with relationships." Brian sees relationships as one important facet of his Christian life. "Here at Patrick Henry, we have a lot of family-type relationships, brothers and sisters in Christ. The girls are my sisters and the guys are my brothers."

Music is a very important part of his life. "I've played piano since I was two," Brian says. "When I was five years old, Mom took me to a Wilmington, Delaware, music school and looked into piano lessons, but there were no openings. Grandfather played violin, and I decided to try that, instead." Music runs in the family, as Kathy plays harp and piano, takes voice lessons, teaches violin, and composes for harp. Tim was a trumpet player in the U.S. Navy Band for four years. "Dad's dream was that we would have a family string quartet, and that happened when I was fourteen," Brian says. "Scott and I played violin, Christie was on viola, and James on cello."

When Brian was eighteen, he was part of the Philadelphia

Youth Orchestra that traveled to Moscow as part of the World Youth Orchestra. "I got a chance to perform with more technically advanced players," he says. "By the time I was seventeen, I was practicing four to six hours a day on average, including orchestra and ensemble practice." His extensive practicing gave Brian a severe case of tendonitis and encouraged another direction, in guitar. He discovered composing and has since written thirty songs. "I'm glad that my parents love music and taught me to love music," Brian says. "There were times when money for our lessons was coming out of the food budget."

Brian has been seriously pursuing his passions, like music, since he was twelve. "I set goals and went after them," he says. "Later I learned to not make goals the end of my life, but also to live *today* in a productive way. This philosophy enabled me to head my own company, develop a project, and much more. They were life lessons that empowered me."

Brian thinks traditional schools take away power. "I see the schools as making everything secure. Everything is fine, it's all laid out. They tell you, 'There's no need to question. We'll help you by never letting you question.' Going to school doesn't raise men, warriors who will fight and risk everything for a good cause. For every guy I know, purpose and significance are directly connected to what he's willing to risk. Young men need help discovering their hearts, confronting their fears, and having the ability to make choices, even if it means they'll possibly fail. To deny failure and choices is to deny the ability to be real."

Through the years, Tim and Kathy's decision to give Brian choices has strengthened their relationship with him. "Not every parent is willing to be real and vulnerable," Brian says. "Even though we're still human beings with problems, my parents have always been friends and confidantes. Now that I see where there are things I don't understand, listening to them is helpful." Kathy says homeschooling has, in the past sixteen years, "made me far more creative, far more compassionate, and far closer to my children than I ever dreamed possible. It is amazing to me what the heart will take on out of conviction and love for one's family. It's crazy, but it has stretched me and taught me so much."

Brian also finds that he has been stretched. "I worked really hard to get into college," he says. "I worked harder in high school to get in than I'm working now in college. When I was younger, I put being prepared for life above living and enjoying things today. Now it's more of a moment by moment adventure."

Shaisa, Matt, and Jennifer.

Fourteen

Working Their Dream Careers

Family:
Jennifer (39), Matt (40), Shaisa (SHAY-suh, 13).

Location:
Moline, Illinois (one of the Quad Cities) a metro area of about one million.

Best advice:
Relax, you have plenty of time! Figure out what *your* goals are, not the school's, not your mom's.

Worst advice:
Put your child in school so you can get a *real* job.

Favorite quote:
"The world is divided into people who think they are right." (Peggy Seeger)

Favorite resources:

The Teenage Liberation Handbook by Grace Llewellyn, Lowry
   House Publishing.
What Do I Do Monday? by John Holt, Heinemann.
How Children Learn by John Holt, Perseus Press.
How Children Fail by John Holt, Perseus Press.
Dumbing Us Down by J. T. Gatto, New Society Publishing.

Jennifer B.-N. read about homeschooling and self-directed
learning when she was fifteen or sixteen, and she wanted to
try it herself. "My parents said 'No way,' but I decided to keep on
learning anyway," Jennifer says, smiling. "I also planned to
homeschool my own kids if ever I had some. I informed my future husband, Matt, on our third date that, by the way, if this
worked out and we got married and had kids, they would be
homeschooled. What could he say?"

Jennifer, Matt, and their daughter Shaisa believe in learning
together as a family, "One of our goals in homeschooling is to
live with people who are interested in learning as a lifelong activity and who are passionate about their interests," Jennifer says. "I
also hope that Shaisa becomes a kind, loving, ethical individual
with a deep sense of connectedness to this world and the beings
in it. I hope that she is an integrated person in whom spirit, body,
mind, and emotion are balanced parts of a whole, and that's also
what I am working towards."

To this end, Jennifer and Matt made the difficult decision to
leave conventional jobs and pursue their own passions. "We are
both artistic, and another one of our main goals for Shaisa is to
have her grow up and make a living at what she loves to do," Jennifer says. "The best way to teach her that is by example. That's
one of the reasons we decided to try to make our main money
from music and the arts."

For two years, Matt was an electrician's apprentice and hated his work. "I thought it was a *bad* example to all of us," Jennifer says. "I was afraid it would probably kill him, and then we'd really be in trouble." Matt quit his job and decided to pursue a full schedule in music. He currently plays piano with dance bands and for two churches. He also accompanies the high school and junior high show choirs and arranges music for them. In addition, he sings tenor and frequently performs in an a cappella quartet with Jennifer and two friends and composes music. Ironically, electrical work is now his hobby.

Like her husband, Jennifer is also talented in the arts. She performs poetry and, with other poets on her team, has participated in competitions against others. She is also a visual artist specializing in small-scale sculpture and collage. "A lot of my art is concept-based," she says. "I did a sculpture with a base of driftwood and used red and metallic paints, polymer clays, tobacco, and thyme seeds. It's called 'Seeds of Time in the Womb of the Tree of the World.' I take images and combine them carefully so that they seem to be all of one piece until you look at them and see the discrepancies." Jennifer is a member of Midcoast Fine Arts, a nonprofit agency made up of artists who actively seek opportunities to display their art.

In addition to her work in music and art, Jennifer is employed at the Youth Transitional Housing Program, where she works with formerly homeless teens, helping them to "get their lives together," find and keep a job, and function on their own. "It was supposed to be part-time but turned into full-time," she says. "I wasn't prepared for how much I would love this job and the people who work here. I like the philosophy behind it—working with participants' strengths—and the reality." Jennifer works three night shifts, from 8:00 P.M. to 8:00 A.M., each week. Each of the eight teens in the program has his or her own space in one of four two-bedroom apartments plus access to several other "common" rooms.

Her job provides Jennifer with a generous hourly wage, the option of health benefits, and a surprising amount of free time. "I am able to write and do artwork or practice music a lot of the time after the participants are in their apartments for the night," Jennifer says. "I like getting a salary to work on my various projects! I have to be ready to quit at a moment's notice if a problem comes up, but heck, that's just like being a mom."

Jennifer has learned that many of the teenage participants in the transitional housing program are interested in the arts as a vocation or an avocation. "They watch me do my arts and crafts and are usually surprised at the sheer amount of time that has to be devoted to any art form before it becomes salable," she says. "A frequent comment I hear is 'Man! That *is* real work; I thought it would be easy.' "

Shaisa's home learning revolves around her parents' fluctuating schedules. When Jennifer works with the housing program, Shaisa, a night owl, usually calls her mother around 1:00 A.M. to talk. By the time Jennifer arrives at home, her daughter is asleep. Jennifer sleeps until Shaisa has awakened, done her chores, and completed the schoolwork she can do on her own, around 12:30 P.M. "I get home just as my hubby is leaving," Jennifer sighs, "but by the time Matt returns, Shaisa and I are both awake and relatively functional. She and I are not morning people!"

In keeping with their overall philosophy of life, the family "unschools." "I'd say we don't have much of a schedule," Jennifer says. "We are trying to do some Mortensen Math every day at Shaisa's request, and with her online role-playing gaming, Shaisa gets a lot of additional practice in math. She usually reads quite a bit. We do school year round and never really get a break, since we are learning all the time. It isn't forced or hard; it's a joy." Jennifer says her goals as a "resource person" have become clearer. "I used to have more 'schoolish' goals until I figured out that I didn't have to follow that model," she says.

Jennifer believes in what she calls "healthy power dynamics."

"A lot of the structures in society are sick because they use a kind of power that's overbearing and hierarchical," she says. "I don't want to participate in that as much as possible. I don't want to be in that system. Instead, I want to be more encouraging for myself and the people around me to develop the power from within themselves." This applies not only to Jennifer's personal life, but also to homeschooling.

Shaisa follows her own lead in educating herself, with Matt and Jennifer offering support where needed. "We try to help our daughter pursue her many interests," Jennifer says. "Shaisa has completed a number of 4-H projects involving baking, a scratch board, collage, and a detailed polymer clay dragon." Shaisa helped her dad install a dryer outlet as a basic electricity project. She has taken horseback riding lessons since she was three and studies judo and jujitsu. She draws extensively, especially her role-playing characters (from online gaming), and in Japanese animé styles. She also enjoys singing. In addition, Shaisa baby-sits and has done paid cleaning and volunteer work at a petting zoo.

The family doesn't use a curriculum, per se, relying more on activities and discussion to facilitate learning. "We cover subjects that seem important to us," Jennifer says. "We talk about religion, philosophy, current events, fantasy literature, biology, judo, horses, history, politics, music, art, and whatever else comes up. We are going to have to get a little more structured now, because Shaisa has reached that magic age of thirteen when more formal schooling is developmentally desirable. And she seems to be clamoring for it."

Unschooling philosophy considers "school" to be something that goes on during every waking moment. Because of this, the family finds it easy to meet Illinois's homeschool requirements. "Our state is very easy on homeschoolers," Jennifer says. "You have to school 178 days for 5 hours a day. We school 365 days, 24 hours a day, so no problem. We are considered a private school." Neither record-keeping nor testing is required. "It is important to me *not* to have my daughter tested," Jennifer says. "It is very much against all my parenting instincts and my educational philosophy."

Although Shaisa is an only child, she has many opportunities to socialize. The family belongs to a local homeschool group who meet once a month for a roller-skating party and every other week at a family farm. "Toddlers or babies just join in," Jennifer says. "There are whole families there, not thirty kids all the same age level with one or two adults to 'supervise.' It's like Sunday dinner at Mom's."

The homeschool group provides Shaisa with a chance to interact with all kinds of people. "We have a diverse group," Jennifer says. "Most of us are homeschooling for academic reasons with a few who are doing it for religious reasons. We tend to be the 'outcasts,' those who aren't comfortable signing a statement of Christian faith, for example, or requiring others to do so." Friends of all ages from the group drop by often to play or share activities of mutual interest. Sometimes Shaisa and her friends go on field trips.

Jennifer believes "socialization" is highly overrated. "I am happy that my child lacks the chance to develop peer dependence," she says. "Did you know that it's defined as a mental illness, included in the *Diagnostic and Statistical Manual* of the American Psychiatric Association? I don't want Shaisa to be socially restricted to her very rigidly defined age group within a school setting. By unschooling, she has the opportunity to interact with people of all ages, as well as the opportunity for solitude and quiet reflection."

The family has support from their friends, who "think homeschooling is great," Jennifer says. They do not get much encouragement from family. "My in-laws are neutral, but they are supportive in many ways; they have other grandkids who have been homeschooled at various points," Jennifer says. "My mom hates it. She takes it as a personal criticism of the way she raised me, since she was a teacher in the forties and fifties in K through two and taught in one of the last one-room schoolhouses in our area. But my mom is more a fan of homeschooling when she sees how it allows Shaisa time to be with her family."

Sometimes Shaisa experiences loneliness. "My daughter has days when she would like to 'fit in' better and go to school for the social times with her friends," Jennifer says. "But then her friends bring her back to reality by explaining that they wouldn't see much of each other anyway, and wouldn't be allowed to talk or otherwise socialize. Plus the homework keeps them from getting together after school."

Shaisa likes having occasional homework assignments "so that she can say to her schooled friends that she has it," Jennifer says. "This is a recent development, and I will be glad when it's over. She is also worried that she has not had all the subjects that her schooled friends have had. That's why we're getting a bit more structured in our approach to math. I still consider this unschooling because it is at her request."

Unschooling has not been exactly what Jennifer expected. "It isn't a constant state of obvious learning as I expected. I had this picture in my head, almost like a commercial, of all of us constantly engaged in 'interesting' conversation and 'interesting' activities. And somehow, the house was always clean but no one had to clean it."

Housework is something that most often goes by the wayside, Jennifer notes. "I am trying to change that, since I notice we all get grumpy and unfocused if our home base is too messy. A little disorder is tolerable, but too much sets us all on edge and we get snappy and nasty with each other." To create more balance, the three family members are trying to share housework chores "so I don't feel like the drudge," Jennifer says. "Shaisa can make meals sometimes too. That helps."

When Jennifer gets discouraged, she likes to reread books by

John Holt and J. T. Gatto and *The Teenage Liberation Handbook*. "Then I realize I would never have wanted to send my daughter to school, and I'm glad I homeschool," she says. "We also joke together. When Shaisa does anything particularly silly or unthinking, Matt and I say, 'She's homeschooled. We're so proud.' "

In truth, Shaisa's parents *are* proud of her. "Our daughter reads well, she is a good person, she treats other people well, she gets along with people of all ages," Jennifer says. "I also notice that she has a strong sense of right and wrong, and a deep distaste for injustices. Mostly we have had a good experience. We intend to homeschool all the way."

In order to accomplish their goals of maintaining both homeschool and home-based businesses, Jennifer and Matt have made the decision to live very simply. Some time ago, the couple paid off all their loans and debts and tore up their credit cards. They bought a second car recently, after seventeen years with just one vehicle, to accommodate Matt's full schedule. "We like to work on our house, a fixer-upper bungalow, and are in the process of installing new windows," Jennifer says, "though we never have time to fix it up as much as we'd like."

Occasionally the simple life-style is an embarrassment to Shaisa. "We don't make enough money and we don't wear the right clothes," Jennifer notes. "And we sing out loud in public, in the grocery store, for example, not just on stage."

There is a down side to having artistic parents, especially those who make their living primarily from the arts. "Nothing is perfect yet," Matt points out. "The work itself is what I want to do, but I still have to put up with people, and people are jerks sometimes, or don't do what they said they'd do. Sometimes the schedule isn't what I'd like. Sometimes there isn't enough work and sometimes there is too much." When both Matt and Jennifer are working long hours, they miss seeing each other and Shaisa.

Jennifer dislikes "the necessary evil" of marketing Matt and herself. "Unfortunately, because I am the one who can write a press release the quickest or put together a publicity packet or write the grant proposal in the most effective way, then lucky me, I get to do it," she says. "I have gotten pretty good at asking for huge chunks of cash. I can now say, 'We charge eight hundred dollars an hour corporate rate for the a cappella group,' and negotiate without choking, laughing, breaking eye contact, or blushing. I am still not good at pricing artwork, but I am getting better at documenting my art through slides so I can actually enter shows and try for gallery space."

In spite of the challenges, having home businesses can be very rewarding. "I love it when Matt has a vacation and we can hang out in our jammies and eat bagels and watch the cats," Jennifer says. (In addition to two cats, the family also owns a husky-shepherd mixed-breed dog, a little lizard and a big lizard, a snake, a rat, a rabbit, and three hamsters.) "Shaisa still lets us goof around with her and hugs us and we all get silly," Jennifer says. "I love those times of us all being together, but they're too infrequent. Yet, if there wasn't much work for Matt and he was home a lot, we'd start to worry."

Shaisa is beginning to show some of her own artistic talents. Her animé drawing shows promise. She has started guitar lessons and talks of being part of a band. She even sang a song with both of her parents at a folk festival. "We told Shaisa that if she performed with us, she would be entitled to a cut of the money," Jennifer says. "That pretty much piqued her interest. She has been around rehearsals at our house for years, but was surprised at how different it is when you're in the midst of an actual rehearsal, trying to stay focused."

Whether Shaisa chooses to earn her living in the arts, as her parents have, or in another field, is totally up to her. "We want to give our daughter the same choices we gave ourselves," Jennifer says, "the freedom to pursue our dreams, daily, through our work."

Front row: Emily, Charlie, Laura, David. Back row: Steven, Cindy, Charles.

Fifteen

Homeschooling with a Down's Syndrome Child

Family:
Charles (45), Cindy (43), Steven (23), David (21), Charlie (13), Emily (9), Laura (5).

Location:
Just outside Kalispell, Montana.

Best advice:
Join the Home School Legal Defense Association. Be open to all resources, and don't be so set that you can't make changes to fit your educational views.

Worst advice:
Put your special-needs child in school so he can be "mainstreamed" and learn more. Let your children choose whether to go to school or homeschool.

Favorite saying:
Anyone can count the seeds in an apple, but only God can count the apples in a seed.

Favorite resources:
Learning in Spite of Labels by Joyce Herzog, Greenleaf Press.
Home Schooling Children with Special Needs by Sharon Hensley, Noble Books.
NATHHAN (NATional cHallenged Homeschoolers Associated Network), P.O. Box 39, Porthill, ID 83853, 208-267-6246, www.NATHHAN.com
Woodbine House Publishers (special needs of all sorts), 6510 Bells Mill Rd, Bethesda, MD 20817, 800-843-7323.
National Academy for Child Development (NACD), P.O. Box 1639, Ogden, UT 84402-1639, 801-621-8606.

When Charles and Cindy S.'s third child, Charlie, was born, physicians told the couple to take him home and love him for as long as they could keep him alive. "The doctors said we'd be lucky if our baby reached six months of age," Cindy says. "Then it was a year, then three years. Today, our son is a healthy, happy thirteen-year old."

Charlie was born with Down's syndrome and multiple medical needs. As a newborn, he had to be taught to suck. "Without this instinct, Charlie was literally starving to death," Cindy says. "We had to feed him on the hour around the clock until, nine months later, he finally learned to swallow and suck." Charlie also had three holes in his heart and a very weak immune system. His urethra had to be reconstructed with grafted tissues from his own body.

But in spite of their son's very tenuous beginning, Cindy and Charles have always believed that God has a plan for their son, and that that is the reason he is still with them. "We have seen many people cheered and touched by Charlie," Cindy says. "He has such a love for life! Our son is wonderfully made just as he is, for reasons many do not understand. He is a vital part of our family."

When Charlie was born, he joined his parents and two older brothers, Steven and David, who were already homeschooling. The boys helped name, love, and nurture their new sibling; they even took photos of all his "firsts." Now Charlie likes to keep his two older brothers' graduation cap in his bedroom, and takes great pride in the fact that he will be the third child to graduate from the family's homeschool. He also has two younger sisters, Emily and Laura.

Cindy and Charles married young, at eighteen and twenty. Charles is self-employed and has his own construction business. Cindy is a "domestic engineer" who is also the Montana representative for the NATional cHallenged Homeschoolers Associated Network (NATHHAN). Charles and Cindy, together, have run the construction business from home for the past twenty years. They've homeschooled for even longer, "from infancy to graduation," Cindy says, "for all our children." They hope to eventually help homeschool their grandchildren.

Steven received a high school diploma from his parents and an A.S. degree in science from a nearby community college. He is out on his own, attending Montana Bible College in Bozeman. Steven has a one-year certificate in the study of theology from MBC, and will continue taking classes both there and from the University of Montana, right next door to the Bible college. His studies will probably concentrate on aquatic science, as he is especially interested in working with fisheries.

Son number two is David, who earned a high school diploma from a correspondence school called American School. Like his brother, he is currently studying at Montana Bible College, hoping to eventually pursue a career in music ministry. He finished an extended apprenticeship in carpentry and makes his living doing commercial construction work in Bozeman. He plans to build his own home someday. David is soon to be married and will live with his wife in Bozeman.

Back home, Cindy is in charge of Laura, Emily, and Charlie. "Laura was born with social skills," Cindy says. "She loves to sing and perform music, to garden, to explore the great outdoors. She's a quick learner." Emily is Charlie's "twin," helping her brother as they work through some of the same schoolbooks together. "She is his interpreter," Cindy says, "always knowing what he's saying even when his speech is not clear." Emily loves music, is now learning both piano and painting, and enjoys hobbies and outdoor activities as well. Incredibly, she recently found a tooth that appears to belong to a new, formerly unknown dinosaur. Both girls take fiddle lessons from older brother Steven.

With only three children at home, life is much easier than it once was. "When the older boys were homeschooling and baby Charlie joined our home, there were many new circumstances that forced us to change our schedule," Cindy says. "I had to be away helping Charlie with medical procedures several times a week, so Dad took over schooling while Mom was away."

The schedule thirteen years ago is similar to the one today. Cindy starts breakfast while the children do chores. The family lives on a small farm, gardening and raising livestock. "We own an assortment of cats, dogs, and goldfish for pets," Cindy says, "and that's just the beginning." Depending on the year, they may also be raising hogs, feeder calves, lambs, goats, turkeys, and/or chickens for sale. Cindy gathers and sells eggs in town, and she often "takes orders" from urban customers who can't raise their own livestock. With animal and farm chores to complete, plus academics, mornings are busy.

When Charlie was a baby, David cleared the table, did the breakfast dishes, and helped with his younger brother while Cindy and Steven worked one-on-one in a separate room.

David read to Charlie for fifteen minutes a day, using his readers, novels, or children's books, giving him valuable read-aloud practice and Charlie a chance to hear many wonderful stories. Then Cindy and David worked together while Steven cared for Charlie.

Next came a time when Cindy, Steven, and David met together for reading, writing, and arithmetic. Cindy added history, geography, language arts, science, art, and other high-interest subjects on a regular basis each week, though not all in the same day. The older boys were also required to keep a daily journal and write short reports about what they read, sharing them with the family. All this time, if Charlie were awake, he would be in the room doing puzzles, playing with toys, or otherwise keeping busy.

The boys learned to be handy in the kitchen, and so were in charge of making lunch. After a midday meal and a break, the family regrouped. Steven and David finished their day's schoolwork, coming to Cindy if needed. "Charles and I believe in teaching our children to be responsible in all things," Cindy says, "and by fifth or sixth grade, they are quite capable of taking responsibility for their own education. As I watch this develop, I become more of a coach than a teacher, though I'm always there for questions and to help solve problems."

As Charlie grew, Cindy needed to spend more time with him in physical and speech therapy. "We simply made the adjustments gradually," she says, "into our already established schedule of study. The older ones watched the physical therapist who came to our home once or twice week. As she worked and taught me, they also learned. So as I continued to work individually with one son, the other one carried out the program—exercises, stimulation activities, teaching sign language—for little Charlie."

Charles, Cindy, Steven, and David worked as a team to encourage Charlie. Cindy made special visual aids, flash cards, and coloring pages for her youngest son to coordinate with unit studies. Charles and the older boys read aloud to Charlie and helped him learn to listen well. "The three Rs are necessary for a Down's syndrome child," Cindy says, "but they cannot be accomplished if a child is struggling in areas of self-help, manners, obedience, and concentration. We tried to work on these areas and watch for Charlie's teachable moments, no matter how small the time slots."

Cindy always has insisted on perseverance in the children's studies. "Charles and I tell all our kids, 'The sky's the limit, so we will work on this together and you will get it sooner or later.' " If Cindy teaches a concept and a child doesn't understand it, she will reteach it. If it's still not sinking in, she may put it on hold for a few weeks and then return to it again. This was particularly true for Charlie. "Charlie does get it, only at a slower pace and with patient repetition and backing off when needed for him and for me," Cindy says. "He continues to reach new levels in his learning and his potential is unlimited. That's why we like that saying, 'Anyone can count the seeds in an apple, but only God can count the apples in a seed.' "

The family's homeschool could be described today, as it was many years ago, as a one-room school. During their time at home, David and Steven were as much involved in teaching as learning. Now Emily, Laura, and Charlie have taken over. Just as it was then, the family's day begins with Cindy fixing breakfast while her three youngest children get dressed, make their beds, do morning chores, and care for the farm animals. At breakfast, the family reads the Bible together and practices memorizing verses. While Emily, Charlie, and Laura wash dishes, Cindy prepares dinner in advance.

Next, while Charlie reads aloud to Cindy, Emily is in a separate room reading to Laura, a preschooler, for fifteen minutes, and helping her with puzzles and toys. Then Charlie spends time with his younger sister while Emily works with Cindy. Together again, the three children learn a math lesson. The rest of the day is filled with Emily and Charlie completing their book work and independent reading while Laura plays nearby with dollies and dress-up clothes, kitchen utensils, and Play-Doh, blocks, farm animals, cutting and pasting projects, and books. Laura is expected to take out one quiet-toy box at a time, then pick it up and put it away before another box is opened. She also knows that she must be quiet and respectful during Cindy's teaching times with her siblings, just as each of the older children learned the same lessons when they were small.

Charlie has made great strides since his early days. He loves books and can read from his large-print Bible at devotion times. His attention has improved and he seldom uses signing any more. His speech, though sometimes still difficult to understand, is much better. He can keep little Laura's attention as he reads aloud to her each day, his special job, and one that he takes seriously.

Cindy thinks the children's interaction is essential not only to Charlie but also to their own progress. "This type of teaching, multiple lessons with multiple grades, can be done once you take time to organize it," Cindy says. "With practice it's very natural. I can spend about fifteen minutes on one subject with one child, and that will produce about fifteen minutes to an hour's worth of work for the child to do on his or her own. So if I spend a thirty to forty-five minute block of time, I can get two to three lessons in with each child in the morning and about the same in the afternoon."

The results of all this cooperation among the children has been not only learning, but also a sense of close bonding. "Our older kids learn to enjoy little-kids things and our little ones learn to be patient doing big-kids things," Cindy says. "It's made for unique friendships for life." In an essay called "What I Like About Homeschooling," nine-year-old Emily wrote, "In the winter I got to sled and make a dinoSNOWasaur. He was six feet tall! My brother David helped me and Charlie build him. This is what I like best about being homeschooled."

Beyond bonding, each student also has had the fulfilling experience of being a teacher. "What a joy it has been," Cindy says, "to see my children's smiles when they have worked with Charlie teaching sign language, and at last he signed back to them! How does one ever experience this in a public school setting? I have learned to never underestimate the worth of my children's capabilities."

Each day, lunch is followed by a check on the animals, afternoon chores, and some outside fun. Quiet time is next. Laura takes a nap, giving Cindy an hour or more with the older children. "I listen to Emily read out loud from her phonics handbook and reading book," Cindy says. "She, like the rest of us, takes a quiet time and will stretch out in her favorite spot with a book of her choice, reading and sometimes dozing off." Meanwhile, Charlie has been working individually, and then reads aloud to his mother.

Cindy uses a variety of curricula. "We do high-interest studies [unit studies]," Cindy says, "and make good use of our own library, *World Book Encyclopedias*, an atlas, and a globe. We like G. A. Henty's books, old classics, stories of Christian character and heroes of the faith, *Favorite Poems Old and New*, biographies, Peter Marshall's books, Bob Jones chapter books, and a wide selection of our own read-aloud children's books. We also rely heavily on our public library." In addition, the children have access to plenty of good supplementary materials, Cuisenaire rods, a variety of felts and visual aids, and carefully selected library videos.

When the family first started homeschooling, Cindy designed her own curriculum. "Then I found I could order through A Beka, which was about the only publisher available for homeschoolers at the time," Cindy says. "I supplemented by reading aloud from the Bible, stories of heroes, and high-interest books. Our library then was the bookmobile service that came to our small town once a month." Through the years, the children have made use of material from a variety of publishers, including A Beka, Calvert, Bob Jones, Alpha Omega, Christian Liberty Academy, and Saxon.

Charlie's academic needs have required special curricula. Cindy prefers to teach with the supervision of the National Academy for Child Development (NACD), an organization that helps families set up individualized programs. Cindy, Charles, and some of the children travel with Charlie to Utah every four months to update his particular program. Staff at NACD evaluate Charlie's progress academically, physically, and nutritionally. They also check to make sure his assigned exercises are being done correctly and test his muscle tone. "I especially like NACD because they don't support labels," Cindy says. "They look at the child as a *child* rather than a 'Down's syndrome.' And they see where the holes are and work to fill them." NACD accepts children of all ages and abilities and disabilities. "They are the only organization in the U.S. that specializes this way," Cindy says. "It's not cheap, but we consider this an investment in Charlie's education. We pay for NACD instead of ordering expensive curriculum for him or enrolling him in a correspondence school."

For training in the three Rs, Charlie uses a second-grade A Beka math textbook. He shares an A Beka phonics and language arts book with Emily, and is supplemented with *Alphaphonics* workbook pages and *A Reason for Writing* penmanship assignments. "Charlie is just starting at the beginning of phonics," Cindy says, "and understanding the basics of adding and subtracting."

Cindy does physical therapy with her son at home, and Charlie has worked hard to develop the marshmallowlike muscles below his thumbs. "He is so proud now that he can use a pencil and eraser!" Cindy says, beaming. Charlie's lessons move at a slower rate than the other children's, but he is making steady progress. "At NACD's suggestion, we work with a lot of patterning in the brain, repetition and review," Cindy says. "Yet he also thrives on challenges."

Charlie is able to speak orally but also uses sign language. "Even when he was only twelve months old, I saw my son's frustration in not being able to communicate," Cindy says. "My little one-year-old had begun to rock and sometimes bang his head because he had poor muscle tone in his mouth and couldn't talk. The banging was unacceptable behavior, and I had to do something to help him. I used the book *Signing Exact English* to teach him signs, and in less than a few weeks, Charlie had learned six. The rocking and banging left once he could express himself."

Cindy tries to finish school by 3:00. Afterschool activities vary from day to day, like a once-a-week trip to town that includes speech therapy for Charlie, piano lessons for Emily, and a library visit, or work around the house and garden. The family raises much of their own food and "puts it up" as well. "We do have typical and nontypical days," Cindy says. "But *all* are educational days."

Through many years of homeschooling, Cindy has learned to take one day at a time. "I have tried to become agreeable with the changes as they arise," Cindy says, "not getting upset if our school day needs to end early. It's better, I think, that Mom and the kids still love each other at the end of the day, rather than to insist that a course of study is completed. Don't get me wrong, I need good solid plans. But then I need to be able to see Plan B, C, D, or even X if necessary. Though we always try to cover Bible, reading, writing, and arithmetic, I cut back wherever I have to in order to preserve my sanity and good humor."

Cindy has no problem with rearranging the schedule. If all is running smoothly she may occasionally double up on lessons. The children might complete an entire course of study in history before going on to science studies, or cover all their math for the week in one day, with the rest of the week spent on reading. Sometimes Cindy arranges days off, if needed. Once, when she was in town running errands during regular school hours, a clerk asked David why he wasn't in school. Four-year-old Emily quickly and politely asked the woman why *she* wasn't in school. The clerk replied that she already had done school. And Emily said simply, "Well, we already did our school, too, and now we have errands to do."

Just as she has to be flexible in scheduling, Cindy also has learned to manage with whatever home base is available to her. When Steven was eight years old, Charles's work took the family to California for the winter. As Cindy and the children traveled with Dad to be near him, school was held in a tiny camp trailer. "We used the trailer's small table for meals, school, and then as a bed at night," Cindy says. The family also lived for several years in a 20-foot-by-20-foot log cabin home that served as both a one-room house and a one-room school. Now that Cindy has a large denlike area available in a large home, she greatly appreciates her "school space."

The family also appreciates the material luxuries they now have, most of them hard-earned. When the older children were young, Cindy and Charles worked together to build their own home. "We had no electricity, and water had to be carried in, until years later when we had saved enough to have a well dug and electric run up our mountain," Cindy says. The family settled in a section of Montana that's close to both a small town, Kalispell, and Glacier National Park. They are located only sixty miles from the Canadian border. The view of the mountains and surrounding scenery is spectacular.

There is always plenty of work to do around both the house and the farm. "I learned early that one person could never do it all," Cindy says. "The children were expected to start taking on responsibilities when they were very young. I know my children can do anything I can do: washing clothes, drying and folding and putting them away, even ironing, for example. I only need to be willing to teach and discipline them, and I do teach all the children tasks that will lighten my load. We have always helped each other where needed and the children never questioned this."

Most days wind down around 6:30, with evening chores, animal care, supper, and bath time. One important bed-time ritual is Daddy's story hour. Charles is well-versed in tales of adventure, true characters, and tall tales, and makes up many stories on the spot. Bed time is officially 8:30. "But that may change if the older boys are around. We share such good times all together, with so much to catch up on and new tunes and tales to hear," Cindy says. "Because our family is close, our priorities are based around family togetherness."

To allow for more flexibility, Cindy and the children homeschool year round. "This gives us leeway for those slow-start days and interruptions," Cindy says. Adjustments always are made for a new baby, such as a three-week break when Charlie was born, and half-days for some time afterward. "We have all enjoyed these 'baby kind of days,' " Cindy says, "and worked up to full loads as each baby grew and weaned, and time allowed." The family tries to maintain a schedule of nine weeks on, three weeks off. "I don't make a habit of taking too many days off in a year, or walking away from a tough situation in life," Cindy says. "But I do know when these break times are necessary for both me and the children."

Charles makes a point of giving Cindy regular breaks as well. Because the family business is home-based, Dad can take over homeschooling whenever Cindy is sick or needs a day off. "Charles supports me one-hundred percent," Cindy says. "There are times I've taken a special quilting class or a homeschoolers' workshop, and he knows the necessity and worth of this for the overall well-being of our home. We are teammates in this lifestyle of educating and raising our children at home. I would not be homeschooling if I did not have his full support and encouragement in doing so."

When Steven was young, Charles had had doubts about homeschooling, so Cindy and Charles sent their firstborn to public school kindergarten for two weeks. Cindy was relieved when Charles agreed with her conviction to bring Steven home. "The drive to town was long and difficult, fifteen miles on a dirt road with poor conditions," Cindy remembers. "Then came a hard winter. For the sake of safety as well as education, Charles simply told me that he felt we should homeschool Steven. And we both believed strongly that, as Proverbs says, 'Train up a child in the way he should go, and when he is old he will not depart from it.' By the time Steven was halfway through his first month of public school, Charles was sure of homeschooling and he never gave it another thought."

Charles's roles in the family include those of school administrator and financial supporter. When there were two school-age sons in the family, Dad was also a coach, involved with Little League baseball, soccer, and some basketball games, and a faithful spectator when the boys ran track. Charles became involved with hunter education as a lead instructor when the older boys were young, teaching gun safety and outdoor and survival skills. He continues to help even now, with Charlie by his side as a junior instructor. Charlie goes with Dad to different classes and demonstrates a proper survival pack.

Charles is also a leader in AWANA, an international children's club that teaches the Bible in an entertaining way, and Charlie, Emily and Laura are active in the group. Finally, Charles takes time, when needed, to help with his children's math assignments, science experiments, and field trips.

The family business integrates Dad into a teaching role on a regular basis. Charles, a licensed general B contractor, is currently teaching Charlie the trade his father taught him, and Steven and

David learned when they were younger. "All the boys began helping when they were about eight years old, sweeping, picking up cords, cleaning up after a job, and learning how to conduct themselves in front of customers," Cindy says. "Our older sons have been around construction, even on job sites, since they were infants. It's now become like second nature to them. By the time they were in junior high, they were very capable of working whenever Charles needed them to fill in existing crews of carpenters." Eventually the boys worked up to being their father's top carpenters, earning good money in their spare time.

On the days when Steven and David went to work with Dad, they did their schoolwork on-site, started it in the morning and finished in the evening, or spent their Saturdays hitting the books. They were accountable for completing assignments on time. "If the boys didn't keep up with their schoolwork, the penalty was hard," Cindy says. "They simply didn't get to go to work with Charles. My boys enjoyed working and earning money, and they paid for their own vehicles, ski lift tickets, most of their own clothing, some groceries—even ice cream treats for the whole family." As they grew, Steven and David became more and more financially responsible while also homeschooling and learning a valuable trade. "My teenagers were happy young men," Cindy says, "keeping busy and full of love for life. And now they are happy, productive young adults."

In addition to construction, Steven and David also worked several other jobs while growing up. Steven, a gifted musician, started teaching fiddle (violin, old-time style) lessons from home when he was fifteen, and still teaches fifteen students. Together, when they were young, David and Steven did yard work, snow removal, and handyman chores to earn extra money. Later they were able to take on snow plowing and more complicated repair work. "They had several small business ventures on their own," Cindy says. "I think the one I loved most was their S & D Tree and House Service.

What the boys did was to take scrap lumber, then cut, paint, and detail it to make miniature trees and houses for Lionel electric train-track layouts. I still have all the ones they couldn't sell, and they can be seen under our tree at Christmas, making a whole village and forest for our trains." The boys also raised hogs and rabbits for sale. "My homeschooled boys knew how to market and make money in very creative ways," Cindy says.

To help prepare her sons for future careers, Cindy conducted two separate career studies with Steven and David when each was in seventh grade. "We did this all year," Cindy says. "We made trips to places that were implementing the boys' top career choices, and they actually got a day or two on the job." Apprenticeships often followed, like Steven's experience in assisting a biologist at the Department of Fish, Wildlife, and Parks; he worked for several years helping to imbed radio chips in trout, use a laptop computer to track fish from an airplane, and set traps for trout in the river. The apprenticeships in turn yielded excellent recommendations for the boys' college applications.

These career studies were a big plus, Cindy says. "They helped Steven, David, and me to see areas where they were strong, to give us direction for the high school years. At eighth grade we thought of our sons as being finished with academics, since they tested on the twelfth-grade level. Their final years at home were to prepare them for the next phase of life." Steven was ready to graduate when he was fifteen and a half years old. "Dad and Mom were not so sure about this," Cindy says, grinning. "Being our first child, we had no example or manual to follow. So Steven worked full time with the family construction company and continued to live at home."

Having raised two children to adulthood, Charles and Cindy have strong opinions about how they want to raise the others. Both parents expect their children to be highly accountable and work hard. In return, they are given a great deal of freedom.

Though Mom and Dad made final decisions on curricula, for example, their older boys had much input on their preferences. "We were able to keep a balance in our teens' education because we allowed the boys to be a part in its planning," Cindy says. "I discovered that my teens were natural goal setters. I tried to direct them and keep them busy and interested in what they could do well. We were partners." Even as adults, Steven and David often call home for advice and help in decision making. In a letter to Cindy, Steven wrote, "I'm a grown man and to this day I still learn things from my parents. I believe this is what separates me from others in my generation."

Interaction among family members leads naturally to socialization. Although the children consider their siblings to be their best friends, all the family members are out and about, working and playing with others through 4-H, community service and volunteer work, hunter education, and the construction business. In the past, David and Steven were AWANA leaders and volunteers in the DREAM ski program, serving as "buddies" for handicapped people and helping them to ski successfully. Charles and the older boys often play music together both in informal jam sessions at home and for paid performances, and have led worship music at their church. "We also make time to have friends over," Cindy says, "and we host potlucks, sledding parties, camping and fishing outings, *American Girls* history parties through a local support group, and so much more." The family does not watch TV, but there is always plenty to do. "We share games, talks, books, jokes, and riddles, and many home projects and crafts," Cindy says. "We're never bored."

Bored, no. Discouraged, sometimes. Cindy and Charles are all too aware of their human frailities. "But we believe strongly that we should not allow a negative thought or deed to fester into a 'bad experience,' " Cindy says. When this does occasionally happen, Cindy remembers inspiring Bible verses, and prays. "I may also break and regroup," she says, "or attempt to understand what is causing the discouragement, or work on changes needed. Some days we just take off. I try to see these as growth days."

In spite of occasional bad days, Cindy and Charles think of themselves as blessed. They are very proud of their two young daughters and two grown sons. "Steven and David know proper conduct, have strong religious beliefs, share in many family traditions, and have learned to have a calm and reasonable attitude, accepting things as they are and making the best of them," Cindy says. "They have a love of wisdom and pursue it." Charles, Cindy, Steven, and David remember their homeschooling years, to date, with great warmth. "Sharing times together . . . what fun we all had!" Cindy says.

Both parents also recall, with profound thankfulness, the gift God gave them in Charlie: "I only need to remember my tiny newborn babe as the doctors told me how severely retarded he would be, if he even survived at all," Cindy says. "I remember all the surgeries—nine in all, through the years—and countless medical procedures. I took the doctors' advice to 'take him home and love him,' not as they intended, though. I did take him home for good, and with prayers and love he is here and thriving from being educated at home."

Recently Charlie wrote an essay about his education. "I like doing my schoolwork at home. I like being with Mom and Dad. I like to work with Dad. I like to play with my sisters Emily and Laura. I like my homeschool."

And Charlie, the miracle baby, is now drawing close to his own homeschool graduation. When Steven, the oldest grandchild, graduated from high school, Cindy's parents drove one thousand miles from California to surprise the family. At David's graduation, the grandparents, several aunts and uncles, and even Cindy's grandfather were present. "The extended family are waiting for the announcement of Charlie's graduation," Cindy says. "What a family party that will be!"

Caitlin, Daniel, Clare, and Grace.

Sixteen

Laying Down the Law

Family:
Mark (45), Christine (44), Clare (10), Caitlin (9), Grace (5), Daniel (3).

Location:
Wheaton, Illinois (a Chicago suburb).

Best advice:
Relax and enjoy homeschooling!

Worst advice:
Make your plan and stick to it no matter what.

Favorite quote:
"He settles the barren woman in her home as joyful mother of children." (Psalms 113:9, the Bible)

Favorite resources:

Educating the Wholehearted Child by Sally Clarkson, WholeHeart Ministries.

Seasons of a Mother's Heart by Sally Clarkson, WholeHeart Ministries.

Family Matters: Why Homeschooling Makes Sense by David Guterson, Harvest Books.

Homeschool Digest magazine, Box 374, Covert, MI 49043.

A Mom Just Like You by Vicky Farris, Loyal Publishing.

A few years ago, Christine F. lived what most people consider a fulfilling life as a successful lawyer. First she worked for six years as a prosecutor. Then, for two more years, Christine had her own office, specializing in civil litigation and general practice. For some time she was single, divorced, and very much enjoying her work. Then one day she met Mark, the chief of administration in a sheriff's office, at the courthouse. "We shared some of our early experiences with a bad marriage, plus our individual dealings in the court system with families who were dysfunctional and had done everything wrong," Christine says. "The more we talked, the more we began to have a vision for what it would be like to raise a family the right way, with character and values."

Christine and Mark were married a few years later. When they were ready to have children, the couple discovered they were "secondary infertile": one of Christine's fallopian tubes was blocked, and the other partially blocked, making pregnancy extremely difficult. But she did become pregnant, and shortly afterward discovered that a baby girl would soon be available for adoption through Christine's law practice. Sadly, Christine miscarried. But two weeks later the couple adopted three-day-old Clare. Within a year Christine was pregnant again, and delivered Caitlin seventeen months after Clare's arrival.

All this time, Christine was busy at work. Her marriage reached a crisis point when Mark was offered a new position as chief of police in a Chicago suburb, Wheaton. "His job change would have meant a move nearly one hundred miles away," Christine remembers. "And it also meant I would have to give up my practice. This was an overwhelmingly difficult time for me." They finally agreed that Mark would accept the new position, with Christine changing her career. "My friends and family thought I was nuts to leave my practice," she remembers. "I also regularly questioned my own sanity, but could not ignore the longings of my heart."

The move officially took place in May 1991, though Mark had been commuting the long distance for three months before this. Christine spent an additional three months winding down her practice, driving the girls with her to a home day care near her work, then making the long, difficult, almost-one-hundred-mile commute back to Wheaton each evening.

A crucial turning point came one night when Christine was driving home from work with her two young daughters. Her car ran into the back of a wrecker. "The kids were screaming, the man in the wrecker was laughing at me, and I was so stressed out! I finally asked myself, 'Why am I doing this? Who am I trying to prove something to?' I decided that my colleagues and clients could always find another lawyer, but these girls couldn't find another mother." Christine made the move to full-time motherhood when Clare was two and Caitlin was six months old.

Settled into a new routine and a new city, Christine says she never looked back. "When Caitlin was over her colic, Mark and I were ready to have more children. But biologically, nothing was happening." The couple went to private adoption agencies and were discouraged by seven- to eight-year waiting lists. They eventually decided to try international adoption. An organization called Bethany Christian Services (www.bethany.org, 616-224-

7610) helped Mark and Christine complete the paperwork to adopt a Korean baby.

While waiting to get a referral, Mark's sister tragically was murdered by her ex-husband. The day of the funeral, Mark and Christine were in Michigan at his parents' home when they received a call from their social worker. "The agency had a newborn baby girl and wanted to know if we would adopt her," Christine says. "The timing was perfect, because my in-laws were grieving over their daughter's loss, but then they started focusing more on the baby." Five months later, little Grace was escorted to the United States from Korea. As experienced parents of three, Mark and Christine decided to try for one more child. "We applied again to adopt through Bethany Christian Services, and had one referral fall through," Christine says. "The following week our social worker came with a picture of Daniel, a beautiful, healthy Korean boy. This time when we made the trip to the airport to pick him up, there were three big sisters anxious to greet their new brother." Shortly afterward, the growing family moved into a huge old house only three blocks away from Mark's office.

Today, Christine is a homemaker and mother to Clare, Caitlin, Grace, and Daniel. She is also the author of five books, *Coming Home to Raise Your Children*, *Should You Adopt?*, *A Field Guide to Home Schooling*, *Life Skills for Kids*, and *Help for the Harried Homeschooler*, and a columnist for two homeschool magazines. She also speaks at local, regional, and national conventions of homeschoolers, adoptive families, and stay-at-home mothers.

In addition to mothering, Christine is a homeschool teacher. Mark and Christine's decision to home-educate was based on several factors. "We went from being a two-career, infertile couple to having a pack of kids," she says. "And once the prospect of raising a family became a reality for us, we sought ways to do it which would be pleasing to God. Homeschooling was the logical option. In addition, at one time our oldest daughter was very peer dependent," Christine says. "We wanted her to be independent, while spiritually grounded, and that would be impossible for her to accomplish with the distraction of peer influences." Christine says the family also "just plain enjoys being together. We all want the good parts of the kids' days, not just the dregs of leftovers after school."

When asked what a typical homeschooling day is like, Christine laughs. "There often seem to be no normal days because young children change and grow so quickly. What works this year, or semester, may not work next year because the ages and abilities of my children have shifted, changing the equilibrium of the whole family." Christine likes to get up between 5:30 and 6:00 A.M. in order to have some time alone. Mark leaves very early for work, before breakfast. The children wake up, the youngest two first, then the older ones. The children and Mom have breakfast, memorizing Bible verses together while they eat. Then it's time for morning chores and schoolwork.

The family often alternates chores with academics. While Christine is working on reading skills with Grace for twenty minutes, for example, Clare may be folding laundry and Caitlin teaching colors to Daniel. During the next half hour, Christine might work with Clare and Caitlin while Grace plays with Daniel. Then while Mom has special time with Daniel, Grace may be cleaning her room while both Clare and Caitlin work independently.

Christine believes in having a schedule, but also in bending it if necessary. "When your home is the center of learning, home learning is more than phonics. It is about living and learning in life, which is not always predictable. Children get sick, the phone rings with callers who need your help, and family and friends experience crises." Rather than a rigid list of time slots, Christine prefers to set a flow for activities of the day in blocks of time. "I try to accept the fact that life with children is full of interruptions and distractions. Whenever I go to the bathroom, I think my kids have a sensor that goes off as soon as I sit down. I hear a *bang*, and suddenly at least two little people appear at the door."

Ideally, lunch is served around noon. With his office close by, Mark usually comes home to join the family. Soon afterward, Grace and Daniel nap or play and Christine works with Clare and Caitlin. The older girls have daily goals for completing a certain amount of work, and continue until their goals are reached. Both are voracious readers.

The family uses A Beka and Bob Jones packaged materials and textbooks as the foundation of their curricula. "We feel very strongly that in the early years, the children need a firm grounding in the basics, academics as well as practical life skills," Christine says. "We take a pretty traditional approach to education, focusing on phonics, for example. As the children grow older, we think it is important to give them an overview of knowledge."

Christine has learned the hard way that not all curricula work for her. "The worst year of homeschooling we ever had was the year we tried to do a full-blown, individual program with each child," she says. "Each had a separate Bible lesson, a separate math lesson, different topics in science and every other subject. I would dart from one child to the next, answering questions, teaching a snippet of a lesson, all the while trying to simply maintain the baby. Daniel wasn't very stimulated or enriched during that time. He was barely noticed."

The family struggled through seven weeks of diligently following the detailed lesson plans. "It was unsatisfying and frustrating for all the children and it was exhausting for me," Christine says. "I began to ask myself, 'Is this method the best for our family?' The children were only minimally interested in their lessons and the strain was wearing on our family's closeness. I was so focused on getting everyone's work completed that I was skimping on my role as Mom."

Soon Christine returned to A Beka. "Because I enjoy reading, writing, and researching, I would love to write my own program, but the reality is that I do not have time to invest in that," she says. "Rather, we have used prepared curricula, including Calvert, from a few suppliers. We supplement with reading good books, taking relevant field trips, doing appropriate experiments or art projects, and watching high-quality movies or videos." Clare and Caitlin also use the computer for typing lessons, word processing, and for drilling math and geography, and Grace plays with phonics and numbers programs. "Then, when one of our children expresses a deep interest in something, we run with that interest until it is satisfied," Christine observes. "It's resulted in some delightful forays into music, science, nature, and art. This approach has worked well for us."

Two years ago, a couple of mothers at Christine's church started a homeschool cooperative. "This year the co-op had classes meeting every other Friday for three hours at a time," Christine says. "We've offered arts and crafts, P.E., Spanish, scrap-booking, a book club, and a club for girls to learn home-making skills. All the moms take turns teaching and helping out. This summer, classes were taught in crochet, canning, and quilting a nine-patch pillow." In the fall, Christine will lead a group in music and art appreciation.

The family purposely avoids a great deal of running around. "Someone once said that the hardest thing about homeschooling is staying home," Christine says. "I could plan an outing for each day of the week, if I chose to do so." Instead, she tries to apply Dr. James Dobson's three-part test when evaluating outside activities: Is it worthy of our time? What will be eliminated if it is added? What will be its impact on our family life? "We have also found it helpful to ask whether the activity is going to deal with skills or knowledge which we could pursue together as a family," Christine adds. "If we can do it at home, we don't need a group and a schedule and a car pool to enrich our children's lives with that experience." With that in mind, the family has chosen to be involved in the co-op, Pioneer Girls at church, and sporadic ballet classes. Clare, Caitlin, and Grace have all danced twice in a local production of *The Nutcracker* as soldiers, cherubs, bonbons, or party girls.

With a full schedule and young children underfoot, Mark and Christine have agreed to lower their housekeeping standards. "Everyone who lives in our house is responsible for helping to take care of it," Christine says. "I start early, training our kids to help, though I find it interesting that they *want* to do chores when it is least convenient for me, like when they're two years old and have few skills." Christine has learned that if you begin training a two-year-old, by the time a child is six or seven, she is truly helpful. "I tell myself that my house will be clean when all the kids move out," she says. "Mark would rather see me spend my energy on the children than on cleaning. While we're so busy with home-education, the world won't come to an end if our houses are not perfectly tidy."

To deal with household chores, Christine tries to be as organized as possible. "I use the notebook method to organize my recipes," she says. "I put recipes from many different sources into notebooks, slipping each sheet into a plasic cover and sorting them with dividers. Taking my notebook, I plan a week's menus and note every ingredient on a shopping list. Then I photocopy these and store them in a plastic sleeve until I want to use them again." Christine handles laundry while doing something else. "Do you know how to tell a veteran homeschooler?" she asks, grinning. "The length of her lesson is determined by when the timer on the dryer rings."

Mark and Christine use what they call a five-finger system for chores with their young children. "We draw each child's hand on a piece of paper and designate one morning chore for each finger: eat breakfast and clean up after yourself; get dressed; brush teeth and wash up; make bed; and, pick up your room. Instead of having to ask whether each job is completed, we simply ask, 'Did you do all your fingers?' We also made picture charts for pre-readers."

There are days when housework seems overwhelming. "Some mornings I wake up, look around my messy house, and begin to feel a sense of dread," Christine says. "My life feels like drudgery. And then, as I set about my work, I'm grumbling. On a really bad day, I lash out at the children." She finds comfort in the words of Brother Lawrence, a monk who wrote *The Practice of the Presence of God*. Whether scrubbing pots or peeling potatoes, he advised, "During your meals or during daily duty, lift up your heart to Him [God], because even the least little remembrance will please Him. You don't have to pray out loud; He's nearer than you can imagine." "I try to remember these words when I'm doing laundry or changing diapers," says Christine.

Once after a severe storm hit their area, Christine was tempted to go outside to the yard and begin gathering up fallen tree branches. Caitlin suggested they stay on the couch and pray. "At her bidding, we prayed for Daddy and for others who were out in the storm, asking God to keep them—and us—safe," Christine says. "I whispered my own silent prayer of gratitude for the great God who gave me this sensitive daughter. She reminded me to put His priorities first in my life."

Mark's job, with all its responsibilities, does not keep him from being home for dinner almost every night. (Two nights a month, he lectures around the country about ethics in law enforcement.) Dad makes it a point to read out loud to the children and supervise their memorization of scripture. He is also in charge of teaching some important values. "We spend six minutes at the dinner table each night on a character quality or wisdom we want to impart. We spent several evenings talking about fairness, for example, and one night on dialing 911. Mark plans and leads these 'six-minute solutions.' "

Christine and Mark believe good character must be instilled first, before academic subjects are taught. Still, their children's academic levels are excellent. Though Illinois does not require testing, "we did test the two oldest children the past two years and they were way above grade level," Christine says. "Now that we've done it, I don't think we'll do it again for a while. It was reassuring to know that while we were focusing on their souls, hearts, and character, God was blessing our efforts by developing their intellects as well."

Character development is also a priority for Mom. As much as she loves and enjoys her young children, Christine finds them challenging, stretching her patience and parenting skills. "The babies and toddlers have always seemed to have a goal of disrupting everything else I am trying to do," she says. To cope, the family has set up a play area near their desks with special "school stuff" for Daniel, the youngest and now a toddler. Included are a school bag with coloring books, markers, and special toys (allowed only during school time), dish pans filled with children's board books, and five boxes of toys to be opened one at a time. Daniel can easily carry these items and is responsible for putting them away. "Balancing babies and toddlers has made me feel crazy sometimes, but I try to remember that the baby years are of limited duration," Christine says.

To help the older children work with their youngest sibling, Christine designed "Danny Do Cards" last year. Each card lists an activity which an older child can complete with Danny, simple but interactive and educational. One card reads, "Play Head, Shoulders, Knees, and Toes," and another, "Name the colors on the color poster with Daniel." "I put fifteen cards on a ring and switched them around regularly," Christine says. "This idea worked splendidly. The older children enjoyed having something concrete to do with the two-year-old, instead of simply being told, 'Go watch your brother.' Daniel benefited from the wisdom and knowledge of his older sisters, and Mom had a much smoother morning while trying to teach phonics to yet another child."

Daniel adds many bright spots to the day. "He loves to recite the Pledge of Allegiance, and he holds up various objects and nags us all until we recite with him," Christine says, laughing. "We have 'pledged allegiance' to rakes, pencils, and forks at the dinner table! Most of the time, I look at my young children as a blessing. The short years when they are annoying will be a time to learn much about patience, kindness, and cooperation as a family."

Different as each child is, all are blended together into a loving family. Clare is very artistic and sensitive, with a giving and loving heart. Caitlin is analytical, task-oriented, and loyal. Grace is "sweetness and light," her mother says. "And Daniel is full of beans! He's everywhere and into everything." Like all children, Clare, Caitlin, and Grace have both good and bad days, especially regarding homeschooling. "Sometimes they love it and sometimes they hate it," Christine says. "They do know that this is what Mark and I believe is the best choice for them and they have confidence in our judgment. Sometimes they thank us and sometimes they complain about it. We are secure enough in our decision that we let them express their feelings, both positive and negative."

Christine admits that her new career has not been easy. "I never expected the fatigue of managing a home and homeschooling. That has surprised me. And sometimes I miss my law practice. Just this last year, I had two opportunities to practice on a limited basis. I turned them down as I looked at the reality of adding another ingredient to our already full life." There have been pleasant surprises, too, "especially the joy and peace this has brought my heart," Christine says. "It has been a faith-building, family-strengthening experience for us. Although it is really hard work to homeschool, maintain a home, and keep some outside interests, it has been the most rewarding experience of my life next to knowing and loving the Lord. If I could relive my life, I would unequivocally choose homeschooling."

Christine and Mark also would choose adoption. Earlier this year, Bethany Christian Services asked them to keep a foster baby for two to three days. The time lengthened into two weeks. "Then the thirteen-year-old birth mother wanted us to adopt her son," Christine says. "Everyone was excited about the possibility until the reality of waking up seven or eight times a night—and trying to balance the needs of another human being—set in." The child was ultimately placed with a loving family, their first baby. "I still miss him," Christine says, "but I am deeply committed to raising my brood, my blessings, with energy and enthusiasm. At my age of forty-four, four children require about all the energy and enthusiasm I can manage!"

Seventeen

Motorcyclists, Clowns, and Zookeepers

Family:
Melanie (41), Jorge (42), Kristin (23), Keegan (20), Jorel (13).

Location:
Miami, Florida.

Best advice:
Homeschooling is legal!

Worst advice:
Bring school home and run your homeschool very rigidly, like a traditional school.

Favorite saying:
When it comes to school, there's no place like home.

Left to right: Dave, Keegan, Jorel, Jorge, Melanie, Kristin.

Favorite resources:

Home Education Magazine, 509-486-1351, www.home-ed-
magazine.com

Growing Without Schooling by John Holt, Holt Associates.

Real Lives: Eleven Teenagers Who Don't Go To School, edited by
Grace Llewellyn, Lowry House Publishing.

The library.

The computer.

If you unexpectedly drop by this family's house one day, you'll
never know what kinds of interesting people you might find
there. Two clowns, Melanie B. and her daughter Keegan, may
meet you at the door. Jorge and son, Jorel, could very well be riding their BMX bikes around the backyard. If Kristin and her husband happen to visit, you'd also get a chance to meet two
zookeepers.

Melanie, coordinator of the family's homeschool, is a professional clown. Jorge is a mobile disk jockey for parties, picnics,
and other social gatherings. He also has a lawn maintenance
business and excels in his role as Mr. Fix-It, servicing all his own
equipment as well as taking care of house and vehicle repairs.

Kristin has graduated from homeschool. She now works as the
manager of the Children's Zoo at Miami's MetroZoo, where she
is responsible for a collection of over seventy-five animals, a full-
time staff of three, and the supervision and training of adult and
teen volunteers. Jorge used to tease Kristin about spending a
whole day just looking at a spider or an insect. "Now she basically gets paid to do just that," Melanie jokes, "as well as to present them to other people." Kristin met, fell in love, and married
her husband, a fellow zookeeper, at the zoo.

Keegan is also a homeschool graduate, moving on to study art
and drama at Miami Dade Community College two days a week.
The honor society pursued her when she first started attending

classes and gave her a full scholarship for the first term. Next term, Keegan chose to leave the honor agenda, taking classes that interested her rather than those required by the society. The society offered her another full scholarship anyway.

Like her mother, Keegan is a professional clown, sometimes performing solo and sometimes partnering with Melanie. Since Keegan has attended clown conventions for several years, she has learned a great deal and is highly respected by her elders in the business. She also has a "day job" working for a mail-order motorcycle parts and accessory company, taking and processing orders.

Jorel is still in school, though the family's relaxed approach gives him plenty of freedom in his academic choices. He often helps with the family's lawn maintenance business. One of Jorel's hobbies is bicycle motor-cross (BMX), and he began to ride when he was five years old. He went on to race for a while with Jorge joining in, and both father and son performed well in local and state championships. The family has a dirt track that circles their property, complete with hills and turns. Whenever possible, they practice riding on both their own track and others.

Jorel and Jorge have also moved up to motorcycles (dirt bikes). Jorel owns two Kawasaki KX80 dirt bikes, a 1996 and a 1998, and does most of his own mechanical work on both. Jorge has a 1997 Yamaha YZ125 and Jorel helps maintain it, too. They occasionally run local races and Jorel shows great potential.

In addition, Jorge and Jorel participate in out-of-town racing events. To help with travel expenses, they bought a 1978 Class C motorhome and are in the process of renovating it. Melanie contributed by making curtains of "motor-cross material" for the camper.

Extensive traveling and racing would not be possible without the flexible life-style that flows from both homeschooling and self-employment. "All our professions work hand-in-hand with our homeschooling," Melanie says. "The three kids have learned along with me, for example, in such things as juggling, face painting, balloon sculptures, and making our own costumes. We get to attend the yearly clown convention without worrying about missing school because the convention *is* school. The kids see all aspects of this business and participate as well."

The same is true with Jorge's two businesses. Instead of Dad going away to an office, he's at home, where all aspects of his work are visible. Whether Jorge is servicing equipment, burning a CD, or writing up contracts or invoices, the family is aware of how his work gets done. "We also help with fix-it jobs, and these present many a learning experience for all of us," Melanie says. "Jorel seems to be following in his father's footsteps, with his own fix-it abilities. And we girls are not opposed to getting our hands dirty or fixing a few things ourselves. We are quite a handy bunch."

Whether working on dirt bikes, clowning, or studying math, Melanie and Jorge believe that all life is learning. "Life is your school," the couple says. "It's a natural process. Our goals are to encourage this process in all areas of life. We believe you should give the confidence to the child that he or she is intelligent and has a creative mind. We believe every child starts out this way and we want to allow them to feed on opportunities as they come."

The family started homeschooling thirteen years ago, when Kristin was ten, Keegan was seven, and Jorel was newly home-birthed. "One day during school hours, Jorge happened to drop by some friends' house and noticed all the kids were home," Melanie recalls. "They told him they homeschooled. Jorge was excited to learn that homeschooling was legal and could hardly wait to share the good news with me. He knew right then it was the way to go. I, on the other hand, answered with, 'How am I qualified to do something like this?' " The couple talked and attended some lectures and seminars, and finally made their decision.

Melanie and Jorge chose to homeschool for many reasons, but

religion was not one of them. "Personally, we do not feel the need
for a 'middle man,' or to follow any dogma," Melanie says. "All of
us are nature-connected and try to live by the Golden Rule. We are
very open-minded with our spirituality, much the same as we are
with our learning."

At first, Jorge and Melanie "brought school home." Next
they "homeschooled" and then "unschooled." "Basically we are
life learners, learning all the time," Melanie says. "We don't tell
the kids everything, we help them figure things out for themselves." Jorge agrees. "Traditional school seems to take away
opportunities and tries to make kids *follow* a certain path rather
than *lead* their own learning," he notes. "My wife and I see our
goal as helping them find the maps that have all different paths
so that each child's creative mind can find the path that interests
him. That in itself is what nurtures the desire to continue to
want to learn. Formal education, precollege, seems to kill off
that desire."

Though Kristin and Jorel are ten years apart in age, Melanie
found no problem in homeschooling them at the same time. "I
think this is one of the advantages of homeschool, that you aren't
split up into groups only your same age," she says. "Different
ages at home isn't as big a problem as you might think, except for
the usual sibling rivalry, which in our case was minimal. I held
the baby while I read with the others. Sometimes the older ones
helped the younger ones. Occasionally the younger ones helped
the older ones." Melanie remembers her older children enjoying
times when they sat in on something new with Jorel. "Who says
the child has to learn certain things at specific ages? The different ages can learn perfectly fine together. Later you can spend
one-on-one time if needed."

In this family, that one-on-one time is often shared by father
and child. "Jorge has always been very available to the kids because of the flexibility of his business," Melanie says. "He actu-

ally does the majority of the guided learning with Jorel these days." Jorge is home at many different hours, allowing him to be very active in both family and homeschool life.

A typical day begins with Jorge up first, doing office work and record-keeping for his business. Melanie is next, starting on laundry and other household chores, then Jorel, then Keegan. Breakfast is sometimes a family affair, sometimes casual. Keegan leaves for work or college classes, while Jorge heads back to the in-home office or services equipment. With the help of a few textbooks and several workbooks, Jorel concentrates on math, vocabulary, reading, and writing. He also studies Spanish and American Sign Language. "I've taken about four years of ASL," Melanie says, "and pass on some to the family. It's great to finger-spell words for a different approach to spelling, or to use sign language when we are motorcycling."

Lunch is usually at 1:00, when the soap opera *All My Children* is on; the family often eats together while they watch. "We've gotten into some great discussions stemming from an incident on my soap opera," Melanie says, smiling. Occasionally Kristin drops by on her lunch hour from the zoo. Jorge and Jorel may squeeze in a look at one of their motor-cross videos.

In the afternoon, Jorge might be cutting grass, preparing for a DJ party, working more in the office, or servicing some of the ve-hicles. "By then, Jorel is definitely doing something on his dirt bike, either cleaning from the previous ride or servicing and preparing for the next ride," Melanie says. "Keegan is still at work or college. I could be doing any number of things like sewing, preparing for my parties, or working with plants."

Evening activities vary, as there is no formal weekly schedule. Sometimes the family eats together and watches TV, and some-times everyone goes in separate directions. Jorge and Jorel try to ride as much as they can. Keegan usually does something with friends, and Melanie may go to a class or a lecture at a bookstore.

"We just try to be as productive, year round, as possible," Melanie says.

Productivity, in this case, means natural life-learning, and Melanie and Jorge choose curricula that best help them all learn. At various times the children have used workbooks from an assortment of companies. They've also utilized books from the local public school depository, free to those willing to dig through a warehouse pile, and they take full advantage of the public library. "Our homemade curriculum has everything from baking, sewing, child care, cooking, driver's ed, mechanics, video, and photography, to constructing a haunted house," Melanie says. "Magazines, maps, newsletters, and even utilities bills are part of our curriculum. I firmly believe you can learn from almost anything. We try to let things flow and capitalize on natural learning."

The computer is always on for e-mail, Africam (a website with cameras watching several protected areas for wildlife passing by), or current motor-cross schedules. Keegan has her own website, is often chatting with someone, and has even answered online questions for novice homeschoolers. The family also watches educational TV and videos for everything from yoga to motor-cross. Jorge and Jorel video themselves riding and study their homemade tapes. They also go over purchased, taped-from-TV, and homemade videos to study the better riders, learning how to improve their own techniques.

Florida mandates that homeschooling families keep a log of what they've done throughout the 180 days they are required to school. The children must also be tested annually or evaluated by a certified teacher. Melanie and Jorge have sometimes taken advantage of SAT testing, and sometimes worked with teachers. "Testing is not important to us," Melanie says. "Although our children have always done well on the tests they've taken, we feel it's unnecessary and could do more harm than good in some cases. You can tell on a day-to-day basis where a child needs help."

The children test well, but are they socialized? Like all home-schoolers, the family hears the question often. "People are totally uneducated and blind regarding this subject," Jorge says. "I think homeschooled children are more socialized than others," Melanie adds. "They are not stuck all day in a room with kids and a teacher they may or may not get along with. Besides, don't you get in trouble for socializing in school?" The children in this family, as in most homeschool families, interact with all ages and all kinds of people. "They are not afraid to spend time with a younger child for fear of being called a baby," Melanie observes. "They can hold a conversation with adults on various subjects. They are more in the *real* world just by not being lumped to-gether with only their same age group."

Socialization, like learning, has been a natural process, a part of day-to-day living. "You have friends in the neighborhood, at get-togethers, on homeschool field trips with a group, in sports, clubs, any number of things," Melanie says. "Most of the friends our children have are through some particular interest they share, or just mutual friends of friends."

Throughout the family's homeschool years, the girls have been involved in a variety of activities offered both privately and through the public school system: dance lessons, gymnastics, and an environmental science program at the community college de-signed especially for a homeschool group. Jorel has participated in a Spanish class for homeschoolers, roller hockey, and of course, BMX.

All three children began earning money when they were still young. (Jorge and Melanie have never paid the children for household chores.) One of Kristin's first jobs was baby-sitting, and later she worked at a skating rink and a pet shop. From there she found her career as a zookeeper. Keegan has tried baby-sitting and waitressing at a sidewalk cafe. She began her clown-ing career when she was fourteen. Jorel's first official pay was earned repairing a neighbor's lawnmower. "All of these jobs have been learning situations in and of themselves," Melanie says.

Though the homeschooling life-style has been a very positive choice for the family, it was a choice that was not supported by anyone in either of the extended families. "They did us the favor of not saying too much," Melanie recalls. "My father has told me that at first he was very much against homeschooling and thought it was wrong. Now he has seen the results over the years and thinks it's the best thing we ever did."

Jorge and Melanie say they will continue to homeschool as long as they are living and breathing. Still, Melanie has felt discouraged from time to time. "It was especially bad during the bring-school-home days," she says. "Jorge never wavered. I would discuss it with him, and he always stood strong and made me feel confident. I would get encouragement from fellow homeschool moms too." Melanie thinks homeschooling has been everything she and Jorge expected and more. "The rewards are never ending," she says. "It's the same thing as being there for your baby's first step. You get that over and over as they grow and do new things. You see the lightbulb go on when they learn something new."

Jorel enjoys homeschooling because he says it allows him to be himself and not so heavily influenced by his peers. "I like being able to be home a lot," he says. "I can go places with my mom and dad. I can be with my family. You get to do more things." Academically, Jorel appreciates the availability of more personalized help. "If you need something, not like in a classroom, you can ask what you want and you don't have to be embarrassed," he says. "You don't have to deal with people showing off to impress their friends."

Keegan says that with her personality, she's better off because of homeschooling. "I don't think I would have dealt well with the controlling environment of school," she says. "I think if I had gone to school I would have become one of two things: a really bad kid rebelling against being told what to do every minute of the day, or more quiet, just going along with what I was told, repressing my own creativity. With the way we have done high school I've pretty much been able to go at my own pace. At times I needed to be pushed because I was lazy, but I had the freedom to learn what I needed to learn when I was ready."

From her own experience, Keegan has noticed that homeschoolers are able to observe and experience many things that kids in school don't get to see until later, "anything from watching the cable guy hook up the cable, going to the bank, waiting at the DMV or marking your lunch hour by Mom's soap opera. You get to miss the lines at the museums, and groan every time you see a school bus pull up because you know the school kids will act up and get yelled at."

Kristin was the experimental child. "I went to public school up until fourth grade," she says. "Fifth through eighth, I was homeschooled, then decided I wanted to go back to high school to be a 'big girl.' I quickly realized that was the wrong decision, but in the long run it has given me a good perspective on homeschool versus traditional school." Kristin thinks that school forces children to choose between conforming to the norm, acting like a bully, or being shy. "By the time they are ready to make friends outside the family unit, in the neighborhood, or through other activities, homeschool children are already comfortable with being themselves," she says. "At home, a close family like ours knows who you are and loves you anyway. That builds a strong base of confidence, which makes it easier to say no to the things you don't want to do and yes to the things you do." Kristin says that for her and her siblings, "homeschooling worked really well. It's what my husband and I will do with our children."

Because of so many shared experiences, the family is very tightly knit. "We truly enjoy having our kids around," Melanie says. "We think they're three well-rounded, self-confident, multitalented children." Jorge says that one of their greatest successes is in "seeing the difference between our kids and others."

Jorge and Melanie are proud of Kristin's prestigious position at MetroZoo, noting that the knowledge she's gained, relating to her career, has all been self-motivated. The couple is proud of the respect given to Keegan in her profession of clowning, and her success in college. They are proud of Jorel's ability to completely rebuild and service his go-cart, the weed eaters, and the dirt bikes.

Jorel, like his sisters, has had the chance to pursue his interests when he's been ready to learn more. All three children were also given the opportunity to direct their own learning and to schedule their days. Melanie can't say enough about the flexibility of homeschool. "You can be doing your laundry and helping your kids with their math," she explains, "or involved in a wonderful discussion while your kids are cleaning their room. Jorge might be paying the bills while Jorel is studying vocabulary. And the whole time you can be in your pajamas or bathing suit, listening to your favorite music, and have your dog or snake right there with you. It all goes hand in hand."

This flexibility extends to travel opportunites, too. Melanie has had the chance to attend a Native American powwow in Georgia with Keegan, a silent weekend program at the School for the Deaf and Blind in St. Augustine with Kristin, and a day trip to Islamorada to visit the Wild Bird Rescue Center with Jorel. "These are just a few of the wonderful activities our home-school schedule—or lack of one—has afforded us," she says. "And we can be out of town during the week, avoiding the hustle and bustle of weekend crowds."

Jorge and Jorel have also had their share of traveling together, especially to races. One particular adventure, in Dade City, Florida, was their first trip in the family motorhome. "It was the weekend of Jorel's thirteenth birthday, a great time until both of the bikes broke down," Melanie remembers. "But Jorge and Jorel kept a good attitude." While at Dade City, Jorel had the opportunity to meet and "hang out" with the fourteen-year-old number-one national BMX rider, James Stewart. "Jorel has videos of James that he watches all the time," Melanie says. "He got to talk with and see how down-to-earth this boy is. Several of the riders they've met are also homeschoolers." In spite of the setbacks, Jorge and Jorel watched the race and thoroughly enjoyed their weekend. "That's one of the best lessons Jorge has passed on to Jorel," Melanie says. "To make the most of a situation, whatever happens."

"For us," Melanie continues, "with diverse careers and interests in BMX, motorcycling, clowning, repair work, lawn maintenance, disk jockeying, zookeeping, and more, all life is a learning process in and of itself," she says. "We believe in going with that and making the best of it."

Front row: Jon, Daniel, Mike, David. Back row: Becky, Bruce, Joe, Don, Saimon.

Eighteen

Life with Six Boys

Family:
Bruce (49), Becky (43), Donald (18), Joseph (16), Jonathan (13), Michael (11), David (9), Daniel (8).

Location:
Rural Port Orchard, Washington.

Best advice:
1. Love your child's mother/father.
2. Turn off the TV and read to your children.
3. Progress in a child's character development will happen a little at a time. Keep your eyes on the bigger picture of character development and it will help you get through the difficult times in homeschooling.

Worst advice:
Don't organize any formal academics, and don't get locked into a schedule.

Favorite quote:

"Never doubt in the darkness what God has revealed in the light." (Bill Gothard)

Favorite resources:

God's Word (the Bible).

Saxon Math by Hake and Saxon, Saxon Publishers.

Open Court Phonics Program, SRA/McGraw Hill Publishers, 1-888-772-4543.

A Beka materials, 1-877-223-5226.

A list of the one thousand most misspelled words of the English language (books of such lists are available through most libraries).

Bruce and Becky H. and their six children live a busy, rather ordinary life. What sets them apart from most others, though, is that their six children are all active boys. "It is wonderful raising sons, though the challenges are quite different than with daughters," Becky says. "I've talked to other parents with both boys and girls, and they agree."

The family lives in the country outside Port Orchard, a small town in Washington. They moved there three years ago, to 4.6 acres, where they brought in a four-bedroom manufactured home and planted a flower and vegetable garden. An area has been cleared and seeded with grass for a baseball field, which the boys use nearly every day. There's also a large loop driveway where they can run a go-cart, and woods for a game of hide and seek.

Bruce is an inspector on Trident nuclear submarines, a civilian employee of the navy. He is an elder in the family's church and the board chairman for the church's school. Becky is a former registered nurse who retired when her fourth child was born. In 1992, Becky was diagnosed with multiple sclerosis and had to depend heavily on others' help for the next two years. Now she is basically in remission, although she still has many difficult days of weakness and exhaustion. She is supposed to take a one-hour nap every day and follows a very strict diet with virtually no fat. Sometimes she is able to function almost normally, although Bruce describes her energy levels on good days as about half of what they once were.

The family's homeschooling began when Don, their firstborn, was a preschooler. "We observed our friends homeschooling and noticed the lack of peer dependence in the children, their far above usual love for each other and their parents, their academic precocity, and their sensitivity and love for God," Becky says. "Also, I just plain loathed the idea of sending my precious little boy away from home, where I would lose the privilege of enjoying his companionship, where I would forfeit watching him read his first words, and where he would be so vulnerable physically, emotionally, socially, academically, and spiritually, compared to home."

Homeschooling has provided special teaching experiences that draw out the boys' gifts. "If we notice a child is interested or skilled in one area, we will provide opportunities for the development of this," Becky says. Don is drawn to politics, so as he was growing up, his parents gave him a greater than average amount of reading in history, government, and economics, then allowed him to serve as a Washington State Senate page. Jon enjoys cartography and found a related interest in participation in the National Geography Bee. "Joe sensed God might want him to work someday with the Navajo Indians," Becky says, "so Bruce took him to Arizona to visit a mission, local churches, and pastors, to see the work firsthand."

Becky thinks homeschooling parents have a unique opportunity. "In a conventional situation a teacher may be very familiar with a child's academic material but lacks the opportunities to guide the child in applying it to real life, such as business or nature," she says. "A parent is with the child in real-life situations and *could* help the child apply what he knows . . . but the parent usually isn't in touch with the school materials. A parent who is a homeschool teacher has both advantages."

Bruce and Becky have thought carefully through their philosophy of homeschooling, concluding that "our primary goal is to raise sons who love God and others, and who are able to perform well in life," Becky says. Bruce believes his most important job is "to train my boys to be excellent citizens, exemplary workers on the job, loving husbands, and sensitive fathers." Bruce tries to meet these goals by striving to be an excellent example at all times. "I also love my boys' mother," he says, "which leads to a secure atmosphere wherein teaching and learning can be maximized."

Much of the family's homeschool revolves not only around academics and social development, but also around spiritual development, including knowledge of the Bible, daily prayer, and church involvement. "We are in church three to four times per week," Becky notes.

The weeks are busy. Monday evenings, Bruce and all six boys attend a men's Bible study. Tuesday nights are reserved for baseball with the church league team; Bruce, Don, and Joe play, and Bruce also coaches. Each Wednesday, there's an evening prayer service and choir practice for Dad, Mom, Don, Joe, Jon, and Mike; during practice, David and Daniel sit by a family member in the choir and "rehearse," too, or keep busy with quiet homework activities in a nearby pew. Thursday evenings include meetings of AWANA Club, an organization something like the Boy Scouts that stresses Bible memorization and application. On Friday afternoons, the family often swims at a community pool, where Becky instructs them, and every other week, Don, Joe, and Jon attend youth meetings on Friday evenings with Dad. Weekends are also filled with activities.

During rare free time, the family reads aloud together, gardens, or follows the Seattle Mariners's baseball games on the radio. "We don't watch TV," Becky says. "TV eliminates the need to create a picture in one's mind. We want our children to develop their imaginations and think for themselves. We hope they will love books all their lives, and so far, they do." The family does watch videos, and the boys' favorites are home videos of vacations, birthday parties, and similar events. Another important source of recreation is music. Don and Joe love to play the piano and guitar and the family sings together.

Becky tries to follow a school schedule on weekdays, though she says there's no such thing as a typical day. She prefers to rise around 6:00 A.M. and "spend time with God" until 6:30. As the boys awaken, they are expected to get dressed, groom themselves, make their beds, tidy their rooms, and have a personal prayer and Bible study time. Then comes breakfast, some housework, and a short family devotional. Formal study begins at 8:30. There's a break for lunch and outside play, weather permitting, at 11:30. Then comes more study and play, dinner around 5:30, and various evening activities.

The family homeschool covers all traditional subjects, including math, writing, penmanship, spelling, reading, history, geography, astronomy, science, music (informal piano lessons given by Becky, and voice lessons through the church choir), keyboarding with typing software, and Bible. Becky prefers textbooks from Saxon, BJU, and A Beka, and Fastype for typing lessons. She doesn't hesitate to change curricula if necessary, or to make adjustments. "Much of A Beka's material is quite advanced," Becky says. "We're comfortable using it a year or so behind what the program recommends, depending on the child and the subject." The family takes three months off in the summer, but if a boy doesn't finish his work, he will continue "as long as it takes" to complete a course of study before fall.

Each student has a calendar with his individual assignments noted on it. The children and Becky often sit at a table together, with Mom between two boys for math. On Tuesday and Friday mornings, a retired teacher, eighty-two-year-old "Grandma" Beulah, comes and helps for a couple of hours. "I often take one boy who may be struggling with a subject to a bedroom to work one-on-one when she comes," Becky says. "Beulah demands a good measure of traditional classroom behavior, a balance to my more relaxed tendencies."

Another adopted family member, "Auntie Liz," provides personalized spelling instruction and helps with special projects, such as preparing the boys for upcoming spelling bees. She gives homework, and the boys go to her home at random times, usually depending on when they finish their other assignments.

Beulah and Liz are two of the many friends and family members who support the family in homeschooling. Becky's father is in a nearby nursing home, and Bruce, Becky, and the boys often visit him there. Several of Bruce's relatives live in the area and help in many ways: a sister-in-law, for example, handles grocery shopping, a very physically taxing job for Becky because of her multiple sclerosis.

The men and boys of Bruce's extended family like to get together to go hunting. When Joe first accompanied his dad and uncles at the age of twelve, Bruce once set him up at a strategic point on a deer trail and showed him exactly where Dad would be, some ninety yards away. Bruce took great pains to creep silently back to his hiding place. Moments later, with his father gone, Joe began to feel frightened. "He had never been in the woods somewhere feeling so alone, and even though he knew his dad was near, he felt he just had to hear his voice," Bruce recalls. "He began calling quietly at first, "Dad . . . DAD! . . . DAD!!! louder and louder." Bruce had no choice but to answer, and that was the end of hunting for the day; all the deer for many miles around now knew exactly where the hunters were hiding. "Through experiences like these the boys learn more than just facts about animal behavior," Becky observes. "They learn about courage, common sense, and most importantly, how they should handle difficult and disappointing situations, through their father's example of patience and love."

Bruce is actively involved in teaching all of the boys important skills and lessons, though on a more informal level than Becky. "Bruce includes them in everything from planting a garden to shopping to fixing the car," Becky says, "utilizing every teaching opportunity on the way." He also leads either morning or evening devotions with the family, depending on his schedule. He works odd shifts, currently ten-hour days, 2:30 P.M. to 1:00 A.M., Thursday through Sunday; the hours change every four months or so. In his free time, Bruce takes the boys to the lake to swim, coaches and plays baseball, helps lead church groups that include his children, and makes sure the family stays informed of current events.

Everyone, including Bruce and all six boys, pitches in to help keep the household running smoothly. "Every week, we rotate our sons' responsibilities—kitchen jobs, sweeping, vacuuming, bathrooms, dusting, et cetera," Becky says. Each boy is in charge of his own laundry, and this includes ironing and mending for the four oldest. Becky sometimes cooks thirty extra meals over a week's time, freezing the entrees for future use, and Bruce and the boys offer plenty of assistance in the kitchen. "This is obviously helpful for our sons in learning to be better husbands and fathers someday," Becky says.

Bruce and Becky both meet the state of Washington's requirement that homeschool teachers must have had at least one year of college. The couple keeps mandatory samples of schoolwork and standardized test results, plus a scrapbook of the boys' accomplishments. Children taught at home must be tested annually, and Becky arranges this through the family's church school or with another retired teacher. "Testing is important to us," she says. "It helps us identify weaknesses and trains our children in the skill of test taking, which they will need later in life."

The boys have plenty of social interaction with the six of them, plus parents, sharing a house measuring 1,770 square feet. In addition, there is often at least one other person living with the family. Becky was an exchange student in Japan in high school, and returned to Japan for a summer mission term when in Bible college; as a result, she is fluent in Japanese. Mike is studying Japanese and hopes to work in Japan teaching English. With all this interest in the people and the culture, they have had many Japanese guests. A twenty-one-year-old student, Saimon, has been part of the household for several months. His brother, Aisaku, fourteen, joined him for six weeks, and his sister, Seira, twenty, also visited; she may live with the family for two to three years while attending college nearby.

Both Bruce and Becky enjoy their busy life-style, and home-schooling is an essential ingredient. "Home-schooling has definitely been a good experience," Becky says. She has been surprised, through the years, to find teaching to be "pretty straightforward, not overly difficult, as I'd expected. The hard part has come in being generally consistent and sticking to a good schedule, having the personal discipline to constantly manage time wisely."

Becky sometimes fears her own inadequacies. "I hope they are no more than those of any teachers my children might encounter in the conventional school system," she says. "But I certainly don't want to have negative effects on our children." When she gets discouraged, "I try to see the bigger picture," she says. "I pray. I sing. I read the Bible. I talk to my husband, children, friends, and spiritual mentors. And I work on getting good sleep and adequate rest, especially since I need more than most people."

The family can point to many tangible successes in their homeschool. Joe and Jon have won and placed in area, district, and regional spelling bees. Don's achievement as regional spelling champion (out of eighteen thousand students from public, private, and homeschools), when he was fourteen, earned him a berth in Washington, D.C., as a competitor in the National Spelling Bee: He placed 160th in the 1996 National Bee, which drew from ten million children. Bruce, Becky, Joe, and Jon were able to fly to Washington with Don. "It was an educationally excellent field trip!" Becky says. "Washington, D.C., has a wealth of history to offer."

Even more important than spelling skills and history lessons, "we have all learned what it means and what it takes to spend all one's free time on an enormous project," Becky says. "High placements in the bees require the boys to deny themselves pleasure and fun in order to study. We've learned commitment and self-discipline, and how hard work and long hours are necessary in order to accomplish tough goals."

Becky started a geography bee in her area after contacting the National Geographic Society for information. Unlike spelling bees, the winner of a local geography bee is given a written test; the one hundred top scorers go on to the state competition. Jon and Joe have each made it. Mike and David have competed also and, with Daniel, hope to win in years to come.

Another success of the family's homeschool is Don's graduation. When he was to become a junior in homeschool high school, he participated in a program called Running Start. Washington state students who pass an entrance exam and receive their parents' permission can take their final two years of high school at a community college. "In effect, the public school system paid for the first two years of college for Don," Becky says. "He graduated with both an associate arts and sciences degree and his homeschool high school diploma last spring." Don's outstanding grades in college qualified him for the national dean's list, and he graduated with honors. He plans to commute to Bates Technical College in the fall.

Don works full-time at a dentist's office cleaning clients' teeth, assisting with root canals, and relining dentures as well as acting as a "do-all boy." By the time he is nineteen, the family's oldest son will have already bought much of the basic equipment he'll need to become a dental lab technician or a denturist. "Don became interested in this profession after taking a blacksmithing class with a friend," Becky smiles. "He really likes the artistic challenges of crafting dentures and corrective appliances." Don hopes to continue to live in Port Orchard, contract with dentists, and work from home or eventually open a denture clinic of his own.

Bruce and Becky have always wanted to be on hand for their boys' "firsts" from babyhood through adulthood. "I was there for each child's first breath, for his first hug, first tooth, first step," Becky says. "I knew that no one on Earth could be as overjoyed for these firsts as one of their own parents."

Six times Becky and Bruce have observed their sons experience a brand-new world opening to them. Becky marvels, "There is nothing comparable to watching the mental lights go on, the wonder spreading across your own little boy's face as he sounds out his first word, realizing what the magical process of reading is all about, and seeing him excited by the prospect that he *can* read. I wouldn't miss this! Experiences like these rank among the most fulfilling of my entire life."

Today, as they watch their young men maturing, Bruce and Becky see the fruit of homeschooling. "When I think about success, it's watching Joe get up behind the podium at church in front of two hundred people, sharing about the Navajo ministry and leading prayer," Becky says. "Noting that it's as natural for our children to freely interact with ninety-five-year-olds as with their own peers. Having all his brothers cheer when Don comes home from work or his classes at the junior college, because they miss him. Listening to my boys share insights beyond their years during a Bible study. Witnessing two brothers make up after some kind of problem between them, each asking the other's forgiveness. Observing our sons' good attitudes in both victory and defeat when competing in spelling and geography bees. Watching a younger son climb on his older brother's knee for love and togetherness."

As the only female in a household of males, Becky has discovered that her men and boys "are just plain fun! They're interesting and fun and it's an adventure discovering what makes them tick and how they think and feel and respond to situations." Having six homeschooled boys has been "quite an experience," all right. A very, very good one.

Brian and Cari with Mary, Brendan, Michael, Gabriel, Daniel, and Rebekah.

Nineteen

Homeschooling in Alaska's Back Country

Family:
Brian (33), Cari (32), Michael (10), Gabriel (7), Rebekah (5), Mary (3), Brendan (18 months), Daniel (6 months).

Location:
North Pole, Alaska.

Best advice:
Enjoy homeschooling. Read a lot to your children.

Worst advice:
Don't worry about it, they'll "get it all" eventually.

Favorite quote:
"To be Queen Elizabeth within a definite area, deciding sales, banquets, labors, and holidays; to be Whitely within a certain area, providing toys, boots, cakes, and books; to be Aristotle within a certain area, teaching morals, manners, theology, and hygiene; I can

understand how this might exhaust the mind, but I cannot imagine how it could narrow it. How can it be a large career to tell other people's children about the Rule of Three, and a small career to tell one's own children about the universe? How can it be broad to be the same thing to everyone and narrow to be everything to someone? No, a woman's function is laborous, but because it is gigantic, not because it is minute." (G. K. Chesterton)

Favorite resources:
The church.
The sacraments.
Homeschooling for Excellence by David and Micki Colfax, Warner Books.
A Survivor's Guide to Home Schooling by Luanne Shackelford and Susan White, Crossway Books.
Catholic Home Schooling by Dr. Mary Kay Clark, founder of Seton Home Study, 540-636-9990.

Cari and Brian M. were childhood sweethearts. They grew up together in Louisiana, married, and moved to southern California when Brian was in the army. Cari ran a computer company that designed medical software for doctors' offices. "I was also pursuing a career in law enforcement and had worked as a reserve deputy sheriff for three and a half years, part-time," she says. "I had just been hired by the Riverside Police Department when I found out I was pregnant with Gabriel." The couple already had one son, Michael, who was nearly three, and they hoped to have more children. Cari made the difficult decision to leave her career and go home to full-time mothering.

Meanwhile, Brian had been discharged from the service and got a job as a deputy sheriff in Riverside County, California. The couple bought their first home in the forest of the San Bernardino mountains, and Brian commuted an hour each way to and from work. They had two more children, Rebekah and Mary. Their lives were settled and stable.

Yet both Cari and Brian harbored a strong desire to get away from their urban environment. "I was somewhat burned out on law enforcement in California," Brian says. "My job was very fast-paced and lots of tragic incidents occurred. I wanted a career change and a life-style change." The couple had always dreamed of a back-to-basics life-style where they could provide for themselves. They kept telling themselves that one day, they would move to Alaska's back country.

When Brian turned thirty, he and Cari took the first step toward fulfilling their shared dream. "We thought, if we were ever going to do something, we needed to do something now," Cari remembers, "so we took a family vacation to Alaska to check out the possibilities. We loved it." Getting a job was the next problem: The couple knew they must move to Alaska before Brian could find employment there as an Alaskan state trooper, since the job requires residency.

While vacationing, Cari had picked up an Alaskan newspaper and brought it home with her. "I was looking through the want ads and found an open position for a caretaker at a remote fishing lodge," she says. "At first Brian and I laughed about it, you know, thinking, 'Wouldn't that be the perfect job for us? Right.' Then we thought, 'Maybe we *could* do this.'" Cari called the number and learned that the owners, in the process of building the unfinished lodge, needed someone to stay there during the next several months. Brian flew back to Alaska the next week to check out the location and the job.

As a married couple with four young children, Brian and Cari were not typical candidates for a caretaking position. In spite of this, they proposed that the owners of the lodge provide them with fuel and food for the winter, free rent, and a loaned van and snowmobile as their only payment for basic maintenance duties. The owners agreed.

By August 1998, Brian had turned in his resignation as a deputy sheriff. Seven weeks later, he, Cari, and the children were the offi-cial caretakers of the fishing lodge on Lake Aleknagik (ah-LEK-nah-gik), Bristol Bay area, Alaska. The family were to be the only occupants of an island, two and a half miles across the lake from Aleknagik, a village of 250 in the summer and 75 in the winter. They sold most of their belongings, including their car, and the rest went into storage in California. Brian, Cari, Michael, Gabriel, Re-bekah, and Mary flew to their new home October 6. Winter weather was already beginning.

The lodge, a brand new structure with six bedrooms and a huge dining room, was enclosed but still incomplete. It was hardly a cozy place to live. "The windows didn't sit right in places, and there were cracks where the wind blew in," Cari says. "We moved our beds into one bedroom and all of us slept in there, in sleeping bags. We closed off the rest of the building to help conserve energy."

The lodge was furnished with an oil drip heater, a boxlike con-traption about two by four by four feet in size, that burned fuel oil. Every two or three days Brian had to go into the village to buy fuel oil, pumping it into a big fifty-gallon drum, bring it home on a sled pulled by the snow machine, and pump it into a fifty-gallon barrel outside the wall that fed the heater.

The unfinished lodge had no electricity. Every morning a bat-tery had to be carried outside to a generator, hooked up, turned on, and brought back into the house. Every evening, the generator was shut down.

To get water, Brian and the boys chipped a hole in the lake's ice; sometimes it grew to be five feet thick, requiring the use of a chain saw. Michael also helped lay out the water lines, hook the water pump to the lines, and crank the portable engine to pump water. "When it got really cold we couldn't use the water lines," Cari says. "Brian had to load a big garbage can onto the back of the sled, fill it with water from the lake, run it on the sled back up to the house, and pump water from the can into the 250-gallon holding tank. It would take Brian eight trips to fill the tank." There were toilets in the lodge, but the family used something called a "honey bucket" instead, which they had to empty every day. "That saved us five gallons of precious water for each flush," Cari says. "We used minimal amounts of water for dish washing and did most of our laundry in town."

The family's new home became increasingly isolated as a bitter winter set in. Snow began to fall in mid-October. "We were able to get in and out to the island by skiff until the week of Thanksgiving," Cari recalls. "The lake had started to ice all around us, but it hadn't completely frozen yet. Boats could still go into the lake, but they couldn't get to us and we couldn't get to them." Fortunately, they were well stocked with supplies, as it was impossible to leave the island for three weeks.

Brian and Cari were not prepared for extremely cold weather. "In Aleknagik, zero degrees was a warm day," Cari says, smiling. "When the temperature dropped below zero, we all had to wear snow pants inside the drafty lodge. We could see our breath inside." Though the couple had lived in the mountains of California and owned winter clothes, they needed better equipment. "We ended up ordering a ton of stuff from a catalog," Cari says.

By December, temperatures had continued to drop and the lake froze over completely, though the ice was still thin. Four days before Christmas it was thirty degrees below zero. The next day, however, the temperature shifted dramatically to forty degrees above zero. The lake started to melt. When Brian and Cari observed native Alaskans out on the ice, they decided to make a fast run into town to buy Christmas presents and supplies before the ice melted completely. "We made a wild ride across the lake on the snow machine, hoping we wouldn't fall in," Cari says, shuddering. "Brian, the four children, and I were out on this two-and-a-half-mile trip across the lake, and I could see the blackness underneath me. There were puddles of water everywhere, and I couldn't tell if it was open water or just overflow, melting water on top of the ice. That was the scariest thing I ever did in my life."

The return trip was just as frightening. "On the way back, we saw one older native couple pulling a sled across the ice," Cari remembers. "Later we talked to some of the younger native guys and they said, 'We wouldn't go out on a snow machine on ice that thin, that's too scary.' Fortunately, by then we were safely back at home."

In spite of the cold weather and isolation, Brian, Cari, and the children were happy with their new life. "Loneliness was not an issue for us," Cari says. "Our family is really close and has been that way for some time. We never felt cut off from society." A local radio station sent an interviewer to ask questions and ice fish with Brian and the boys. "Every time we went into town after that, people said, 'Oh, are you that family on the radio?'" Cari says. "They played excerpts of our interview for two weeks straight. Out in the bush, the local radio station is a big deal."

To pass leisure time indoors at the lodge, the family often played games and read. (Rural Alaska television consists of one channel that features a conglomerate of shows picked from major networks, but Cari and Brian always have preferred to not watch any TV.) Outside, everyone spent free time playing with their pet, an Alaskan timber wolf/Alaskan malamute hybrid named Miko, walking, sledding, ice fishing, and enjoying the scenery, including an occasional view of the northern lights. Brian liked to go jogging in snow shoes across the lake. "He'd come home looking like the 'Ice Man,'" Cari says, grinning, "with frost all over his beard and mustache."

By now, living in Alaska had put Brian into a position where he could apply for work as a state trooper. He received word in February that he had been accepted into the program and was required to go to a seven-week training school beginning May 8.

Meanwhile, Cari was pregnant with their fifth child, due June 10. It was necessary for her to leave the island before her due date, because once the ice began to break up, travel over the lake would again be impossible for some time. The couple resigned their caretaking position in May. Cari and the four children moved into an apartment in Anchorage to await the fifth baby's arrival while Brian flew to the training school's town, Sitka, 450 miles away.

Cari went into labor unexpectedly early, on June 1. Her mother-in-law, scheduled to fly from Louisiana to Anchorage on June 9, could not get another flight for at least twenty-four hours. Brian was unable to leave the training school without forfeiting his position; had he left, he would have been required to reapply and start over again. "So I showed up at the hospital in the middle of the night with all the children," Cari says. "I didn't know anyone in town. There was no one I could call." The hospital staff tucked Michael, Gabriel, Rebekah, and Mary into fold-out beds in the same room as their mother, where they dozed throughout the night.

Cari was in touch with Brian by phone, but urged him not to come. Still, "I was really starting to worry," Cari says. "I said a prayer, 'Dear God, help me. What will I do with the children?' Right after that a nurse walked in and came over to me. She said, 'I know you don't know me, but I'm a Christian, and I feel like God is telling me I should help you with the children. I've worked at the hospital for fourteen years and I have never done this before!' She offered to take the kids for me while I was having the baby. I said, 'Thank you, God!' " Cari called Brian and he agreed to the plan. The children went home for the day with the compassionate nurse.

Soon it was afternoon. Cari's labor was progressing slowly, and she was tired. "I asked the nurses to give me something to help me get my second wind, just an injection of a pain medication," Cari says. "By mistake, I was given a syringe of full-strength Pitocin, a drug that helps women have contractions." Because of the pressure from the uterus's intense squeezing, the baby's heartbeat disappeared. Cari began a series of nonstop contractions that eventually would have ruptured her uterus. "All of a sudden a nurse yelled, 'Code Blue! Come to OB stat!' " she says. "They put me under general anesthesia and I had an emergency C-section to deliver Brendan, our fifth child." Thankfully the baby, mother, and siblings all survived the ordeal, and Cari's mother-in-law was soon on hand to help out.

Brian didn't meet his newborn until June 28, but by then he had completed his training and secured a job as an Alaska state trooper. He was assigned a position in Fairbanks as a patrolman. Today, he works from the same office but now spends three days a week, sometimes more, flying out to remote outlying villages to handle law enforcement problems. "He has a forty-hour workweek, and when the forty hours are up, he's done," Cari says. "There's not much crime, and he likes his work."

The family lives in an area just southeast of Fairbanks in a suburb called North Pole. "We're kind of out in the country on a one-acre plot," Cari says. "We have a cooperative garden with a growing season from June through September. Because of the extra daylight in the summer, plants up here can grow really huge. One cabbage can be eighty to one hundred pounds." The family goes berry picking each year, and Cari cans the berries as well as producing jams and jellies. "The children help with all of this. I consider it part of their training in practical homeschooling."

In addition to gardening and berry picking, the family currently raises livestock, including six chickens and a rooster. Earlier this year, they butchered their own pig plus two turkeys for Thanksgiving and Christmas dinners. "Basically everything 'country' we've done, Cari and I have gotten a book and read up on it," Brian says. "Once when we raised New Zealand white rabbits, one of our good breeding does had grown a cyst on her neck and was withering away. Cari read up on it and talked to people at the feed store. Then she did surgery with a scalpel and removed the cyst. The rabbit healed up fine and had several more litters. We're into that do-it-yourself kind of thing."

Brian and Cari have access to rather unusual food sources. The fish hatcheries around the coast, for example, raise salmon for the eggs only, and by law the fish cannot be discarded. Instead, the salmon hatcheries give away salmon—five silver salmon per person, and as much pink salmon as requested—in different areas of the state. "These fish are a couple of feet long, and twenty-five of them provide enough fish to last us a year," Cari says, "but if we can't get them, we also fish for ourselves."

Occasionally moose wander through the family's backyard and they sometimes hunt them. In addition, "there's a policy here that if somebody in a car hits a moose, the meat is given to a charity," Cari says. "If the charity doesn't respond, the troopers need to find someone who will take it right away. An average moose weighs seventeen hundred pounds, with about eight-hundred pounds of usable meat." Cari recently got an offer to pick up a freshly killed cow. "I had watched a video earlier in the year on how to field dress a moose, so I knew I could handle it. I took Daniel [the family's latest addition, now six months old] and Michael and went to pick up the moose and skin it." Brian had been injured at work the day before and so stayed home with the other children. Fortunately, two men helped Cari and Michael lift the cow via a backhoe and field dress it.

Homeschooling, whether in practical arts or academics, is a major part of the family's life-style. "We do have to hit the books, but the children learn so much from everyday living, things we would not be able to do were they off at school," Cari says. "We feel that we can and do provide the very best education for our children. And we can keep our children from being negatively influenced by today's society. We can raise our children with correct morals, not watered down by society's lack of morals."

The family are devout Catholics. "Our Catholic faith is *the* most important thing to us," Cari says. "We teach the children that everything revolves around our Catholic faith and our belief in Jesus Christ. Our faith is in everything that we do and everything we learn about. We are successful in teaching that to our children, and without homeschooling, we would never be able to do so."

Cari and Brian chose Seton Home Study because "the flavor of our faith is evident throughout the curricula," Cari says. "In English lessons, for example, when the children are learning about sentence structure, the text might mention stopping at the church to talk to Father, or not eating meat on Friday, things of that nature. It's the same thing with reading selections; they're stories about Catholic families or saints or just good, wholesome stories." Cari has never changed curricula, though she likes Calvert and has incorporated many of their suggestions and ideas into her homeschool.

When Cari researched various curricula, she was impressed with Seton's track record. "They turn out more homeschoolers with either perfect or near perfect SAT scores every year than any other curricula I found," she says. "The course is very demanding, comparable to that of a good Catholic school. They use older textbooks that are synonymous with good education and teaching children the faith."

As part of their Seton training, Michael, Gabriel, and Rebekah learn religion, math, English, reading, science, history, phonics, vocabulary, P.E., music, art, spelling, and handwriting. Cari and Brian also teach animal husbandry, home economics, auto mechanics, woodworking, and other practical skills. "The children will eventually learn Latin," Cari says. "We attend a Latin mass, and the priest reads the scriptures first in Latin and then in English. We say prayers along with the server in Latin, with the English translation in the missal [a small book containing the order of the mass, including prayers and Bible readings]."

The family's Catholicism is woven into their daily life. All eight attend daily mass whenever possible. On Fridays, they try to visit their church's stations of the cross, a series of sculptures or paintings that depict scenes of Jesus' journey to his crucifixion. On Saturdays, Brian, Cari, and Michael attend confessions with the priest. Each day begins with family prayers, and each night ends with a recitation of the rosary and acts of contrition. "We all reflect on our day and talk about how we lived it for God," Cari says. "I jog the kids' memories with questions like 'Could you have helped one another more? Did you do your chores willingly?' I ask them to think about these things and decide what they'd like to do better the next day. Then they say individual prayers."

Day-to-day life is predictable but hectic. "A typical morning for me starts with waking up, usually way too early," Cari jokes. "Someone always wants to be up early, and someone always wants to stay up late, too." The children start the morning by completing chores of sweeping, vacuuming, taking out the trash, straightening the coat and boot closet, dishes, laundry, making beds, cleaning rooms, general personal hygiene, and feeding the animals. Other day-to-day chores are handled as the opportunities arise, "when I have a moment to wipe down a sink or fold laundry," Cari says.

P.E. is next, a family affair with Dad, Mom, and all six children participating in a routine of push-ups, sit-ups, leg raises, squats, pull-ups, and running on the treadmill. Brian hoists the youngest ones up to the bar to try chin-ups. Then the children have play time until lunch, the big sit-down meal of the day.

Brian leaves for work at 1:30 P.M., but while he's home he participates in homeschooling in many ways. In addition to leading P.E., Brian instructs the children in karate. He also teaches particular subjects or plays with the little ones as needed.

With Dad gone, the house quiets down as Mary, Brendan, and Daniel take naps and Michael, Gabriel, and Rebekah start on school assignments. Cari teaches the subjects that require her most undivided attention during times when the little ones are napping. She also gives piano lessons to Michael, Gabriel, and Rebekah. To handle teaching children of different ages, Cari gets one started on a project and a second child on something else, then works with the third. She rotates from child to child until everyone's finished. When Mary awakes from her nap, she gets involved in very relaxed preschool work. Cari tries to keep the babies and toddler busy with blocks, Legos, books, a chalkboard, the computer, toys, and coloring books while she schools. The family sometimes watches educational videos together or plays computer games.

Late afternoon, it's time to tidy the house, eat dinner, and take baths. If the three oldest children have any remaining schoolwork to be done, they finish up and are then free to play until evening prayer time. "The children are supposed to be in bed sleeping before Daddy comes home from work between ten-thirty and eleven," Cari says. "Then I get to spend time with Brian before bed. We school on the days when Brian is working, usually Tuesday through Saturday."

Academic work continues throughout the year, with plenty of breaks. "We keep schooling until we are finished with the course, sometime during the summer," Cari says. "We take off a few weeks and then start the next year in September, depending on when berry picking ends." Cari had started homeschooling Michael and Gabriel when the family lived in California, and stopped temporarily when they moved to Alaska. She also took a break before she gave birth to Brendan.

Each of the six children has a distinct personality. Michael is both athletic and inventive. A bookworm, he reads at least one book (the length of a *Hardy Boys*) a day.

Gabriel is an animal lover, artistic, and imaginative. For his birthday, Brian and Cari made him a costume of his favorite character, Zorro. He is the official baby-sitter for the younger children.

Rebekah is "a girlie girl," Cari says. "She likes to dress up and be a princess." Rebekah taught herself to read.

Mary is the family's mischief maker, into everything and curious about everything. "Whenever Brian is working on a project or building furniture, Mary is always there in the middle of it, wanting to play with the tools," Cari says. "She is the happiest person you'll ever meet."

Brendan and Daniel are very content to follow the other children or allow their sisters to pick them up and carry them around the house. Both like it noisy. Cari has noticed that when the house is too quiet, Brendan and Daniel start to wonder what's wrong.

Cari has had the school-age boys tested and found that they far exceed national standards. "In Alaska, you homeschool however and whenever you want," she says. "Residents here just aren't as concerned about homeschoolers, not like they were in California. A lot of people here *have* to homeschool because they have no other choice."

To solve the education problem for many of Alaska's rural residents, the state proposed a novel solution. Interior Distance Education of Alaska (IDEA) arranged for homeschoolers to sign up as "distance learners" through a tiny school district in the bush near a village called Galena. This district now claims thousands of "homeschool" students.

IDEA provides Alaskan homeschoolers with school age children eight hundred dollars per child per semester, seven hundred dollars for kindergarteners, and two hundred dollars for preschoolers. "I can go to Kmart and buy notebooks and pencils and puzzles, and pay for it myself, send the receipt, and get reimbursement," Cari says. "Or if IDEA has a contract with a supplier, I fill out a paper and turn it in, and they purchase the materials for me and ship them directly to me." Brian and Cari bought a complete set of *World Book Encyclopedias* through this program. They also have used the money to pay for swimming lessons for the three oldest children, family passes to practice swimming, and for general school supplies. IDEA dollars provided the family with both a laptop and a desktop computer, a print/scanner/fax machine, and an additional printer. The only restriction is that government money cannot be used for the purchase of religious materials.

The IDEA program is just as beneficial to schools as to homeschoolers. The Galena, Alaska, school district is paid a certain amount of money per registered child from the state government, and this totals much more income than the funds paid to its homeschoolers. That's why Galena, a city of only 450 people, has a first-rate school. "It's a win-win situation," Cari says.

Although they have considered a traditional Catholic boarding school for some of their children's teen years, the family intends to homeschool through high school. Cari's extended family has been supportive of this choice, though Brian's father, a renowned chemical engineer, has concerns about how Cari will teach chemistry or advanced algebra.

When people ask Cari about socialization, she asks for a definition. Cari thinks socialized children should be able to converse and get along with other children and adults respectfully and happily. "My children visit with other children and adults at church and in various areas of life and are comfortable doing so," she says. "But to be socially indoctrinated by thirty or more children of their own ages in a public school setting, no, we don't do that. I really don't believe in that kind of socialization, and I am always willing to tell people about it. I ask them to just look around and see how well it works for most other children."

Surprisingly, many people congregate around swimming pools. "In Alaska, there's usually a pool at every local school," Cari says, "even in most rural districts." Still, much of this young family's socialization comes from working and playing with each other.

Michael and Gabriel also keep busy with entrepreneurial projects. Michael builds birdhouses and crochets slingshots, which he calls David's slings, to sell. Each child receives a monthly allowance, and the boys are always looking for additional money-making jobs such as raking leaves and shoveling snow.

Michael likes homeschooling "a lot" and Gabriel likes it "a little." Michael says his mom is a good teacher. But Cari concedes that it has been rough going at times, particularly when she's in the early stages of a pregnancy, the children are sick, or there's a newborn in the house. "It's also hard for me to stay focused when the first snow of the year falls," she says, "or when spring comes in Alaska. I do feel discouraged, as I feel everyone does. But I have a wonderful husband to whom I can talk about anything, and he encourages me to be the best that I can be. If I had it to do over again, I would definitely homeschool."

Cari, Brian, and the children would also definitely choose Alaska as their permanent home. "I think Alaska is wonderful," Michael says. "I think it's better here. In California it was always hot with no snow, and we lived on a busy street. Up here, after my dad got rid of the snow machine skis, he gave them to me and Gabriel. We sat on them and went down this hill and we were able to turn and go really fast." Gabriel likes living in Alaska "because there's more steeper hills." Rebekah enjoys the snow and says she liked it when her family first moved to Alaska and were "sleeping all together."

Their dad thinks living in the fishing lodge on Lake Aleknagik was the "best seven months of our lives. Rarely a day goes by when we don't reflect on our time out there. It was rugged, very rugged. But even during one of the very worst days, when the generator went down and we had no electricity, Cari asked me, 'Would you do it again, moving up here?' and I answered, 'In a heartbeat,' and she said, 'So would I.' Everything you work for here is so tangible, not like some of my work in law enforcement."

Brian remembers bitterly cold days at the lodge when he'd be chipping a hole in the ice and ice pellets were stinging his face. "I'd look out over the lake and there was the mountain range," he recalls. "I'd say, 'Thank you, God, that I live in Alaska.' "

Twenty

Aunt and Grandma as Homeschool Teacher

Family:
Lynda (53), Frank (45), Derek (17, son), Timothy (16, "acquired child"), Kirk (13, grandson), Krystin (9, granddaughter).

Location:
Eureka, California (exactly halfway between the borders of Mexico and Canada).

Best advice:
"Believe because you do know," from Lynda's grandfather. "Follow what you think you know because you really do know it. Go with your gut feeling."

Worst advice:
" 'They'—the doctors, the schools, the politicians—know best."

Favorite saying:
"If ignorance is bliss, why aren't more people happy?"

Krystin, Derek, and Kirk.

Favorite resources:

The library.

The Internet.

The local community, a source of nearly endless people and places from which to learn.

Friends.

The children themselves.

Lynda D. was only nineteen years old when she first began homeschooling. "Because of a sister-in-law's medical emergency, my husband and I temporarily acquired five children ages ten, eight, seven, six, and two," she says. "The kidlets were stressed to beyond the breaking point and I decided that changing schools, along with the whole public school experience, would be added stress. Instead, I basically unschooled them."

Homeschooling was a new and rather radical concept back in 1968, even in radical California, but Lynda knew just what she wanted to do with her nieces and nephews. "We spent lots of time playing games that were really aimed at the youngest, but each of the older kids evolved to their own 'grade' level," she remembers. Lynda made child number five a large felt board, and the two of them played with it. "The other children thought this was great fun, so I made circles, squares, and other math-related things for them to use on the board," she says. "We also made animals and habitat scenes."

When the children were studying animals and habitats, they made several library searches for the information. "I know the librarian thought we were nuts," Lynda says, smiling, "with kids coming up to me and saying things like, 'Auntie Mom, I found a vulture, yuck! They eat dead people!' and that sort of thing." From library research came other activities: drawing and cutting up magazines to create whole environments for favorite animals, much reading, and even math problems, such as calculating the distance a snowy plover flies to the Arctic Circle.

Lynda's nieces and nephews went everywhere with her and were exposed to all sorts of ideas and experiences. It was the 1960s, and "the kids got quite a few living history lessons from hanging around Berkeley," Lynda says. "They met some folks who later became quite famous—or infamous—as I went to junior high and high school in Sonoma County with Nancy Ling Perry, a member of the Symbionese Liberation Army who was killed in a big fire-bombing in L.A. We'd all go down to People's Park and there were lots of group get-togethers." Many of Lynda's former schoolmates fought in Vietnam and were returning to the States about this time. "Quite a few decided to drop out and live alternatively," Lynda says, "and communes were big. Six guys and girls I knew moved to this little island owned by someone's uncle, planning to live 'as nature intended,' naked. That lasted until monsoon season. Then they all decided that clothes and civilization weren't so bad after all."

After one year of some very unusual homeschooling experiences, all five nieces and nephews returned to their mother and father. "The schools insisted on testing before promoting them to the next grade level," Lynda says. "They all tested far beyond where they needed to be, and in some subjects, like reading, they were ahead by several grade levels. We all did an in-your-face happy dance."

Two years later, Lynda and her husband started their own family with a daughter, Kassondra, and a son, Alexandar. "Unfortunately, I ended up plugged into the philosophy of believing I had to send my children to public school," she says, "and I had a husband and in-laws who were very unsupportive of homeschooling. I did make life hell for my kids' public schools, though, because I knew the rules, the law, and what should have been done. I was constantly on the doorstep. I probably did most of the real teaching myself."

Lynda's marriage of ten years ended in divorce. She was remarried for only a short time and had a second son, Andrew. "I named him after my grandfather, whose influence was pivotal to my homeschooling philosophy," she says, smiling. In 1981, Lynda married Frank, and the couple had Derek.

Meanwhile, the three older children had graduated from high school and moved on, leaving only Derek at home. "About seven years ago, when Derek was at the end of grammar school, I finally reached my saturation point with public school," Lynda recalls. "One day I said, 'I just can't do this anymore.' I had gotten into a routine and kind of forgotten who I really was and what I really wanted."

Lynda realized she had put aside everything she had learned many years earlier while sitting on the front steps with her grandfather. "As an American Indian, I had let myself become too 'white' and had drifted away from my heritage," she says. "I was doing what was expected of me by white middle-class America instead of what was best for me and my family."

In 1993, Lynda began to take charge of her life again when she and Frank moved back to Humboldt County, the home of Lynda's ancestors. The next year, Frank, Lynda, and Derek moved into a solid redwood Victorian cottage on a small lot in Eureka, California.

Eureka is a rather unusual place. A city of twenty-six thousand, it's the largest metro area between Santa Rosa and Portland. The population has remained static over forty years because little work is available to support more people. Nearby are seven rivers, two lakes, several lagoons, and miles of ocean beach. "We also have chunks of the redwood forest, creeks, and—right in the middle of the city—a seventy-acre park," Lynda says. "Bears and deer walk through town, and ten minutes from my house you can hear mountain lions and see foxes and skunks. A hawk sits outside my window. At the last bird counting, we had more species of birds than anywhere else in the U.S." Eureka's average temperature throughout the year is sixty degrees, rarely varying more than ten degrees hotter or colder.

Before retiring with a disability, Lynda worked in Humboldt County at Table Bluff Indian Reservation, where she was the fiscal administrator. "I used to leave the house, drive through the middle of a golf course in Eureka, and suddenly come upon a bird's-eye view of the bay and the Pacific Ocean," Lynda says. "The reservation was to the south, around the end of the bay and up to the top of a bluff." Two years ago, Frank also retired from his job with a disability from cancer.

Frank and Lynda had lived in Eureka for about a year when Lynda's thirty-one-year-old daughter, Kassandra, called. "At the time, she had two children and was living three and a half hours away from here," Lynda says. "She asked if Frank and I would take her two children, Kirk and Krystin, to come and temporarily live with us." After the initial shock wore off, the couple agreed. Their immediate family expanded to include seven-year-old Kirk and three-year-old Krystin. The temporary arrangement eventually turned into a permanent one when Kassandra granted her parents custody of the children.

When he first moved in with his grandparents, Kirk attended public school. He stayed in the system for several years, through October of sixth grade. Kirk chose to come home after a teacher hit his friend in the head with a math book for talking in class. By that time, Lynda says that "he was so far behind and school had made such a mess, it was more or less like starting over. 'Deschooling' took quite a long time, and he still thinks in 'public school mode' sometimes."

Krystin enrolled in public school kindergarten "because all her little friends were there and she wanted to go and finger paint," says Lynda. Krystin soon discovered that next year, first grade would mean sitting at a desk all day, "doing what the teacher wanted, when the teacher wanted it," as Lynda puts it. Following kindergarten, Krystin joined Uncle Derek, and later Kirk joined the two of them, in unschooling at home.

As a grandmother and mother, Lynda still believes in the same basic philosophy she held as a homeschooling "Auntie Mom" thirty years earlier. "We have child-led learning here," she says. "We're more unschooling than homeschooling." Krystin picked up reading from watching the *Wheel of Fortune* television show. "She never had to just sit and learn," Lynda says. "She started bugging her uncle and brother and saying she wanted to read a Disney book, a book on tape, and it just flowed."

Frank, who grew up in a rigid public school system that required both uniforms and uniformity, has found unschooling difficult to accept. "My husband is from Massachusetts, where people are much less accepting of things than they are here in California," Lynda says. "This whole way of learning has been very hard for him, though he says we're contagious. The more he sees the more he believes. We've converted him because he sees that homeschooling works."

Frank taught himself to play drums, guitar, and music by ear, plus basic car repair and home maintenance. "It took the longest time to convince Frank that he was already an unschooler," Lynda says. "Something that we've all heard at least a million times from him is, 'I'm best if you just leave me alone and let me learn it by myself.' I finally said, 'Frank, this is unschooling!' "

Unschooling is a family affair and more, with Lynda, Frank, Derek, Kirk, Krystin, and one "acquired child," Timothy, who lives with the family temporarily when his home life becomes unbearable. "Timothy has been with us six months this time, five months before this," Lynda says. "School was part of his problem. He was told he was stupid—and this is a child who likes to read Shakespeare and university-level psychology books—and was put in the alternative school. But he's made great strides and we have great hopes for him." Timothy wants to study to become a psychologist.

Derek hopes to make his career in veterinary medicine, so much of his studying centers on science topics. "Right now we're doing chemistry and haven't blown up the house yet," Lynda says. "We frequent used-book sales to find college textbooks, plentiful in a town with two colleges. We've bought all sorts of books on science, and the most we've ever paid for a book is $2.50." From Lynda's personal experience, you don't have to be rich to homeschool. "While we spend quite a bit for 'extras' like model engines and solar panels, that is a personal choice," she says. "Home-schooling can be done on less than one hundred dollars a year."

In addition to textbooks, Lynda also has discovered a number of helpful online science courses for Derek through the use of the Google and Dogpile search engines. "When Derek wanted to study dissection, I came up with hundreds of sites," Lynda says, "some animated, some with photography of a person actually dissecting, one allowing you to use a virtual knife to do it yourself." Lynda and Derek also have found free online courses such as a biology class, complete with text, offered by the University of Arizona.

The family's youngest son lives a busy life. He has a job and works an average of thirty hours a week or more at an "uncommercial" fast-food place doing cashiering, order taking, and miscellaneous work. As a sports enthusiast, Derek works out at a nearby gym and enjoys basketball, baseball, soccer, and football.

Derek seems to have been "born an unschooler," Lynda says. "He does what tickles his fancy. He taught himself to ride a bike at the age of two. As something grabs him or there's something he needs, he goes online and finds the answers to his question."

Derek doesn't hesitate to go to public school as needed, especially if he wants to compete in organized sports. "He'll attend classes long enough for his team to compete in the championship, and then he'll walk out," Lynda says. "The schools are required by law to allow this. He usually doesn't turn in the work, what he calls the 'brain-numbing day-to-day crud,' and then he aces the test." When Derek is in public school, he usually maintains a B average.

Grandson Kirk plans to become a sports lawyer. He hopes to someday be successful enough to buy all the houses on Lombard Hill, known as "the crookedest street in the world," in San Francisco. "Kirk plans to tear down all the houses on the street except for the one he's going to live in," Lynda says, smiling. "He's in love with the city and in love with that street." Kirk already has bought law books and begun to study. One of his favorite workbooks is *You Be the Judge*, a collection of cases where the reader makes the decisions, just as a judge would do. "We've had whole-family discussions over those cases," Lynda says.

Kirk loves reading and Nintendo. He's interested in martial arts and wants to take lessons. He also thinks pigs are the greatest animal invented and that everyone should have one.

Krystin says she's going to grow up to rule the world, starting with the job of U.S. president for practice, or she may decide to become an organic restaurateur. "My granddaughter is a typical little girl in a houseful of boys," Lynda says. "She loves Barbies, teasing her brother and uncle, and throwing out dollar-bill words in the middle of family discussions."

Krystin taught herself piano. She likes to play Elvis songs together with Frank, whom she calls Frank-pa. She took ballet lessons for two years and starred in two productions, once as an elf and another as a jewel under the sea in *Anastasia*. She has played peewee softball and wants to try gymnastics next.

All four have participated in Little League baseball. In the fall they'll join 4-H and are picking up entry forms for craft projects for the county fair. Kirk and Krystin share the job of delivering newspapers, a joint project in which Krystin folds and Kirk rides his bike and delivers the papers.

Through part-time jobs, extracurricular activities, and various friendships, the children of the family get plenty of socialization. "We always have kids running in and out of the house," Lynda says. "In fact, several are now homeschooling because their parents have seen what it has meant to our kids." Derek, Kirk, and Krystin all have friends of various ages. Some homeschool, but many are enrolled in public or private school.

In addition to socialization skills, Lynda is proud of the way her "kidlets" have developed a social conscience. Last year, the younger members of the family initiated a project called Stop the Frostbite. Derek, Timothy, Kirk, and Krystin were concerned when they learned that the incidence of frostbite on Indian reservations in both the Southwest and the Dakotas is one in every four to five families; only one in seven to ten houses on the reservations have heating systems, and the number of deaths from freezing is appallingly high. The whole family crocheted afghans and collected coats, jackets, and blankets—a total of twelve boxes full—then sent them to some of the reservations before winter. This year the Stop the Frostbite project continues, and the family is also making quilts to send.

Lynda's family has a special interest in helping American Indians because of Lynda's Wiyot (WEE-ot) ancestry. "I am Indian," Lynda says, insisting that "Indian" is the correct term for her ancestry, not "Native American." "I feel it, I understand Indian humor, I run on Indian time. Two of my sons definitely inherited this. Being Indian is a sense you're born with. A piece of paper doesn't make you Indian, nor does being raised on a reservation." When a person has an African heritage, Lynda points out, everyone can see it. "It's different when one is Indian," she says. "Most people think of Hollywood stereotypes. But there are hundreds of different tribes, just as there are many different European countries, and an Irishman wants to be thought of as Irish rather than European. Tribes within the U.S. are very, very different. We don't all live in tepees and we don't all look like the Indian who cries on the TV commercial."

"To me, being Indian means attempting to preserve a future for one's children," Lynda continues. "Being a tree-hugger is not a negative. It means trying to live the philosophy that what you do now affects seven generations, an Indian philosophy. It means an ongoing war with ignorance."

Lynda has made it a high priority to teach her children and grandchildren about their Indian heritage, passing down stories she learned from her grandfather. "This area of the country was not even discovered by white men until 1850," Lynda says. At that time the Indians were living on prime real estate, the area around the bay where there was abundant game available through fishing and hunting. By 1860 there was a nearby community of white people, and the businessmen of the town decided they wanted the Indians' land.

"The prevailing viewpoint at the time was 'The only good Indian is a dead Indian,'" Lynda explains, "and white settlers decided to wipe out the local tribes." Each year for three hundred years, all the Wiyot and surrounding tribes had held a renewal celebration in the last week of February on one of the islands in the bay. "The townspeople knew that all the Indian men would leave to replenish supplies, and the only ones left on the island would be women, children, and the elderly," Lynda says. "The 'militia,' a group funded by local businessmen, started at the far north end of the island and systematically murdered all the Indians they found." A one-night killing spree on February 26, 1860, yielded a total of one to two thousand casualties.

Lynda's two great-grandmothers, who were sisters, survived

the massacre. On that fateful day, not wanting to disturb others, both had walked to the far west side of the island to care for their fussy babies. Their description of the white men's arrival was one of "weasels crawling on their bellies." Later, the "mothers," as they were called, gathered up a total of thirteen surviving children, including their own, placed them in a salvaged canoe, and swam the canoe across the bay, where they went into hiding in the Freshwater Valley.

The next morning, the army from Fort Humboldt arrived at the island to bury the dead and found one more living child who was lying under his lifeless mother. Later that day the soldiers were ordered to round up all the surviving Wiyot and take them to the fort. "Cattle had been turned out of their pens, and these pens were used to 'house' the Indians," Lynda says. "Next they were moved to the North Jetty, a sand spit that separates the bay from the Pacific, to survive among the dunes. The following spring they were rounded up and placed on a ship where they were listed as cargo, and for six days they had no food, water, or blankets. Two hundred and sixty-four died before they reached their destination, the Smith River."

After a year at Smith River, the remaining Wiyot were marched in winter across the mountains to Hupa Valley. "Only about half survived the march," Lynda says. "Among those who died were many of the mothers' brothers, sisters, uncles, aunts, and cousins."

Stories such as these have been passed from generation to generation. "It is one way to keep our sense of identity alive," Linda notes. "My children have also learned Indian crafts like basket weaving. They know about foods, like tomatoes and chocolate, that came from the Americas. We visit places that have historical significance. We talk about our heritage."

Home-schooling seems to have been an important part of Lynda's personal heritage. "My great-grandfather's daughter decided she wanted to learn piano," Lynda says, "so her father sent to San Francisco to have an organ *and* an instructor sent up here. When Great Uncle Henry decided to learn a musical instrument, Great-Grandfather sent to San Francisco again. The second time, he ordered a violin that was a 'Stradivarius knock-off' and an instructor whose father had trained in Europe under Stradivarius himself." Uncle Henry went on to a career in making violas, violins, and cellos, and some were played by members of both the San Francisco Philharmonic and the Boston Pops. Lynda says one of her most cherished possessions is the first violin Uncle Henry made.

In Lynda's grandfather's and mother's generations, Indian children were removed from their homes and forced to go to boarding school. "I think the government had determined that the best way to get rid of Indians was to remove their heritage," Lynda says. "All the children were given Buster Brown haircuts, boys and girls alike, and made to wear white uniforms. Some of them were shipped far away, as far as Arizona and New Mexico. Children were punished through beatings and starving if they spoke their language, thanked Mother Earth for her bounty, or apologized to an animal that was killed to feed them. They were expected to become 'good little Christians.' "

Lynda's grandfather rebelled against the government edicts. "He took my mother and her siblings out of boarding school," Lynda says, "and told the authorities, 'Send me to jail.' They didn't. But everyone except my mother—who was too young and had not been in boarding school long enough—was negatively impacted from his or her experiences at school. My aunt didn't claim her ancestry until she was in her early fifties."

Much of Lynda's philosophy of life comes from her Indian heritage. "My main goal, my priority, is to nourish the human flower," she says. "Some kids need structure, some kids wither with too much structure. We won't do anything that vaguely resembles public school." Recently Kirk tried to convince his sister Krystin that she should attend school. Her reply was, "I'm not going to be locked up in kiddie-prison for eight hours a day!"

Giving her children and grandchildren the freedom to choose their own course ties in with an Indian approach to spirituality. "Religion for most Indians isn't the same as the European concept of religion," she says. "It's not about anybody leading or telling, or going to church on Sunday. It's about spirituality within yourself. Two of my sons are uncomfortable with 'white' religion, they feel different."

From spirituality to day-to-day living, Lynda and Frank "go with the flow." Chores, for example, are completed based on whatever needs to be done. "Whoever is in the room at the wrong time, I say, 'You're the one to do this job,' " Lynda says. The family's life-style is full but also relaxed. "The kidlets have a million activities going. Derek has gone to more proms at both public and private schools than most kids his age would even dream of."

Lynda and Frank have had few complaints about homeschooling. Lynda finds that dealing with teens can sometimes be exhausting, but usually has enough energy to cope. "Sometimes I feel frustrated because all the stuff that was pounded into the kids when they were in public school comes floating to the surface again," she says. "For example, someone will say he 'has to do thus and such instead of something else,' or 'it has to be done in a certain way.' I say, 'No, why do you say you have to do it this way? Why does geometry, for example, have to come before algebra two?' And I sometimes feel close to burnout when fighting math phobia. I think this is taught by public school."

When Lynda needs support, she goes to friends on the Internet. "We no longer have immediate family, since both sets of parents are deceased," Lynda says. "I have three sisters, but we have little or infrequent contact. Local friends and support groups are not really important to us. I have enough trouble explaining being an Indian, not to mention explaining unschooling. The people whose opinions I value are friends on the 'net."

California itself offers a kind of support system. "We're real lucky in being up here in northern California, because we don't run into a lot of narrow-minded bigots," Lynda says. "We've never been verbally attacked. Ninety-nine out of one hundred comments have been positive." In addition, state requirements for homeschoolers—that they turn in a form saying they're a private school—are minimal, and testing is not required.

Overall, homeschooling has been positive. "I'm a realist, and the homeschooling experience has been what I expected," Lynda says. "I've seen my children bloom instead of being put in pigeonholes. I didn't want lemmings. My expectations were simply that everybody be happy and that they not be forced to be unhappy simply because they weren't old enough to vote."

If Lynda could relive her life, "I would take the knowledge I acquired along the way and not make the same mistakes," she says. "I wouldn't have listened to my first mother-in-law, and I never would have put any of my children in school. I would have always done what I'm doing now."

First a homeschooling aunt, next a homeschooling mother, and now a homeschooling grandmother, Lynda says she'll "homeschool as long as each child chooses because that is what unschooling is all about: children taking control of their own destiny."

Front row: Courtney. Middle Row: Don, Ben, Pat, Kelley, Stacey, Kimberly, Matt. Back row: Jonathan (Kelley's new husband), Tony, David, Jonathan.

Twenty-one

Real-Life Homeschooling

Family:
Don (51), Pat (45), Kelley (20), Stacey (18), Tony (16), David (14), Jonathan (12), Kimberly (9), Matt (6), Courtney (4), and Ben (2).

Location:
Rural Bristol, Tennessee.

Best advice:
Don't be too structured or stressed about school. Realize that life is learning. Seize the moment.

Worst advice:
Put them in school.

Favorite quote:
"If there is no God, nothing matters. If there *is* a God, nothing *else* matters." (H. G. Wells)

Favorite resources:

The Bible.

The Elijah Company catalog (free), 1-888-2-ELIJAH, www.elijahco.com

Learning in Spite of Labels by Joyce Herzog, Greenleaf Press.

The Successful Homeschool Family Handbook by Raymond Moore, Thomas Nelson.

The Relaxed Home School by Mary Hood, Ambleside Educational Press.

As a young mother in Tallahassee, Florida, Pat W. never even considered homeschooling. In fact, she and her sister-in-law used to make fun of homeschoolers. "We'd say, 'Why in the world would mothers decide to keep their kids at home just at the age when they finally had a chance to ship them off to school?' "

Pat changed her mind after an intense conversation with a fellow churchgoer, a very convincing woman who had helped to pass the law making homeschool legal in Florida. "She shared a lot with me," Pat says, "from our responsibilities as parents to how you might endanger or harm your children's eyesight giving them board work too early. She also gave me some information by Raymond Moore. I read a lot, thought a lot, and prayed a lot." Pat and her husband, Don, talked it over and made the decision to begin teaching at home.

Together with their nine children, Don and Pat moved from Tallahassee to a mountaintop home in Tennessee. The family has been home-educating for fifteen years, and their philosophy has changed considerably during that time. "When we began homeschooling, our educational goal was to emulate the school system and to fill our children full of information they could spit out. We didn't give it much thought."

Now all are much more oriented toward what could be called

"real-life homeschooling." "One of my goals is to make my children desire knowledge all of their lives, to be inquisitive, to want more," Pat says. "Our society stifles that in children. We also want to equip them with the experience and materials to find the information they need when they need it. And we want them to be able to verify and use the information they find. If we help children master this three-part process, I think we can say we've done our job, and our kids will be lifelong learners. Then, technically, our job is through. The rest of the time, we can help our children pursue their interests and develop skills in other areas like practical arts. This will help them function in society as responsible adults."

Learning practical skills is an area where Pat's family excels. The family owns a business, D.P.&K. (Don, Pat and Kids) Productions, that includes a staggering number of endeavors. Don is a real estate agent and does construction work. Pat is coeditor of a money-saving newsletter, *BIG Ideas/Small Budget*, and has written and self-published a book by the same name. She also has produced two unit-study books, one on the Civil War and one called *Inventions, Inventors and Entrepreneurs*, plus several workbooks labeled *Information Please!* Between the two of them, Don and Pat have had extensive experience in a number of businesses, from multilevel marketing—selling Amway and Excel long-distance phone services—to mystery shopping, where the family is hired to secretly evaluate businesses and report on their service to company headquarters.

Pat considers involvement in home business to be an absolute essential of her family's homeschool, real-life experiences that can't be duplicated in book learning. To this end, her children have been actively included in making money by selling lemonade from a street corner, house-sitting, picking pecans, teaching craft classes at a Ben Franklin store, delivering phone books, operating a lawn business, pressure-washing houses, teaching gym classes at a local YMCA, cleaning houses, entertaining as clowns, helping to organize and put on birthday parties, stuffing envelopes, selling products door-to-door, working for other entrepreneurs, "sitting" with elderly persons recovering from surgery, doing yard work and other odd jobs on an estate, being camp counselors and assistant directors at a church camp, and entering data into a computer for a candy-making company. The children also work for pay in D.P.&K. Productions, binding Pat's books, filling orders, and helping as needed.

Working with their father, the older boys have taken an interest—and developed great skills—in several areas. David owns his own gas edger, blower, trimmer, and lawn mower, and bought them all with his own money to use in his lawn business. He also has some automotive talent and can change the oil, brake pads, and shocks in a car, plus rotate the tires and do other related work. Tony, David, and Jonathan have helped their dad tile, roof, rewire, frame, layout, plumb, and put down concrete. When David was twelve, he put together a Pentium computer from scratch.

The girls' and younger children's interests have led them to other skills. Kelley worked with handicapped children. Also, "my daughters have taken clothes to consignment shops in order to earn money," Pat says. "They know what to buy at yard sales in order to get a good return for their money." The children also have rented booths at flea markets to sell homemade crafts, and have hosted several yard sales, where they sold drinks and home-baked goods as well as secondhand items.

Pat and her family started a jewelry-making business after two of the children discovered there was money to be made by selling Cokes and candy to Florida State University football fans en route to the game; the walking path happened to go right by a friend's house, where the kids had set up a booth. This inspired a brainstorming session. Pat and the children had done a unit study on Native Americans and developed some beautiful hand-crafted earrings. Pat adapted their original design to fit the colors and style of the Seminoles, FSU's football team, and soon these new earrings began to attract attention. The family sold some directly from their booth to passersby, and then in stores, including an FSU store. "Within two years, we had our jewelry in ten stores, and we sold over five thousand dollars worth in a four-month period," Pat says.

Age is no handicap in earning money. Jonathan, age eight at the time, once collected twenty dollars taste-testing two new cough syrups at a survey center at the mall. The children also are paid piecemeal for assembly-line work when Pat or some of the siblings are producing earrings and other craft projects, so even preschoolers have the opportunity to earn a penny for every bead placed on a strip of leather, or a dime for attaching leather to earrings.

All this work experience has made the children fearless entrepreneurs. David and Jonathan have purchased two gumball machines and plan to place them in stores; each time they're emptied, the boys will pocket fifty dollars profit each. Once when Kelley was selling earrings outside the stadium of an FSU football game, she spotted a man who was buying and reselling tickets. Kelley asked her dad's permission to try this herself. "Sure," her father said. "But you have to risk your own money. If you end up with tickets by game time, you can treat us to the game." At the next home game, Kelley started with forty dollars in hand, and within half an hour had cleared one hundred dollars profit.

Pat has discovered that her children learn as much from disappointments as successes. At the height of their earrings' commercial success, Kelley asked her mother if she could purchase her own materials, make the jewelry, sell it herself, and keep all the profit. Pat agreed, with the condition that she must find her own accounts. She also explained that, again, Kelley would have to bear the risk herself, including the expense of leftover materials and unsold product. Although Kelley enjoyed her project and made a profit, she soon realized that there was more to production and marketing than she had realized. In this case, she could make more money working for her mother with much less hassle, and returned to that. Tony started work as a cafeteria worker for minimum wage when he was fourteen. Since then he has decided this is *not* what he wants to do for the rest of his life. "It's been a great learning experience," Pat says.

The family is not entirely business-oriented, and believes strongly in the value of volunteer work. "Our kids do everything from sorting food for the Salvation Army, feeding the homeless at shelters, volunteering for campaigns, baby-sitting for free, visiting nursing homes, helping set up or clean up at church functions, and buying presents for the needy at Christmas, to mowing grass for the elderly," Pat says.

The children also do their share of academic work. Pat has no formal schedule. "Usually we have daily goals," she says. "I tell the kids, 'This is what you need to have accomplished by the end of the day, and you won't be riding the four-wheeler until it's done.' " Pat says she doesn't have "typical" days. "Sometimes the day will break because we have a field trip or we'll have to go to town. So I say, 'Let's get this much done, and when we come back we'll do the rest.' "

Pat prefers to get up early for quiet time to herself, and often takes advantage of the wee morning hours to complete necessary book work for her business. The younger children wake up before the others and they toddle around until everyone is up. Then comes breakfast, followed by a quick clean-up time: While some clear the table and do dishes, the others start laundry, dress the little ones, and declutter. After clean-up the family has devotions and Bible study.

The rest of the day may take one of many different directions. "If we are in the middle of reading a really good book and everyone is able to listen," Pat says, "we may begin by reading while the little ones play. If one of the preschoolers becomes disruptive, then he can play alone in his room for a while."

The children have their assignments and proceed, coming to Pat for help when needed. Sometimes the older ones teach the younger their lessons. "The children love to keep in touch with friends and family via e-mail," Pat says, "and they are allowed on the computer for that as well as learning software, including typing lessons, with time limits set. Many days some of the kids will stay with their dad, helping out with a current project."

When some schoolwork and chores are complete, lunch is next on the agenda. Afterward, the younger children rest and the others are occupied with either business, unfinished schoolwork, or physical activities like jumping on the trampoline, chopping wood, riding the minibike and four-wheeler, hiking, and running. "If orders need to be filled and prepared for mailing, we do this in the afternoon," Pat says, "and projects that involve science experiments or crafts, when the little ones are resting. The older children may leave to attend classes or work. If we have to run errands, we will do that after naps, often combining trips to town with visits to the library and a playground. Supper time is usually around six, and rarely are all eleven of us present because of jobs, sports, or classes."

The family might spend their evening finishing up chores or business projects, watching a video, or playing outdoors. Wednesday nights are reserved for youth group functions at church. The older children are allowed to stay up later than their set bed time each night if they are reading.

For a few hours after the younger children are in bed, Pat works on her current projects, like writing articles for her newsletter or producing new unit studies. She is able to save much time that might be spent in record-keeping, as she pays ninety dollars a year to an "umbrella school" to handle the paperwork required of homeschoolers by the state of Tennessee. "I send in attendance reports and other records of what we're doing, and they keep track of it," she says.

None of this schedule is set in stone. "I go with the flow," Pat says. "I tell my kids, 'Life is learning. There are opportunities every day.' If we're using the summer to travel to curriculum fairs, we'll go to the museums and other attractions. It's year-round learning, it's not necessarily year-round books."

In order to fit in all necessary school subjects, Pat decided years ago to incorporate unit studies. "The more children I had, the less hours there were to divide them into grades and subjects. It only took a few school-age children to realize that." Now, Pat chooses a topic and centers most subjects, including language arts, history, and science, around it. She likes to make use of the most exciting books she can find, either from the local library or the family's extensive collection, as resources.

Pat wants to make sure her children thoroughly understand all the fundamental academics. "When I came out of high school, I didn't know the solar system, geography, continents, capitals, the presidents of the U.S., basic knowledge," she says. "And I went to a research and development school associated with a major university." Beyond understanding, Pat also stresses that her children must know how to research and use information. "I want to give them knowledge that they'll not only remember, but is also of interest to them, and applicable to their lives," she says.

The children learn language arts by doing plenty of writing, then correcting their grammar, spelling, and mechanical problems. Pat doesn't worry about timing. "I expect my children to learn to read and write," she says, "but that can come at very different times of development. My two oldest daughters learned when they were four years old. Some of the boys struggled, and weren't reading until a much later age."

Math is studied through math supplements and textbooks, mostly Saxon, for the older children. Kelley took the math software of the SAT prep test to learn what she needed to know for college. "For logic and thinking skills, we use games like Boggle," Pat says. "And we're on the computer a lot. Our VCR tapes are often reserved for helping my little ones settle down, though our VCR is usually broken!"

Don participates most in the hands-on, life-skills teaching. "He's also a math wizard," Pat says, "so when the kids have problems with math, they go to him. And he helps them with their devotions and Bible study." Don taught a worldview class one year to several teenage homeschoolers in the area.

The family takes advantage of many kinds of classes, like homeschool offerings in algebra and biology. Also, "in Florida, you could take college classes while you were in high school, and all you had to pay for were books," Pat says, "so Kelley and Stacey signed up for Spanish and computers. In Tallahassee, there were several homeschooled children who finished their AA degrees by the time they graduated from high school."

When the family lived in Florida, they were actively involved in a homeschool cooperative with four or five other families, meeting once a week. "We would prepare for these group unit studies several days in advance, because the kids had assignments that they had to present orally before the group," Pat says. "The youngest children were kept in another room with some of the parents, and we adults rotated responsibilities like baby-sitting, being in charge of crafts, and presenting materials. We covered research, history, literature, almost every discipline except math. My kids enjoyed being with other children, learning in a group situation, and sharing." After each co-op meeting, Pat and other parents arranged all the homeschoolers' reports into a weekly newsletter, a portfolio for each participant to keep.

Pat thinks the co-op is one example of real-life academic

learning that equipped her children with practical skills. "My oldest daughter won a statewide speech contest and got a fifteen-hundred-dollar scholarship her junior year," Pat says. "Looking back, I think the reason she could stand up before three hundred strangers and give her speech was because week after week at co-op, she'd present her oral reports. It gave her the confidence she needed."

The children have not been formally tested, but Pat and Don are not concerned. Kelley began college with an almost-full scholarship her first year. "Her grades were excellent," Pat says. "By the second semester, Kelley had an A minus average in spite of carrying sixteen hours, living at home with eight siblings, playing on the college basketball team, and helping around the house after I had had surgery."

Kelley isn't the only family member who can help around the house. In order to cope with all the daily responsibilities, Pat requires her children to "do an awful lot of the daily household chores. I handle most of the cooking and conduct my business, but I do very little housework. Stacey does the laundry; that's her job. She's good at it, and she likes it. One time she wasn't keeping up, so I switched her to dishes, which horrified her. For a week she did dishes. When she went back to laundry, then she was *really good*," Pat says, laughing. "We alternate when I feel someone needs to learn another chore, or when the little ones get old enough to take someone else's chores."

Don and Pat see great value in chores, book learning, and business experiences, but their number-one priority is to instill good character in their children. Pat quotes Joyce Herzog in her book *Learning in Spite of Labels:* "If your child is the most intelligent, gifted, learned person in the world, but has a terrible personality, is miserably self-centered, sees no purpose in life but the moment, have you been a successful teacher?" "I think there are some things," says Pat, "that are more important to me than their education, a lot more important, like their spiritual up-bringing, their character. There have been times when we have not worried about anything in the books for a while, as we worked on these other areas."

The couple also makes sure their children have plenty of social interaction. "Who says it's the school's responsibility to social-ize?" Pat asks. Her children have been involved with homeschool band and regularly attend church and youth group functions, in-cluding mission trips to Mexico. They've always participated in sports, including soccer, baseball, and basketball, either through the schools, a homeschool group, or city leagues. At one time, four children were competitive gymnasts.

Kelley and Stacey were both part of a basketball team that won the national championship in their division. At the championship game, these two sisters made history. "One of our daughters did a flip-flop while the other daughter made a basket, helping to win the game," Pat says. "Someone filmed their play, and about a month later, it was featured on CNN as the play of the week. Later, *Good Morning America*, and then *The Today Show*, also aired the play. Then *Real TV* picked it up and turned it into a segment."

Home-schooling has been full of surprises, Pat says. "It's been a great experience. We've had our ups and downs, but I'm convinced this is what we should be doing. When I started I didn't have any expectations. It's been more than I expected, in that I have been so pleased with it. I love the fact that homeschoolers can take advan-tage of late-night PBS specials, or take a few days off to go view a visiting exhibit, or attend a Civil War reenactment."

Still, Pat admits that she sometimes feels overwhelmed. "There are moments when I think, 'Boy, if they were all in school, I'd have a peaceful day and time to myself,' but that's not what I really want. And there are times when the kids are giving me trouble, and I just have to deal with that." On bad days, Pat can't help but question her homeschooling. "I think, 'Am I doing a good job? Could I be doing better? Am I slighting them some-how?' That's when I try to take a moment to sit and contemplate, or pray, or go back and reread Raymond Moore's book, *The Successful Homeschool Family Handbook*, or back issues of *Practical Homeschooling* magazines. Then I'm always refreshed and deter-mined, and I think, 'Yes I'm doing what's right, the best I can do with what I have.' "

The family thinks it's important to give themselves some breaks. "Sometimes we all hop in the van and go somewhere, like to a museum or a playground," Pat says. "It helps us to refocus." The family also schedules in a time of recreation on either a Sat-urday or Sunday afternoon. "We take hikes, ride bikes, or go to parks. Sunday is reserved for church, naps, visits with friends, and overall relaxing."

Pat loves her life-style. "Having the family together, the sib-lings together, working out relationships, being home for much of the day—for the most part, we are really close," she says. "Our kids do act like normal teenagers and withdraw somewhat when they hit adolescence, but then they come out of it. It's very re-warding to have each of the oldest two say, 'Mom, I'm glad you stuck in there, even when we begged to go to school. I'm glad you didn't send us. I see why you homeschooled, and I'm going to homeschool my children.' "

To Pat and Don, the joy of homeschooling is directly related to their "real life" philosophy of education. "Some may say that our children have missed out on possible academic advantage," the couple says. "To that we would answer that education is not the most important factor to us. If we've shorted our children ac-ademically, they aren't ruined for life. If we've *not* taught them how to function in this world as mature, reasonable, loving, de-pendable adults, with the life skills necessary to succeed in what-ever endeavor they pursue—*then* we would say that we have failed them."

Afterword

When I wrote the introduction to this book some months earlier, I posed the following question: "When someone says 'I homeschool,' what does that really mean?" I thought at the time that I knew the answer to that question. After all, I'm a veteran homeschooler, I read extensively on the subject, and I have met and talked with hundreds of homeschoolers from many different states.

Continuing in the introduction, I mentioned that "in interviewing twenty-one families, I have been astonished to discover a variety of life-styles and teaching philosophies that are just about as diverse as you can get." That statement, written well before I finished all the interviews, has proved to be even more true than I could have imagined.

This book is all about diversity, and from the beginning I purposely chose families who were different from one another. The diversity has taken several different forms:

Diversity in geography

I found it refreshing to see how homeschooling works equally well for Sandy and Chuck's family on Kwajalein, a Pacific island, and Cari and Brian's family, who prefer the rigors of outback living in Alaska. The interviewees in this book also live in cities, suburbs, small towns, and the country, all over the United States.

Diversity in family life-style

Many families featured in this book are well off financially, but some have very low incomes. Some prefer a busy, hectic life-style, and some need a generous dose of peace and quiet. It was fascinating to interview the parents of large families, and also to learn how some parents teach their only child.

You may have noticed that I selected families with babies, young children, preteens, teens, and/or adult offspring. The various stories demonstrate that it is possible to deal with the challenges in each stage of child development and still homeschool successfully.

Diversity in philosophy and worldview

There are many answers to the question as to why people choose to homeschool, and the primary reason often comes back to philosophy and worldview. You will remember that many of the interviewees, devout conservative Christians, began homeschooling because of their heartfelt belief that this is what God called them to do. I hope that I have fairly represented families of faith by letting them tell their own stories; it seems to me that such people are often misrepresented in the media.

It is my sincere hope that the stories in this book show that homeschoolers of all philosophies and worldviews share much common ground. By reading about each others' ways of life, perhaps it will help us all to recognize that we have a great deal to discuss and learn from each other.

Diversity in methods of teaching

Writing this book helped me to understand the wide variety of teaching methods available to homeschoolers. Naomi and Rod use a video school program, Bobby and Nina prefer textbooks, Pat and Don like unit studies, Susie and Mark teach from an eclectic assortment of materials, and Lori and Roy "unschool."

Did you note how many of the interviewees said they started out by "bringing school home," and then relaxed as the years went by?

Diversity in goals desired through homeschooling

I thought it interesting that some families homeschooled primarily for academic reasons, but many more thought religious training, character development, family closeness, and other reasons were just as—or even more—important goals to be reached.

Diversity is everywhere in this book. That proves to me, at least in this somewhat limited sphere, that homeschooling works. Geographic location, family life-style, philosophy and worldview, methods of teaching, and desired goals are widely varied within the stories of these interviewees, and within the homeschooling movement as well.

And now a few words of explanation about other issues raised.

This book is not meant to be a how-to manual, but simply a book of stories.

I wanted to tell stories because, in reading through much homeschooling literature, stories always have been the most helpful to me. It's refreshing to connect with a real family where the nuts and bolts of homeschooling are actually being carried out, concept by concept, day by day. A story helps me to visualize how people live and make it all work.

How-to books can be an invaluable aid in homeschooling, but I encourage homeschoolers to beware of anyone advising only one "right way" to homeschool. A vendor once told me that novice homeschoolers often come to her table in tears, asking advice on the "right" materials to buy. The answer is that there is no one right package. It's hard to remember this, brushing past dozens of skilled salespeople at a curriculum fair or paging through a two-hundred-page catalog, and advice on what to buy and how to teach varies widely. Instead, families must sometimes try a variety of options before they find what works best for them.

Real-Life Homeschooling does not present a totally balanced, demographically accurate picture of homeschoolers throughout the United States.

It is impossible to present such a view. The number of Jewish homeschoolers like Joan and Aren, for example, is probably a tiny proportion of the overall population. Angie laments the lack of fellow African Americans involved in the homeschool movement, though there are indications that minority participation is increasing. I doubt that five out of every twenty-one homeschoolers, nationwide, unschool.

Rather than keep the stories rigidly balanced to certain percentages, my goal in writing this book has been simply to profile an interesting assortment of people.

Homeschoolers are not as consistently cheerful and content as they may sometimes appear to be in this book.

Writing the stories of twenty-one families, using mostly their own words, posed an interesting problem. On the one hand, when I wrote down everything these homeschoolers had accomplished, many of them were surprised at how successful they've been. Unfortunately, the writing process also tended to sanitize the genuine sorrow, frustration, occasional boredom, and persistent irritations inherent in day-to-day living. It was sometimes hard to make each of these families' problems seem real, and interviewees were naturally none too eager to dwell on their failures and faults.

(I did make several attempts, with no success, to locate a family who had tried homeschooling and then decided it was not compatible with their life-style.)

Homeschooling does not work for everyone.

As a dedicated but not fanatical homeschooler, I have reluctantly concluded that homeschooling is not for everyone. For whatever reasons, many families decide that the time, place, or circumstances are not right for them to try teaching at home. This book is not meant to be a polemic against public or private schools, nor is it meant to endorse homeschooling exclusively. It is not my place to criticize any family's decision.

Homeschooling is not an easy task, but neither is it an overwhelming task.

One should not even attempt homeschooling with the idea that most children can be put on auto pilot. While some students need minimal help, others require a great deal of tutoring, encouragement and stimulation from the parent/teacher. Prospective homeschoolers should be aware of the challenges and go into homeschooling with eyes wide open. Veterans need to remember that homeschooling is the equivalent of a full-time job, and adjust their other commitments accordingly. Home-schooling, in a word, is *challenging*.

Then again, homeschooling one's children is certainly doable. I once wrote to a newspaper editorialist who had criticized the competency of homeschoolers: "While it is true that home-schooling is sometimes a difficult task, it is certainly not unattainable. I can't see much difference between homeschooling my children as my chosen career, and supervising employees in a corporation or acting as principal of a public school. Let's face it, homeschooling is like many other careers; one simply needs good management skills and a desire to learn the job. That makes a good teacher, as well as a good boss."

Real-Life Homeschooling is designed to be read by all sorts of people: those who are simply interested in knowing more, those who plan to start homeschooling sometime in the future, and both novice and veteran homeschoolers.

This is a book for those who simply want to know more about homeschooling. It is my hope that after reading through several stories, such readers will have a much clearer picture of how homeschooling works . . . and never, ever again ask the tiresome and naive question, "But what about socialization?"

For those who plan to homeschool sometime in the future, may this book help you to understand the tremendous options open to you.

Novice homeschoolers can be encouraged to learn that by simply jumping in and beginning to teach their children at home, much will fall in place of its own accord. As you learn and grow together, your family will discover the right path for you.

Finally, veterans should be inspired to know that others who have homeschooled through high school and beyond have produced intelligent, well-adjusted children. Long-term burnout is not inevitable and can be avoided. Good counsel is readily available. The journey is hard but oh, so worth it in the end.

It's no understatement to say that writing this book, *Real-Life Homeschooling: The Stories of 21 Families Who Teach Their Children at Home*, has changed my life. The stories of these remarkable yet ordinary families have made me consider, reevaluate, and come out better, I think, in the end. I have made several major adjustments to my daily homeschooling schedule, my short-term goals, my long-term goals, and my implementation of homeschooling in general. I hope that you have had a similarly gratifying experience as you read through this book. If nothing else, I hope you simply enjoyed the stories.

I'd enjoy hearing comments from readers, and you can contact me through either of the addresses listed below. Check our website now and then for updates on our family business ventures.

Rhonda Barfield
P.O. Box 665
St. Charles, MO 63302

www.lilacpublishing.com

Index

perseverance, 10, 40
philosophy, diversity in, 294
Physical Fitness Award program, 116
pioneers, hardships of, 33
portfolios, assessment, 50, 90
postsecondary education options (PSEO), 165
power dynamics, healthy, 186–87
Practical Homeschooling magazines, 292
practical skills, 18–19, 74, 216, 258, 283
Practice of the Presence of God, The (Lawrence), 219
prayer, function of, 219
Prayer Organizer, The (Richards), 23
public performances, 37–38
public schools:
   advantages of, 21
   attentance required in, 25–33
   black children's treatment in, 107
   bureaucratic indifference in, 2–3
   conformity learned in, 150
   doubts about, 14, 44, 55–56, 97–98, 141, 153, 271–72, 278
   dropouts from, 47–48
   giving up on, 268–69, 270
   from homeschool and back, 13–21, 233, 273
   labels in, 153
   partnership with, 3, 63, 152, 165, 273
   powerlessness in, 180
   running for the board of, 1–3, 11
   special needs students mainstreamed into, 54–55, 140–41
   standardization in, 90–91, 98–99, 228, 233, 271

Real Lives (Llewellyn), 225
Reason for Writing, A, 114, 201
religion:
   as basis for decisions, 97, 98, 99, 111, 169, 294
   as basis for life, 258, 259
   as basis for relationships, 179
   in curricula, 6–7, 80, 125, 126, 161, 188, 240, 295
responsibility:
   freedom and, 92, 207
   learning, 10–11, 49, 62, 203–4, 243, 283
   for one's own education, 197
   of parents, 48
Rod and Staff, 38
Running Start, 245–46

Sacred Romance (Curtis and Eldredge), 172
Saxon Math, 2, 17, 58, 85, 112, 115, 129, 142, 238, 241, 289
Scholastic Books, 146
school board, running for, 1–3, 11
science, 18, 73, 103, 113, 114, 129–30, 142, 272
Seasons of a Mother's Heart (Clarkson), 212
Second Harvest, 54
Seeger, Peggy, 183
self-employment, 226–27, 263, 285
self-motivation, 234
self-teaching, 45, 85–86, 184, 187, 271, 272–73
Seton Home Study, 258
Signing Exact English, 202
Simply Grammar, 73
socialization, 9–10, 18, 39, 47, 62–63, 79, 88–89, 104–5, 135, 149–50, 165, 188, 189, 208, 231, 244, 262–63, 274, 291
Sonlight, 73–74
special needs, 53–66, 139–53, 193–209
Spelling Power, 73, 75
sports activities, 60, 77, 79, 88, 116, 291
state regulations:
   Alaska, 261
   California, 273, 279
   Connecticut, 90
   Delaware, 177
   Florida, 25–33, 230, 282
   Illinois, 187–88, 220

Biography of Rhonda Barfield

Rhonda Barfield is a professional homemaker, wife to Michael, and mother of Eric, 15, Christian, 14, Lisa, 12, and Mary, 10. She has homeschooled for ten years and, most of the time, very much enjoys doing so.

She is best known as the author of three books: *Eat Well for $50 a Week* (now out of print), *Eat Healthy for $50 a Week* (updated and renamed *Feed Your Family for $12 a Day*), and *15-Minute Cooking*. *Real-Life Homeschooling: 21 Families Who Make It Work* is her fourth book.

Rhonda's books have been acclaimed in dozens of national magazines and newspapers, including *Family Circle*, *Redbook*, *Kiplinger's Personal Finance*, *Woman's Day*, *Chicago Sun-Times*, *Practical Homeschooling*, and *Homeschooling Today*, among many others. She has been a guest on several local, syndicated, and network television shows and radio programs.

Rhonda has written more than one hundred published articles for a variety of magazines and newsletters. In addition to writing, she enjoys speaking to groups of all sizes and has addressed dozens of audiences in the past several years. Finally, she is C.E.O., publicist, secretary, and janitor of Lilac Publishing, the Barfields' family business.